Gangsters Without Borders

ISSUES OF GLOBALIZATION
Case Studies in Contemporary Anthropology

Labor and Legality:
An Ethnography of a Mexican Immigrant Network
Ruth Gomberg-Muñoz

Listen, Here Is a Story:
Ethnographic Life Narratives from Aka and Ngandu
Women of the Congo Basin
Bonnie L. Hewlett

Cuban Color in Tourism and La Lucha:
An Ethnography of Racial Meanings
L. Kaifa Roland

Our Blood Does Not Agree:
An Ethnography of HIV/AIDS Prevention Programs in Botswana
Rebecca Upton

Gangsters Without Borders:
An Ethnography of a Salvadoran Street Gang
T. W. Ward

Gangsters Without Borders

An Ethnography of a Salvadoran Street Gang

T. W. WARD

New York   Oxford
OXFORD UNIVERSITY PRESS

Oxford University Press, Inc., publishes works that further Oxford University's
objective of excellence in research, scholarship, and education.

Oxford New York
Auckland Cape Town Dar es Salaam Hong Kong Karachi
Kuala Lumpur Madrid Melbourne Mexico City Nairobi
New Delhi Shanghai Taipei Toronto

With offices in
Argentina Austria Brazil Chile Czech Republic France Greece
Guatemala Hungary Italy Japan Poland Portugal Singapore
South Korea Switzerland Thailand Turkey Ukraine Vietnam

For titles covered by Section 112 of the US Higher Education
Opportunity Act, please visit www.oup.com/us/he for the
latest information about pricing and alternate formats.

Published by Oxford University Press, Inc.
198 Madison Avenue, New York, New York 10016
http://www.oup.com

Oxford is a registered trademark of Oxford University Press

Library of Congress Cataloging-in-Publication Data
Ward, Thomas W., 1957-
Gangsters without borders : an ethnography of a Salvadoran street gang / T. W. Ward.
  p. cm.
ISBN 978-0-19-985906-1 (pbk)
1. MS-13 (Gang)   2. Hispanic American gangs—California—Los Angeles.
3. Salvadorans—California—Los Angeles—Social conditions.   4. Immigrant youth—
California—Los Angeles—Social conditions.   5. Gang members—California—Los Angeles—
Social conditions.   I. Title.
HV6439.U7L7883 2012
364.106'6089687284079494—dc23   2011051378

Printing number: 9 8 7 6 5 4

Printed in the United States of America
on acid-free paper

To Dr. Bob and Raven

Drawn by an MS gang member in Pelican Bay State Prison.

CONTENTS

....

FOREWORD
....

Malcolm W. Klein
Professor Emeritus, University of Southern California

Professor Ward has given us the first careful, considered, and non-inflammatory view of a huge street gang that has captured American politicians' warped imagination. Ward's description of MS-13 members is not of 'gangsters,' but of complex young gang members. The MS-13 found in media reports and public discourse is a far cry from the close-up look provided in Ward's eight-and-a-half-year immersion in the gang. For this reason alone, this book is must reading for academics, law enforcement, and public officials alike. I'm not sure any street gang has so engaged public attention since The Sharks and Jets sang and danced their way through the streets of New York.

A second major strength of this work is that it has solved the predicament of preserving the identities of its gang member informants while making their complex existence come alive and believable. The use of composite portraits of these 'gangsters' is a clever and credible vehicle for portraying the Mara Salvatrucha subculture of pain and violence, as only an intensive ethnography can.

In assessing the contribution of Ward's descriptions of the gang and its members, some contextualization may be helpful. This is a very special report on a very special gang. And while the author does not share a pivotal moment with his readers, I will do so because it emphasizes something about ethnographic gang research and the temper of those who undertake it. When a loaded firearm was placed next to Tom Ward's head, he had to decide – instantaneously and thereafter – on the value of research and of life itself. That we can read this book is a testament to his struggle and his ability to achieve peace with his street clients and with himself. I am aware of only a few other street gang researchers who were similarly, if not quite so dramatically, confronted with the danger of their enterprise. One was shot, another beaten up, a third targeted for a gang 'hit.' It happens, albeit rarely. Less rarely, police are occasionally confronted by armed gang members and, in a few instances, mortally wounded. That so few truly serious incidents take place is a reminder (again) that the drama portrayed in *Gangsters Without Borders* is atypical. MS-13 is not like most street gangs, and most street gangs are well documented around the world as far less threatening and far less desperate than Ward's composite images. We know some things about the 'ordinary' street gang that place MS-13 in this broader context.

1. MS-13 is one of thousands of street gangs in the U.S. Recent research in Europe describes scores of others there in over fifty cities. Few of the gangs here or there resemble MS-13 in size, age distribution, or levels of violence.
2. Street gangs come in a variety of structures. The extensive and complex structure of MS-13 is typical of "traditional" street gangs, a category that comprises a minority of all street gangs. To generalize from MS-13 to most other gangs would be foolish just as ascribing to MS-13 the characteristics of most gangs would be equally so.
3. Street gangs, MS-13 and others, comprise a minority of youth groups. Street gangs are qualitatively different from most other youth groups and need to be studied and understood as a somewhat separate social phenomenon (as author Ward clearly does).
4. Street gangs are also different from other groups to which the "gang" label has been applied. They differ from prison gangs, motorcycle gangs, drug cartels, and terrorist groups. Attempts to equate them – often noticed in official proclamations from federal agencies and local officials – are misleading and often deliberately so.
5. Street gang members are not simply "thugs" or "hardened criminals" or "purveyors of violence and drug trafficking." They are young people living tough lives in tough situations. The reader should take note, for instance, of Ward's "9 Lessons about Street Gangs" in his appendix, as well as his description of gang members' varied and boring life patterns in Chapters 3, 5, and 6.

At the risk of overstating the uniqueness of MS-13, I want to emphasize several points because this gang has become so subject to official and media exaggeration and extrapolation to other street gangs. Ward's careful work and descriptions should help to ameliorate the situation, but let's go one step further.

- MS-13 was birthed (in Los Angeles) as a result of a violent revolution in El Salvador, unlike any other North American gang.
- MS-13 was magnified by an ethnic rivalry with a large Mexican-American gang in Los Angeles ("18th Street"). This has been a local gang of foreign origin, shaped within the borders of the city and county of Los Angeles.
- MS-13 has been fueled, like no other American gang, by the policies and practices of U.S. immigration officials who thought to deport the problem, only to magnify it instead.
- MS-13 is by now not one gang but a wide nominal umbrella for thousands of gang youth, in a complex and loose network of cliques, many of which know nothing of each other.
- Finally, the reader should keep in mind that Ward's engaging and convincing depiction of his composite gang members is, for the most part, a depiction of hard-core gang members. As he is careful to point out, they are special and not typical of most MS-13 members (to say nothing of most members of most other street gangs).

We do not generalize from these unusual youth to most gang members, nor from this unusual gang to most street gangs. Rather, *Gangsters Without Borders* provides a significant marker against which to judge other, less dramatic gangs. It also provides an almost unequaled example of an intensive, thoughtful, and careful ethnographic journey into a world known to most of us from superficial and poorly documented exaggerations for public consumption. Thus, I have become a fan of Tom Ward.

Los Angeles,
September, 2011

NOTE TO THE READER
....

The title of this book, *Gangsters Without Borders*, may lead some readers to believe that the Mara Salvatrucha (MS) gang is a closely interconnected network of terrorist cells whose members are highly organized and in close contact. While MS is a transnational street gang, its various cliques in different states and countries are not intimately connected, nor are the activities of these cliques in El Salvador, Honduras, Guatemala, Mexico, Canada, and the United States highly coordinated. Although some MS gang members have traversed national boundaries, the ties between the cliques in different countries are loose and are based on personal connections.

The spread of MS from its origins in Los Angeles to other states and across international borders was unintentional. It occurred initially as a result of the secondary migration of Central American families within the United States—moving to find jobs—and later as a result of the mass deportations of gang members back to their home countries in Central America. For these reasons, I would like the reader to know that the title does **not** mean these "gangsters" are "without borders" in terms of being part of a huge criminal conspiracy.

In contrast, *Without Borders* is meant to convey three important aspects of the lives of these hard-core MS gang members. These aspects are geographic, behavioral, and psychological in nature. First, *Without Borders* implies the feeling of being disenfranchised or marginalized, a sense of liminality, or a lack of a feeling of belonging to a particular group or society, as represented by the borders of a nation-state. Second, the title is meant to connote a sense of rebelliousness that knows no bounds, including suicidal behavior. Hard-core gang members, the focus of this book, practice much less self-control than other members of the gang and are extremely opportunistic, free to express their anger and their greed. And third, *Without Borders* refers to their deeply ingrained sense of identification with the gang, even after retirement. The gangster identity is difficult to shake for hard-core members of street gangs and lingers in their hearts and minds long after their retirement from the gangster life. The gang represents a sacred aspect of their lives as rebellious juvenile delinquents—a heart connection without borders.

ACKNOWLEDGMENTS

I would like to thank the people who helped in my academic development and the creation of this book. First, I'd like to thank my undergraduate professors in the English department at SMU, including Willard Spiegelman, John Lewis, Ken Shields, Marshall Terry, and Steve Daniels. I would also like to thank my anthropology professors at UCLA and UC Berkeley who taught me to see through the ethnographic lens. Nancy Scheper-Hughes was my undergraduate mentor, and Robert B. Edgerton served as my graduate mentor and instigator for this research. My debt to Dr. Bob (as we affectionately called him), who supported me in all phases of this research, is reflected in the dedication of this book. Among the many others who contributed toward my understanding of anthropology are (in alphabetical order) Ira Abrams, Gerry Berreman, Walter Goldschmidt, John Kennedy, Keith Kernan, Hilda Kuper, Lew Langness, Sally Falk Moore, Laura Nader, Philip Newman, Douglas Price-Williams, William "Wild Bill" Pulte, Paul Rabinow, and Tom Weisner. I would also like to thank my colleagues in graduate school at UCLA, who shared with me their thoughts on theory and methodology: Joe Graffam, Paul Koegel, Frank Marlowe, Vivianne del Signore, Scott Cooper, Gelya Frank, Silvia Hirsch, Lisa Ryder, and Dana Baldwin.

I would especially like to thank my colleagues at USC who welcomed me into the fold of teaching anthropology: Alexander "Zandy" Moore, who gave me the job in the first place, and the other department chairs, Craig Stanford and Nancy Lutkehaus, who allowed me to keep it. Thanks also go to Joseph Hawkins, Erin Moore, Andre Simic, Gene Cooper, Amy Parish, Lanita Jacobs, Fadwa El Guindi, Joan Weibel-Orlando, Janet Hoskins, Dorinne Kondo, Gary Seaman, Cheryl Mattingly, Tok Thompson, Eric Cannon, and my other colleagues in the anthropology department. I would also like to thank Rita Jones, Sandra Dymally, Dennis Miranda, and Debbie Williams, who have been more than gracious and patient in dealing with logistics. I owe a huge debt to Malcolm "Mac" Klein, and his "partner in crime," Cheryl Maxson, for graciously aiding in my understanding of street gangs. Most of what one needs to know about street gangs can be gleaned from these two eminent sociologists. However, the class on street gangs that I have taught for the past sixteen years at USC gave me the opportunity to meet ex-gang members from several different ethnic gangs and law enforcement officials from the Los Angeles Police Department and the Los Angeles County Sheriff's Department, whose views deepened my understanding of street gangs. With regard to my understanding of MS, I would like to thank law enforcement officials from the FBI MS gang task force, Interpol, local officials from Fairfax, Virginia, Maryland, and Los Angeles, as well as social workers from these cities who shared their views. My understanding of street gangs in El Salvador was greatly aided by law enforcement officials from the PNC (National Civil Police), officials from the U.S. Embassy, Oscar Bonilla of the Consejo Nacional para Seguridad Pública, and Miguel Cruz and Jeanette Aguilar, academics from UCA, the Jesuit University in San Salvador.

I would also like to thank Malcolm Klein, Karen Ito, Joseph Hooper, and Susan Cruz, who reviewed a rough draft of the manuscript and offered useful criticism. On this same note, I'd like to thank the nine reviewers whom Oxford solicited—anthropologists and criminologists whose suggestions for revisions were much appreciated:

- Connie M. Anderson, Hartwick College
- Christopher Fennell, University of Illinois, Urbana–Champaign
- Jodi Lane, University of Florida
- Christopher Melde, Michigan State University
- Phyllis Passariello, Centre College
- Dana Peterson, State University of New York at Albany
- Margaret Rance, Grossmont, City and Mesa Colleges
- Vicki T. Root-Wajda, College of DuPage
- Susan F. Sharp, University of Oklahoma

Needless to say, they take no blame for any errors or deficiencies in this final version. A big abrazo (hug) goes out to my extended family, Mom, Dad, David, Mike, Miriam, mis hijos, Sara "Po" Aguilar and Tonatiuh Perez-Ward, my step-kids, Randy and Jennifer Welty, and my wife and soulmate, Dr. B. Raven Lee, for their love and support during the long years of research and writing of this book. Randy Welty gets extra thanks for providing me with the title for this book, which my editor, Sherith Pankratz, preferred over the others I suggested. Sherith, Cari Heicklen, David Wharton and the other folks at Oxford also deserve my heartfelt thanks for expertly helping me navigate the publishing process. Penultimately, I would like to thank my friend and colleague Donna DeCesare for graciously allowing me to use a few of her artistic photographs for this book. Those interested in seeing more of her photographs can check out her website, http://www.destinyschildren.org, or her forthcoming book, *Unsettled* (University of Texas Press, in press), covering her work in Central America, the diaspora in Los Angeles, and youth involved in 18th Street and the Mara Salvatrucha gangs.

And last, but certainly not least, I would like to give a heartfelt thanks to all the homies who helped me understand a bit about their gangs and so generously shared their lives with me. I can never say enough about my deep debt to these young men and women, who, for whatever reasons, broke bread with me and allowed me into their heads and hearts.

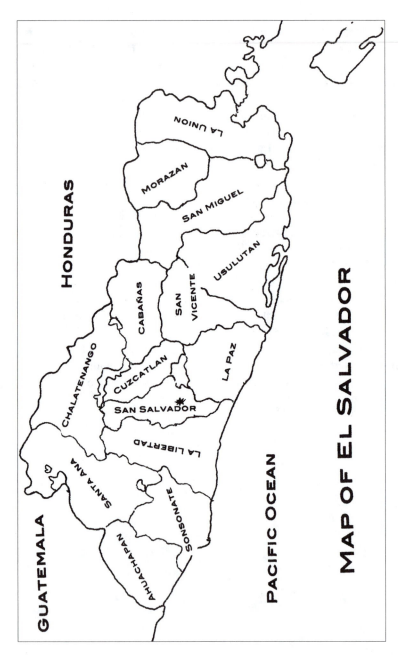

Map of El Salvador.

CHAPTER 1

War Trauma and the Cycle of Violence

Some things you see you can't forget.

— José Amaya

From an early age, José Amaya had become accustomed to seeing dead bodies in his homeland. He was born in 1978 and grew up on a farm in Morazán, an eastern province of El Salvador. During the Salvadoran civil war, which lasted from 1980 to 1992, this was an area controlled by the guerrilla insurgency and therefore one of the worst areas of conflict. The fighting was so bad that José's mother made his brother and him sleep under the bed at night for fear of stray bullets. And when the military arrived as part of the government's counterinsurgency campaign, his family had to flee into the hillside to avoid bombing and mortar attacks. José was familiar with the sounds of warfare—the helicopters, the bullets, and bombs—and was haunted by the sight of the dead bodies of soldiers or civilians in the aftermath. Over time he had become somewhat inured to seeing human corpses in various states of decomposition, which dulled his sense of shock and socialized him to the brutalizing power of violence. Although hardened by the war, he was nonetheless unprepared for the additional trauma of being left behind by his family when he was five years old. One by one, they began fleeing El Salvador and migrating to the United States. For seven years he was separated from his parents and lived with the uncertainty of never seeing them again.

Despite this hardship, when his parents had finally saved enough money to pay a *coyote*, or human trafficker, to smuggle José into the United States, it was *not* a move that he wanted to make. Only twelve years old at that time, José had no wish to be uprooted from his homeland, the only home he had known. But no one asked him his opinion. Bounced around from place to place, he now found himself in a foreign country that considered him an illegal alien, a fact of which he was acutely aware, having endured the hardships of undocumented travel across three borders. In addition to culture shock and the difficulties of learning a new language, José had to deal with the extreme emotional difficulties of reuniting with his parents after what seemed like to him a lifetime. José also became a target for teasing and beatings from his peers at school on the playgrounds and in the barrio.

Partly as a product of his childhood socialization to violence and the traumas of war, partly as a result of his feelings of abandonment, resentment, and alienation, and partly as a response to this new form of oppression, José chose to join a street gang in Los Angeles, one that represented his interests and his nationality. When José joined the street gang called *la Mara Salvatrucha*, he decided to go all out and became a hard-core member, active in serious crime and violence. For José, deciding to join a street gang was merely taking the next step on a long, twisted road that had been formed by a cycle of violence begun by the atrocities of war.

José was one of several hard-core gang members I got to know well over the course of eight and a half years of participant-observation fieldwork in Los Angeles. He represents a tiny microcosm of the world of street gangs, which have become a prevalent and sometimes glorified subculture within the United States. Gangs are an inextricable part of American life that reflects the darker aspects of the urban underbelly and the shadow side of the human psyche. Like a warped, convex mirror, they distort certain aspects of our body politic. Gangs exaggerate or amplify the negative characteristics of human aggression, violence, greed, distrust, exploitation, cynicism, and sexism, which are the by-products of impoverished lives in urban ghettos, where the dog-eat-dog survival street code thrives. *La vida loca*, or the crazy life—the Spanish term gang members often use for gang participation—is an adaptation to harsh environments, and the street gang ideology reflects that harshness.

Survival and a Surrogate Family

Youth like José join gangs as a means of survival and self-defense, as a means of constructing an identity of self-worth, and as a way to create a surrogate family. The fact that the gang family can be as dysfunctional as the biological one it replaces—if not much more so—reflects the lack of positive role models and resources available to marginalized youth. As anyone who has studied gang members can attest, adolescents join street gangs in response to hostile neighborhoods, dysfunctional schools, aggressive (bully) peers, lack of good-paying jobs, and absent, neglectful, or abusive parents or surrogate caretakers. Adolescents also join street gangs as a response to the poverty, racism, and discrimination they experience as the stigmatized and marginalized of society.

Street gangs are part of a deviant subculture, and therefore certain aspects of gang life tend to be shrouded in mystery, which leads to misinformation and misunderstanding. Because they live in a shadow of denial and deception, it is difficult to know what gang members do on a daily basis, much less what they really think and feel. Although partially based on reality, a distorted, stereotypical view of street gangs as highly organized, criminal organizations bent on murder and mayhem has been perpetuated by gang members and law enforcement officials tasked with the attempt to curb their criminal activities. Because it serves their different agendas, these actors have created a mythos about street gangs, which the media is all too eager to report. Despite the vast amount of academic research that has elucidated much of gang life and corrected this distorted view,[1] there is still a large gap between the reality of street gangs and the public perception of what it means to be a gang member.

When I began the research for this book in 1993, like most people I had been conditioned by news, film, and television to believe this stereotype of gang members as tough "street thugs" who enjoy terrorizing others and spend most of their time selling drugs, robbing people, or doing drive-by shootings. While this is partly true for a small minority of gang members, what I found over the course of eight and a half years of fieldwork was much more complex. Although the violence and criminality of gang life have been well documented, and it is well known that some gang members are heavily involved with using and dealing drugs, what is missing from media descriptions of gang life is a holistic perspective that places this behavior in context. The media is not concerned with the fact that there is a great deal of variability of deviance between street gangs and that no two gangs are alike. Likewise, it ignores the enormous variability between individual members and the fact that most gang members are not involved in serious crimes of violence.[2]

Furthermore, the popular conception of a gang career does not consider the fact that the vast majority of members eventually retires from their gang and moves on to a pro-social life.

For those who have had no direct contact with street gangs, what is least known about them is the flip side of their members' aggression and criminality: namely, the altruism or compassion expressed between homeboys and homegirls and the extent to which their gangs serve as adaptations to hostile environments. Street gangs thrive in the poorest neighborhoods in our urban communities. They are highly complex social organizations that serve multiple functions. Some gangs are like deviant social clubs providing camaraderie, excitement, and entertainment, which are an escape from boredom. Other gangs are like paramilitary organizations that provide protection and opportunity for economic gain and positive "gangster" status. Regardless of the type of gang, most youth join street gangs in their search for a particular quality of life, a sense of self-worth, and a sense of belonging to a group that cares about their welfare and survival.

When gang members speak about their group as a (surrogate) *family*, they are referring to this aspect of love and concern for one another. For many, the gang temporarily fills a vacuum of love and respect. Although veterans of the gang life admit that their members usually fall far short of this ideology of sharing and caring for "fellow homies," the fact remains that, for many members, the gang replaces the dysfunctional families and communities that have neglected, abused, or abandoned them in one way or another. Most gang members call their gang a family because, at some level of functionality, it serves the essential purposes of caring and survival. As the gang members intuitively know, the core of any family is *kinship*, and love and compassion are expected by-products.

In order for the street gang to survive, much less thrive, it must provide some degree of safety and comfort to its members, some sense of status, and some sense of belonging. Otherwise, these disenfranchised youth would seek out some alternative to the gangster life. Generally speaking, the degree to which a gang serves this function of family is the degree to which an individual is committed to a hard-core version of the gangster life. He or she sees the gang as an acceptable substitute for his or her biological or fictive kin. For the most hard-core of gang members, the gang is the primary family they know or care about. For them, in addition to the questions of survival and status, the heart of the matter with street gangs is the matter of the *heart*, in terms of solidarity and bonding. The gang as surrogate family gives a person a sense of meaning and purpose in life, however distorted, destructive, or dysfunctional. It took me many years of conversation and observation to understand the complexity of how this played out between gang members over many places and many years.

Beginning the Research

My mentor, Robert B. Edgerton, planted the seed for this study. As a University Professor of Psychiatry and Anthropology at UCLA, Edgerton taught his graduate students that the goal of anthropology is both theoretical and applied. It seeks to further our understanding of the human species and, more importantly, moves us to contribute to the practical solutions of its problems. In 1993, when I sought out Edgerton's advice for a new topic for research, he mentioned a recent local television news report on a street gang in Los Angeles that had been formed by Salvadoran immigrant youth. He suggested I check it out. Initially, I was reluctant because I knew next to nothing about street gangs, and I doubted that I could gain the acceptance needed to conduct intensive, long-term ethnographic research. The dangers involved also gave me pause.

Despite these initial reservations, I decided to investigate to see if this research was possible. This would not be my first venture into anthropological research. At that time that I began the study of MS, I had over fourteen years of experience doing ethnographic research in various urban settings, including four and a half years of participant-observation research on skid row in downtown Los Angeles. This research involved hanging out with and documenting the lives of homeless men suffering with schizophrenia or another chronic mental illness. Some of the participants in this study were also drug addicts—what in psychiatric parlance is called dual diagnosis. Prior to this study of adaptations to homelessness,[3] I had spent over twelve years conducting research in the Salvadoran community in Los Angeles for my doctoral dissertation. During this time, I had learned a good bit of Salvadoran slang, which would serve me well in my gang research.

My involvement with the Salvadoran community began in 1981, as a volunteer at El Rescate, Spanish for *The Rescue*. Founded earlier that year, El Rescate was a social service agency that provided food, shelter, and legal services for Central American refugees fleeing their war-ravaged countries. At that time, the offices of El Rescate were located in a rather dilapidated building on the corner of Union and Eighth streets, just west of downtown Los Angeles. I started work in their legal clinic, where each Wednesday night, tucked into a tiny, cramped, stuffy office with no windows, I would sit behind an old wooden desk piled high with files of legal documents and interview Salvadoran individuals or families to help them prepare depositions for their political asylum applications. Over the next seven years I interviewed over a hundred Central Americans, most of them Salvadorans, regarding their requests for asylum in the United States or Canada.

Having grown up in a sheltered, upper-middle-class white neighborhood in Highland Park, a suburb of Dallas, Texas, I was unprepared for the horrifying stories of these Salvadoran families. As a member of Amnesty International, I had read accounts of physical abuse in other countries, but I had never actually met anyone who had been severely beaten, shot, or tortured, or had family members "disappeared" by paramilitary death squads. At El Rescate I interviewed people who had been subjected to unimaginable torture by the military, the police, or security forces, including one man who had been electrocuted with wires attached to his testicles and inserted into his penis. His work for the poor as a union organizer in El Salvador was undeterred by the threats against his life, and as a result he eventually paid a heavy price. We became good friends and I fondly remember the many conversations over *pupusas*—grilled corn tortillas stuffed with cheese or meat—that we shared together over the years.

Inspired by their courage and tenacity, I decided to document these Salvadoran refugees' problems adapting to life in Los Angeles; the dissertation from this research was entitled "The Price of Fear."[4] In addition to formal interviews, I conducted participant-observation research, which included hanging out on street corners and visiting homes, churches, bakeries, and Salvadoran restaurants, called *pupusarias*. I also attended fiestas, barbeques in the parks, poetry readings, weddings, and *asambleas* or group meetings. I made several trips to INS (Immigration and Naturalization Service)[5] detention facilities for undocumented aliens in Hollywood and El Centro and accompanied Salvadorans to deportation hearings in U.S. Immigration Court, where I served as translator. I visited El Salvador twice during its civil war. In 1984 I visited two camps for people displaced by the war and attended "The First Human Rights Congress of El Salvador" (also, unfortunately, the last). I returned to El Salvador in 1989, driving a large Bobcat truck from Los Angeles as part of a caravan of vehicles carrying medical supplies from the United States, which was sponsored by the Robert F. Kennedy Center for Justice and Human Rights.

My first-hand knowledge of El Salvador, its culture and its people, convinced me that I might be able to get inside this street gang because the adolescents who created this gang were, figuratively speaking, the children of the refugees I had come to know so well. Through the generosity and trust of these Salvadorans in Los Angeles, I managed to make contact with members of Mara Salvatrucha and, over time, gain their acceptance to spend considerable time with them and document the complexity of their lives. The main themes of this ethnography are *survival*, *status*, and *the heart connection*. Survival is what brings these young homies to the gang, but it's the status and the heart connection that keeps them "banging." Ironically, it is the rupture of this heart connection that causes many hard-core gangsters to retire. While the vast majority of MS gang members, as in other street gangs, matures out of the gang and retires from gang activity, hard-core members of the gang are much more likely to suffer the other outcomes of gang participation: hospitalization, incarceration, deportation, or death. Before examining these issues with the hard, fast life of the gangster, I should provide some explanation as to how the study was conducted.

Methodology

As one might imagine, you don't walk up to a member of an LA street gang and say, "Hi, my name is Tomás. I am an anthropologist and I'd like to study your gang." It takes a much subtler approach. To initiate my research on this gang, I first got in touch with my Salvadoran friends and acquaintances to see what they knew about Mara Salvatrucha. I was quite surprised to find that many of these folks not only were familiar with the gang but had friends or relatives who were active members. I was even more surprised to discover that two friends I had known for over seven years were retired members of MS. These Salvadoran friends and acquaintances generously served as my initial inroad to the gang. They arranged for me to meet active gang members, either in their homes or at local restaurants.

A second source of contacts was established through Mike O'Connor, a freelance journalist who had done a five-part series on street gangs for KCBS-TV in Los Angeles, including the report that Edgerton had seen on MS. O'Connor, a seasoned reporter and delightful raconteur, had covered the civil war in El Salvador from 1983 to 1987. He told me what he knew about the gang and suggested I contact Chuck Coleman, who lived in Los Angeles. Coleman, a tall, lanky, very good-natured Native American from Oklahoma, taught for the LA Unified School District and served as director and counselor for a program that he developed, called "Campsite." The program involved daylong or weekend retreats, with workshops to promote tolerance among high school students.

Through his work, Coleman had come to know some Salvadoran gang members and had unofficially adopted them. He encouraged them to go to school and provided them with hot meals and transportation to job interviews or probation meetings, and they used his apartment as a crash pad, where they could shower, sleep for a night or two, and wash their clothes. It was an unusual arrangement to say the least. But Chuck is a big-hearted man and, seeing a need, he opened up his place as a refuge to these troubled kids. I contacted Coleman and explained my research interest to him over lunch at a Denny's restaurant in Hollywood. He arranged for me to meet with five gang members—two girls and three boys—in his small one-bedroom apartment. It is sobering to reflect back on that night and think about the lost potential of these youth. Only one of the five survived the gang relatively intact. Two of the gang members were shot and killed, one became addicted to crack cocaine but eventually broke the habit, and another ended up serving a life-term in prison without the possibility of parole.

Through these two avenues of contact, I began to visit the hangouts of the gang members and attempt to interview them. Socio-cultural anthropologists usually spend a great deal of time—from a year to several decades—with a small group of people in order to study as many possible aspects of their lives. The end result of this holistic, qualitative, longitudinal research is an ethnographic article or monograph, which is a description of the culture, or an aspect of the culture of the group.[6] The primary method for collecting data among ethnographers is called *participant-observation*, developed by anthropology but no longer unique to the field. It is extremely labor intensive and often requires years of living with people, speaking their language, making observations, and participating in a variety of activities from elaborate rituals to quotidian tasks. The advantage of this strategy is that it produces unexpected discoveries that could not be made with other techniques, mainly as a result of the rapport built between the ethnographer and the participants in the study. The main disadvantage of this technique is that it requires a great deal of time and extreme patience and persistence. In some cases, like this, it also requires some degree of intestinal fortitude.

Patience and persistence are requisites for any ethnography, but especially when the people one wants to study are unwilling or uncooperative participants. Members of street gangs, as one might imagine, are extremely suspicious of outsiders, and for very good reasons. An illustrative example of this suspicion was the reception I got from one of the homeboys on a hot summer night in 1993, at the beginning of my research. Risky,[7] a short, muscular, bald-headed member of the MS gang, approached me as I was interviewing a couple of homegirls in a local hangout. Risky walked up to me and, in a threatening tone of voice, asked what I was doing in *his* barrio. I told him that I was an anthropologist and was doing an investigation of his gang. In heavily accented English, Risky replied, "That's real '*spensive*."

"Why?" I asked.

"The information you want is not a confidence; it's like secrecy," he said. "We can't tell nobody. Just people who belong to the neighborhood [meaning the gang] can know about it."

"Why is that?" I asked.

"Because it's something like—" he paused, somewhat annoyed, "How can I explain to you? It's like, let's say you do something bad and you and God are the only ones who know. You ain't gonna tell somebody else. You have to keep it a secret."

"I'm not asking anyone for secrets," I lied. "I just want to find out what makes you tick."

Through the course of our conversation, Risky warmed to me, and I managed to convince him that I meant no harm to anyone. I was surprised that he not only allowed me to continue interviewing the female members of his clique, he also shared his own story with me. Would that it had all been this easy. Given the realistic suspicions of the gang members regarding my motives, it took a little over a year to get MS gang members from various cliques, or subgroups, to fully accept me. It took another seven and a half years to get the data I needed to complete the main phase of this fieldwork in Los Angeles.

Formal ethnographic research began in 1993 and ended in 2001, but a second phase of the study began in 2001 and concluded in 2011. This second, much less intensive phase involved informal contacts with gang members in four settings: Los Angeles County, California state prisons, Salvadoran prisons, and the homes of retired gang members in El Salvador. Beginning in 2005, and continuing through 2011, I made short, periodic visits to El Salvador to visit gang members I knew who had been deported from Los Angeles and to meet indigenous members of the gang. Most of these individuals were from MS, but a few were from other LA gangs, notably the 18th Street gang. These two gangs represent the largest street gangs in El Salvador, both of which are imports from the United States.

During these visits I met and interviewed both active and inactive or retired gang members in restaurants, homes, or prison. For example, Ciudad Barrios, which I visited in 2009, contains some 2,000 inmates, all of whom are members of MS. In addition, in 2007 I served as a consultant for Professor Cheryl Maxson, a sociologist at the University of California, Riverside, on a study of MS in the Washington, DC, area, Los Angeles, and El Salvador.[8] In El Salvador, we interviewed gang members, academics, and police from the National Civil Police force, and INTERPOL. In Washington, DC, we interviewed gang members, social workers, and members of the FBI MS gang task force.

At the beginning of my research in 1993, the gang members would often question why an old *gringo* would want to spend so much time hanging out with them, pestering them with annoying questions. None of these youth had ever heard of anthropology, and it took them some time to figure out my role as an ethnographer. A few of them considered me to be some variant of a priest, or social worker, or journalist. Others thought I was a *wannabe*—someone who flirts with joining a gang—and a few suspected that I was a dirty old man looking to party with homegirls. Initially, most of the gang members suspected that I was an undercover cop, or a narcotics officer. Later, I was accused of being a member of the FBI. At that time, I was not aware that the FBI had formed an MS gang task force, and I laughed and said, "Next, you're going to accuse me of being a CIA agent!" Their doubts as to my authenticity were understandable, however. As a white, male anthropologist, twice their age, wearing ridiculously large round glasses and a Yankees baseball cap, I cut a strange figure in the barrio.

Not all of the gang members approved of me hanging out in their neighborhoods. Some of them gave me a wide berth and refused to talk with me. And a few threatened me in an attempt to get me to go away. Despite these obstacles, after a little over a year, I managed to establish good rapport with many of the core gang members and became close to a few hard-core members. Looking back, I see several reasons why I was able to gain this particular level of trust and acceptance. At our initial contact, I had the backing of Salvadorans they knew well and who had known me for years and could vouch for my character. Nonetheless, some of the gang members launched an investigation to see if what I was telling them about being an anthropology professor at USC was true. I didn't find out about this until many years later, when a homeboy confided to me that they had checked out my story, including making a call to the university. "Had you told us a lie," he said with a wink, "You could have kissed your ass good-bye."

Confidentiality

Promising the gang members complete confidentiality also probably helped toward building trust. At times they tested this principle, for example, by asking me what some other homeboy had said or done. I always deflected such questions, saying, "You know I don't talk about that stuff. And anything you do or tell me will also be completely confidential." The area where this paid the most dividends was the secrets I kept about the sexual dalliances of both the homeboys and homegirls, each of whom claimed the others were less faithful. In addition, in order not to raise their suspicions and so that I would never have to testify against them in court, I never asked gang members about specific crimes they had committed, but generalized my questions in the abstract—e.g., "How does a *jale*⁹ go down?"

If anyone started to confide specific information to me, I'd interrupt and tell them to leave out names, dates, and places. I explained to the gang members that I wanted to insulate myself from such knowledge not only for their protection, but also for my own. Although it only happened a couple of times over the course of fieldwork, if gang members were going to discuss the commission of a crime, like a robbery, I excused myself from the conversation. And the few times that I was invited to participate in such crimes, I respectfully declined.

Regarding noncriminal behavior and activities, I asked them every-thing I could think to ask. I questioned them about their pasts, about their current relationships, and about their hopes for the future. Over ninety percent of these conversations were in Spanish, and it greatly helped that I was familiar with Salvadoran slang expressions. When I told them, "Tengo dos cipotes," using the Salvadoran slang for children, their faces lit up and they sometimes laughed, delighted that this old gringo knew something about their language and culture. However, the main reason I think I gained their trust was because of my character and the way I showed them respect. One can't just talk the talk; one must also walk the walk. I visited them in hospitals and jails, attended their funerals, brought food and drink to their parties, baked cakes for their birthdays, and tutored them in math and English.

During the initial phase of research, which lasted about a year and a half, fieldwork consisted of hanging out, getting to know them, and allowing them to get to know me. I never took notes in front of them, but wrote notes when I returned home from the field. I also developed strategies for taking notes in the field. For example, I would take bath-room breaks, where I would jot down notes, which I would flesh out later that night or the next morning. After gaining their trust, I began collecting formal life histories, some of which I recorded, and then erased the tapes after writing up fieldnotes. I also did formal interviews regarding specific topics, such as gang initiation, reasons for joining, clique formation and structure, drug use, dating, fighting the enemy, unwritten rules of the gang, and gang taboos. These fieldnotes were destroyed after analysis in order to protect their identities.

During this initial stage, I conducted informal interviews with approximately eighty MS gang members from eight different cliques, or subsets of the gang. I managed to get interviews with a wide variety of gang members in order to get a sense of the diversity within the gang as a whole, within Los Angeles. Street gang members can be composed into five basic types of members or recruits: (1) *wannabes*, or those who are not yet members but are flirting with becoming, (2) *peripheral*, or those who are accepted members of the gang but are not active in crime and violence and therefore "peripheral" to gang activities, (3) *core* members, or those who are somewhat active, but still have lives outside the gang, (4) *hard-core* members, or those who dedicate their lives entirely to the gang and are the most involved in crime and violence, and (5) *veterans*, or those who were active but are now retired, or are still active in the gang's activities, and usually have respect within the gang. The majority of my initial interviews were with core and hard-core members of MS, but I also interviewed several wannabes, peripheral members, and veterans of the gang in order to understand their different roles and perspectives.

After completing interviews with these gang members, I decided to focus my attention on the hard-core members of the gang. The reason for this was simple: although they are a small minority of the gang, approximately 5 percent of active members, they are the ones who cause most of the damage and create the reputation of the gang as criminally violent. At this point in the research, I had established excellent rapport with a dozen hard-core members of MS, and so I spent the next seven years following and formally documenting their lives.

When I began the research for this book in 1993, my objectives were open-ended and ill defined, in order to allow me to investigate the broadest range of possible interests. Over time, the theoretical goals of this research evolved into three main ones, each of which is covered in this book:

1. To discover the origin of MS and understand why these particular youth had joined the gang
2. To observe how gang members changed over time as they matured into adulthood
3. To document the career trajectories of hard-core gang members, which averaged about ten years, with a range of six years to life[10]

The overarching goal of this research was to get into the heads and hearts of these Salvadoran immigrants, to understand the motives for their behaviors, and to document their complexity of their gangster lives.

Other Methodological Issues

As I began the research for this book, various methodological issues presented themselves. One of these concerned gender dynamics within the street gang. During the initial stages of research, I made a considered attempt to interview and document both male and female members of the gang. However, I noticed that the more time I spent with female gang members—including taking them to nightclubs—the more the male members of the gang suspected that I was an old man on the make, i.e., someone looking to date impressionable young girls. I eventually realized that if I were going to get full trust and access to the hard-core male members of the gang, I would have to curtail my association with their female counterparts. Jealousy runs rampant within gangs, as it does within society. Fortunately, it was an accommodation that was easy to make, for I had already established enough rapport with homegirls, so that I could follow up with interviews and observations at a latter date. My intuition was correct, and severely curtailing my interactions with homegirls had the intended effect of instilling the homeboys' trust.

Another important methodological concern involved the nature of participant-observation. Given the criminal and violent activities of hard-core gang members, accommodations had to be made. Obviously, I was not going to, as the gangsters called it, *put in work* for the gang— selling drugs, robbing people, or doing drive-by shootings against enemy gang members. It seems more than a bit strange to me now that over the course of research, gang members invited me to participate in all these activities. These invitations were either a test of my loyalties or a testament to their trust in me, or both. Although a few gang members jokingly made me an honorary member of their clique during one night of party-hopping and drunken debauchery, I decided from the start not to join their gang and I told them so. In addition to wanting to preserve my body and my sanity, I thought joining the gang would compromise my role as an outside observer, to say nothing of the ethical issues. For these reasons, I explained to the gang members that I would break no laws, but that I would not judge them for their actions.

An unintended consequence of this wise decision not to join the gang was the degree of trust I gained from these hard-core gang members. As an outsider, they were able to confide intimate thoughts and feelings to me that they wouldn't have, had I been a member of their gang. The most obvious example of this was the taboo that one should never complain about the gang or its activities, which is a sign of the weakness of disloyalty. Had I been a member, I doubt they would have told me about their disillusionment with their fellow gang members and the extent to which their gang failed to meet their initial, rather exalted expectations. Because the story of my relationship with these gang members, and the establishment of our mutual behavioral boundaries, is quite complex, I decided to address them in a subsequent work, tentatively entitled *Kickin' It—Further Reflections on Gangsters Without Borders*.

The principal challenge of the research and writing of this book was maintaining strict and complete confidentiality. How does one relate things that have been told in strictest confidence without betraying hard-won trust? I wanted to avoid writing anything that would embarrass or endanger any of the gang members, as well as avoiding writing anything that would incur their wrath—which would put the academic motto "publish or perish" in quite a different light. It was not simply a matter of giving these hard-core gang members pseudonyms. This would have sufficiently hidden their identities from the public, but it would not have prevented the gang members from easily recognizing themselves and each other by their words and deeds.

After much reflection, I came up with the compromise of creating composite characters. If I thoroughly mixed up the gang members' backgrounds and personality traits with what they said and did, their identities would be suitably disguised and unrecognizable to all. There is precedent for this practice in the gang literature. Dale Kramer and Madeline Karr use composites to tell the stories of three teenage boys in a New York gang, entitled *Teenage Gangs: The Inside Story of One of America's Gravest Perils*.[11] Also, Malcolm Klein uses composites in his book about law enforcement officials on gang detail, which masterfully combines years of interviews, conversations, and courtroom contacts with "gang cops" to create a composite figure of Paco Domingo.[12]

With these precedents, I decided to use five composite characters in order to convey the variety of personalities within the gang and to show how hard-core gang members interact with one another. The main characters in this book are composites based on the twelve hard-core gang members that I got to know quite well. However, their quotes, events, and personality traits are combined and mixed in order to render them completely anonymous. Nonetheless, it should be noted that everything that is attributed to one of these composite characters happened to one of these dozen hard-core gang members. For example—though hard to believe—the numerous injuries inflicted on the gang member I call "Trouble" was the actual litany of injuries suffered by one of these hard-core gangsters. There is one exception to this rule. I have taken the liberty to add a few quotes from other gang members I met from eleven different cliques or subsets of the gang because they eloquently expressed a sentiment felt by others. It should also be noted that quotes are translated from the Spanish and are not verbatim. While I am not completely comfortable with this compromise of using composite characters, I felt that it was the only way I could protect their identities and yet write about things they confessed to me in strictest confidence, usually inebriated. Because they trusted me with their innermost secrets, I made a vow to completely protect their identities.

A word should be said about the importance of naming. What you call something reflects much about its meaning. Words not only have denotations, but also multiple connotations. The terms "gang member," "gangster," and "homie" have different definitions and meanings. The reader will notice that I intentionally alternate my use of the terms "gang member," "gangster," "homeboy," "homegirl," and "homie" in order to convey the shifting connotations of meaning about one particular individual's identity. While the term "gang member" is fairly neutral, "gangster" reflects a criminal mentality, and "homie" indicates a feeling of emotional warmth and connection. Hard-core members of street gangs share all these of these shifting identities.

This ethnography of MS gang members is unique, as it is the first intensive long-term study of a small sample of hard-core gang members from the time they joined their gang until after they retired, died, or became incarcerated or incapacitated. All of these MS gang members are first-generation immigrants, meaning that they were born and grew up in El Salvador during the Civil War. Each of them is a second- or third-generation member of the gang, meaning that they joined MS in the early 1990s, after the gang had already become firmly established in Los Angeles and other cities in the United States. To the best of my knowledge, they are highly representative of hard-core members of this gang. However, it should be kept in mind that these hard-core members comprise but a small portion (5–10 percent) of all members of this gang, which includes *peripheral, core,* and *veteran* members. These hard-core members represent a small but very important part of the gang. They are the ones who commit most of the serious crimes and violence and established the gang's notorious reputation.

Hard-core gang members differ from their counterparts both in terms of their level of activity and their dedication to the gang. Hard-core members are much more active in the gang life, and they are much more committed to the gangster ideology. They live and breathe the gangster life, and embrace it completely. They are the ones who cause the most trouble, commit the most crimes, and are most invested in their gangster identity. As a result, they are more likely than peripheral or core members to suffer the consequences of gang life, including permanent disability, life in prison, deportation, and death. I chose to focus my research on hard-core gang members because, although they represent a small minority of gang members, they are the ones who garner the most attention and cause the most damage to society and themselves. They are also the ones who perpetuate the gangster ideology, promote the gangster life, and serve as role models for other rebellious, disenfranchised youth in these impoverished neighborhoods.

Data gathered from these hard-core members was augmented by contacts with over 150 gang members from MS, 18th Street, and other smaller gangs that Salvadorans had joined over the years, since the early 1980s. This ethnography reveals the complex processual dynamics of gang participation as well as the contradictory thoughts and feelings of its members as they pass through the stages of their gang careers. It shows how and why gang members change over time and place. It explores their reasons for joining the gang, their activities—including nongang activities—and the consequences of their gang participation. And it explains the gradual process of their retreat from the gangster life and their reasons for becoming *calmado*, or retired.

Chapter Summaries

Chapter Two, The Beauty and the Horror, documents the memories these youth have of their homeland and their journey to the United States. It provides the context or the environment and lived experience of these Salvadoran youth. As the subtitle suggests, their memories of El Salvador are a strange mix of comfort and terror. In their recollections, the beauty of their homeland served as a stark backdrop to the trauma caused by the civil war. Their fond memories of this tropical paradise are clouded by the atrocities they witnessed growing up there. For these youth, seeing dead, decapitated bodies had a lasting impact, coloring and distorting their perceptions. It caused them to have a fatalistic view of the world, and it heavily influenced their decision to join a street gang. For these reasons, MS can be seen as a by-product of the civil war in El Salvador. The chapter also examines the psychological impact of harsh discipline on these youth, and the long years of separation from their parents, before being brought to the United States, illegally, and against their will.

Chapter Three, Hard Times—Welcome to America, describes the difficulties these immigrant youth had adjusting to their new home. First among these difficulties was the need to mend the bonds of trust with their parents that had been frayed by so many years apart. After so many years of separation, reunification for them was a strange, confusing experience, marked by anxiety and frustration. These immigrant youth also had to learn English, a language they had never spoken, and one that seemed difficult and illogical to them. Making their successful transition into the American mainstream increasingly difficult, however, was the fact that they were being teased and beaten up by bullies at school and their neighborhoods. The chapter examines the anatomy of the decision to join a street gang from the perspectives of these undocumented immigrant youth. The subsection, La Gloria Brincada—Welcome to the Barrio, describes the typical ceremony for MS initiates, a *Jump In*, which involves a physical beating by fellow members for a prescribed amount of time. This beating is meant to prepare the initiate for harder times to come.

The origins and transformation of Mara Salvatrucha as a stoner gang into a traditional street gang are explored in Chapter Four, From Prey to Predators. MS serves as one example of how street gangs are formed and transformed. All street gangs are adaptations to particularly harsh environments, and MS is no different. Although it began as a group devoted to smoking marijuana and listening to heavy metal music, it quickly evolved into a cholo-style street gang in response to changing circumstances. When MS became a traditional street gang, its members thought of it as a self-defense organization devoted to protecting its members from attacks by other street gang members. However, it quickly evolved into a predatory gang, with the accompanying change in objectives: seeking further wealth, power, and status. A need for survival and protection caused this street gang to transform, but greed is what caused it to become predatory in nature.

Chapter Four also examines the question of leadership, which plays an important role in arrests, convictions, and sentencing. Unlike the stereotypical view of street gangs as hierarchical organizations with clear leaders at the top, MS is a complicated group in which leadership is diffused within the gang in a form I call *democratic anarchy*. This form evolved as a result of the defiant personalities and rebellious natures of its members. Each of these delinquent youth had a deep distrust of authority and cherished the notion of equality. Part of the reason why MS is disorganized is because most of its members are extremely stubborn and extremely rebellious in the face of any authority. Despite this obstacle, some MS gang members with more clout in the gang attempt to lead the gang in one direction or another. This often leads to internal conflicts. Chapter Four also examines the nature of boredom in street gang life. Gang life, like warfare, is often extremely boring, punctuated by moments of excitement, when committing crimes or fighting. Ironically, boredom is one of the major reasons for joining a gang.

Chapter Five, "Girls" in Gangs—On the Margins of Masculinity, explores the complex relationships between males and females in street gangs, which typically encompass feelings of amorous affection, love, jealousy, distrust, and a fatalistic sense of impermanence. For the most part, street gangs are patriarchal, sexist organizations, dominated by an ethos of *machismo*. The only way for "girls" to get respect within a street gang is to imitate the "guys." For this reason, hard-core female gang members doubly violate societal norms: they not only break the law, they break the norms for their gender. The chapter describes the different rules that apply to female gang members, including the sexual double standard, the "Catch-22" of respect within the gang, and the limitations imposed by pregnancy. The chapter also examines in detail the decision of one MS homegirl to join the gang and the natural consequences of her decision. MS is illustrative in its distrust of women, a reflection of street gang ideology. A common tattoo worn by MS homeboys is "trust no bitch." Given this prejudice against women, homegirls must work harder than homeboys in gaining the trust of individual gang members and the gang as a whole. The chapter concludes with an examination of female gang members' crucial and unacknowledged essential role as *caretakers*.

Chapter Six, Live Fast, Die Young, explores the attractions of street gangs as warrior societies and elucidates the hardships of the gang life, including inter- and intragang fighting, hospitalization, and death by drive-by shootings or suicide. Street gangs illustrate the violent natures of some humans, particularly males of the species.[13] We tend to ignore the fact that violence is adaptive in many respects. Street gangs represent a small subset of human violence as a means of survival and progress. Warfare and fighting are endemic to street gangs because it is the main way that its members gain respect. A "them versus us" perspective characterizes the gangster mentality. Gangs thrive on the existence of "enemies," but the notion of an enemy can change completely given a change in context. Chapter Six also examines the fatalistic, suicidal nature of gang warfare, as well as infighting within street gangs, something the gang members downplay or deny because it is counterproductive to the existence and reputation of their gang. The chapter also includes a very brief analysis of the nature of MS violence throughout the United States and the reasons for the gang's notorious reputation as "The World's Most Dangerous Gang."

Chapter Seven, Becoming Calmado, examines the gang as surrogate family, a *matter of the heart*. Street gangs tend to flourish in harsh environments, where there is a lack of protection and caring. Although the gang is a highly dysfunctional family, the group serves many of the functions of a family, such as shelter, safety, love, and affection. While most gang members mature out of their gangs within a few years, large gangs like MS have hard-core members who are much more active and for much longer. Those most dedicated to the gang usually experience the inevitable process of disillusionment with their gang and, if given the opportunity, leave it behind. The subsection Afterlives describes the process of retirement from the gang, what the gang members call becoming *calmado*. This process can take anywhere from several months for peripheral members to decades for some hard-core gangsters. The chapter examines the possible outcomes of gang membership from the points of view of these five composite characters. The chapter ends on a hopeful note that given enough time, most gang members will mature out of their gang life and lead pro-social lives, and we can do much to speed up this process.

Chapter Eight, Epilogue, looks at possible solutions to the problems caused by street gangs. Because the "gang problem" is complex, the solutions to the problem must also be complex and multifaceted. Fortunately, much can be done to help gang members retire from the gang life earlier, and much can be done to give them opportunities to lead pro-social lives.

Notes

1. Cf. Decker, Scott H., and Van Winkle, Barrik. The history of gangs. In *The Modern Gang Reader*, 3d ed., Los Angeles: Roxbury Publishing Company, 2006, pp. 14–19.
2. Cf. Klein, Malcolm. 2005. *Gang Cops: The Words and Ways of Paco Domingo*. Walnut Creek, CA: Altamira Press.

3. Cf. Koegel, P. 1992.Through a different lens: An anthropological perspective on homelessness and mental illness. *Culture, Medicine and Psychiatry* 16: 1–27.

4. Cf. chapter on Central American community in Diego Vigil's *A Rainbow of Gangs*, University of Texas Press, 2005, which cites much of this material.

5. The federal agency is now called ICE (Immigration Control and Enforcement), under the Department of Homeland Security.

6. The term "ethnography" literally means "writing about culture." See, for example, Lewis, S. J. and Russel, A. J. 2011. Being embedded: A way forward for ethnographic research. *Ethnography* 12, (3): 398–416; Brookman, F., Copes, H., and Hochstetler, A. 2011. Street codes as formula stories: How inmates recount violence. *Journal of Contemporary Ethnography* 40, (4): 397–424.

7. All of the nicknames in this ethnography are pseudonyms.

8. Cf. Cheryl Maxson. 2009. Similar but unique: The "peculiar" case of the Mara Salvatrucha (MS-13), April 16, Youth Violence Prevention Conference, UMSL.

9. *Jale* is a slang term that MS gang members use for a "drive-by shooting."

10. This is, of course, complicated by the fact that street gang "careers" are not always clearly demarcated: because many gang members gradually "fade out" of their gang, there can be a great deal of ambiguity regarding whether or not one is an "ex-gang member." This is discussed in the last chapter.

11. 1953. New York: Henry, Holt, and Company.

12. Klein, Malcolm. 2005. *Gang Cops: The Words and Ways of Paco Domingo.* Altamira Press.

13. Cf. Wrangham, Richard, and Peterson, Dale. 2002. *Demonic Males: The Origins of Human Violence.* New York: Mariner Press.

CHAPTER 2

The Beauty and the Horror— Memories of El Salvador

Some things you see you can't forget. One day, a young woman from our barrio disappeared. A week later, some washerwomen found the decapitated body of a pregnant woman in a ravine near the river. These women went and asked the young woman's mother if she could identify her daughter's body, and took her to the place. When she saw the headless, bloated body, the mother replied, "That can't be my daughter, she wasn't pregnant." But when they lifted up the dress of the corpse they made a horrible discovery. She wasn't pregnant; the death squad had slit open her belly and jammed her head inside.

—JOSÉ AMAYA

Fourteen years later and thousands of miles from home, as he lay in a pool of his own warm blood, five bullets from an Uzi submachine gun having ripped holes in his flesh, José would vaguely recall that distant afternoon in Morazán, when his grandmother, Josephina, his mother, Lupe, his father, Elfago, his sisters, Marta and Lizabeth, and his brother, Juan, had evacuated their two-room hut minutes before the mortars shook the ground of the hillsides, announcing the arrival of government troops, who were launching another counterinsurgency campaign in the countryside in order to "drain the sea" to catch some rebels. What he remembers most, besides the terrifying fear, is the deafening sound of the mortars that sent shock waves through the ground. At that time, José was only four years old, much too young to know why Huey helicopters would strafe his home, or why the military considered his campesino father part of some subversive network of support for guerrillas fighting to overthrow the government. In truth, Elfago, like most of his poor peasant kindred, had been straddling the political fence as best he could, with his fragile hope of surviving the bloody civil war that had torn apart his country for the past two years.

The year was 1982, two years into the Salvadoran civil war that would last another ten years, cost the lives of over 75,000 people, including those tortured or "disappeared" by government security forces. The war also caused the forced relocation or displacement of over a million Salvadoreños, within their homeland and living as refugees in countries as far-flung and disparate as Canada, Australia, and France.[1] This military attack on José's village in Morazán was but a very small part of the government's counterinsurgency plan.[2] It was the first of three such raids, which would eventually force José's family to permanently leave their home. These flights are called *guindas*, and they were the only way to survive for those, like José and his family, who lived in one of the many zones of conflict during the civil war.

The twisted dirt road that led José from his country farm in the easternmost state of Morazán to a Latino barrio of Los Angeles, the City of the Angels, was circular in terms of violence. Having narrowly escaped the ravages of war in El Salvador, José was thrown into another battle, which was fought on the city streets of southern California. Outwardly, José had become inured to the atrocities he witnessed in his homeland and therefore was well prepared, or emotionally steeled at least, to deal with the gang battles he would encounter in LA. The seven years he lived in El Salvador without his parents, who fled to the United States, leaving him behind with his grandmother and older sisters, had also psychologically toughened him up. As the youngest member of the family, he would be the last to be smuggled into this country, a fate he would accept like all his subsequent fates, with a shrug of resignation.

José learned to deal with pain of all sorts, which would serve him well in his gang life. During his gang career, José was shot six times—in the leg, the back, the hand, and twice in the head—stabbed thirteen times, and severely beaten twice, once with a lead pipe, and once with a baseball bat. Having been attacked and injured so many times, atypical even for a hard-core member of MS, José's fellow homeboys considered him a cat with nine lives. José was a survivor, and it was partly for survival that he joined this gang of Salvadoran immigrant youth. He chose Trouble as his *placaso*, or gang nickname, not because it followed him like a dark shadow, but because he embraced and developed a taste for it. His broad shoulders, chiseled tattooed arms, and quick feet always seemed to be moving José toward opportunities toward fighting. His nickname did more than portray an image he wished to promote—it became a self-fulfilling prophecy. "I don't have to look for trouble," he told me with great bravado, "I *am* Trouble!"

Trouble, like the Salvadoran youth who created his gang, was a product of the civil war in El Salvador. His memories of his childhood are a strange mix of the horrors of the war[3] and the beauty of his country and its culture. He and his compatriots recognize that although, as the saying goes, poverty and repression were as common in El Salvador as beans and tortillas, their homeland also gave them their language, their *pupusas*,[4] their taste in music, and their love of dance. Coexisting with their memories of death and destruction are their memories of El Salvador's beautiful landscape, its endless variety of tropical fruits, its long sandy beaches, and the warm waters of its Pacific Ocean.[5] "The water is so warm," Trouble told me, "When you're in it, you can take a piss and not feel the difference."

El Salvador is divided into fourteen states, or what they call departments. During the civil war, which lasted from 1980 to 1992, Salvadorans shared a sardonic joke about their country's predicament. "Do you know why there are only 12 departments in El Salvador? Because in our country there is no *peace* or *unity*." The punch line was morbidly funny only to Salvadorans and anyone else who knew that the names of two of their departments are *La Paz* and *La Union*—peace and unity. And it goes without saying that during their civil war, their homeland lacked both.

The most densely populated of the five republics of Central America, El Salvador is the smallest, and thus its nickname, *El Pulgarcito*, or the tiny thumb. Sandwiched between Guatemala to the north and Honduras to the east, El Salvador has approximately 7 million people squeezed within its borders. At the time of the war the population hovered closer to 5 million. The country is about the size of the state of Massachusetts, or approximately 8,000 square miles, much of which is volcanic in nature and uninhabitable. With 230 miles of coastline along the Pacific Ocean, El Salvador was a former tourist spot for surfers, with some of the longest uninterrupted beaches in the world, whose colored sands range from jet black to purest white. Its tropical climate affords year-round enjoyment of its environs. Trouble affectionately remembers his family's trips to the beach. "We bought fish, fresh from the ocean," he recalled. "And the vendors would cook it

FIGURE 2.1 La Libertad, El Salvador, 2010. A homeboy serves up freshly caught oysters. Copyright © T. W. Ward, 2011.

for us right there on the shore. The water was warm and the sand was hot." He paused for a second, and then laughed, "Almost as hot as the girls in their string bikinis!"

Cuscatlán, Land of Riches

El Salvador seems like a tropical paradise in Trouble's recollections of his early childhood, before he became fully conscious of the civil war. Appropriately, the indigenous name for El Salvador is Cuscatlán, which means land of riches. This feeling is conveyed in a poem written by Joker, a close friend of Trouble and a fellow gang member. Tall, skinny, and wiry, Joker, who grew up in Ahauchapán, in the western part of El Salvador, was a teaser, full of good spirits, and thus his nickname. As part of the research for this book, I asked—or more accurately, pleaded, cajoled and bribed—gang members to write poems about their lives. This poem relates Joker's feelings toward his hometown.

Mi Pueblito	My Little Town

Tranquilo pueblito,
    mi Atiquizaya
	Peaceful little town,
	    my Atiquizaya

bello, habitado de arboles
    y ríos de
	beautiful, inhabited with
	    trees and rivers

aguas frias (San Lorenzo)	with the cool waters of San Lorenzo
y Aguas Calientes	and the hot waters of Aguas Calientes,
corrientes de los volcanes	the currents of volcanoes,
donde he pasado tantos gratos	where I spent so many wonderful
momentos, viendo caller el sol.	moments, watching the sun go down.
Nunca quería salir	I never wanted to leave.
siempre pensaba llegar a mi vejez	I always thought I would grow old
allá, con toda mi familia	there, with my family,
pero por destino	but destiny had other plans
y estoy aquí entre personas	and here I am, among strangers,
con una cultura diferente	with a different culture,
donde no saben de mi pueblito	where they don't know about
tan chiquito,	my little town, which is so small,
tan bello.	and so pretty.
	—Joker

The names San Lorenzo and Aguas Calientes (Hot Waters) refer to rivers near Atiquizaya, where Joker would go with his friends and family to swim and play. The waters of Aguas Calientes are warmed by one of El Salvador's fourteen volcanoes. Izalco, the most famous of these volcanoes, was continually active until 1957 and was called the lighthouse of the Pacific by seamen who piloted their ships by the fire and white-hot rocks it spewed continuously for almost 200 years.[6]

Izalco and the other volcanoes make up two extensive mountain ranges that cover El Salvador from end to end. It would be only a slight exaggeration to say that all Salvadorans have a volcano in their backyard, lending an air of uncertainty to their lives. Joker echoed with this sentiment, saying, "It's been a long time since a volcano erupted in El Salvador. But nobody knows when the next one will blow."

Flores del Volcán	**Flowers from the Volcano**
Catorce volcanes se levantan	Fourteen volcanoes rise
en mi país memoria	in my remembered country ...
catorce volcanes de follaje	fourteen volcanoes of leaves
y piedra	and stone
donde nubes extrañas	where strange clouds
se detienen	linger ...
Quién dijo que era verde	Who said my country
mi país?	was green?
es más rojo	It is more red,
es más gris	more gray,
es más violente	more violent.
el Izalco que ruge	Izalco roars
exigiendo más vidas	demanding more lives.

—Claribel Alegría[7]

The last eruption of Izalco, in 1932, coincided with a rebellion of the peasantry in the western region of El Salvador. Like its volcanoes, the history of El Salvador is one of smoldering government oppression and the intermittent eruptions of peasant revolts. Since the earliest days of the Spanish conquistadors, who invaded in 1524, El Salvador has experienced one bloody rebellion after another. It took fifteen years for the Spanish to subdue the indigenous population because Cuscatlán was made up of small independent city-states. Each of these city-states had to be conquered and reconquered separately—for even after being subjugated, the Indians would frequently revolt.[8]

Revolution in El Salvador

> In El Salvador, the buzzards eat better than the people do.
>
> —Psycho (quoting a popular refrain)

Psycho was another of Trouble's friends from El Salvador, from the town of La Reina, in Chaletanango. Psycho's nickname was meant to convey a particular state of mind, and he did take risks, actively participating in serious crimes and violence. But although he was a danger to himself and others, he was not clinically insane. At 5'6" tall, he was of slight build. But he made up for lack of physical prowess with his aggressive demeanor and his gangster appearance. Like Trouble, Psycho grew up very poor in one of the many zones of combat of the civil war. The tribulations he suffered—hunger, living in a relocation camp, dodging bullets and bombs, and seeing human corpses—partially account for his cynical attitude and his tough demeanor. Psycho was not as tall or strong as Trouble, but he was just as willing to fight. Like his compatriots, he was a survivor. When I bribed Psycho to write a poem about his past, he responded with this bit of bombast.

Bicho Belicoso	**Tough Kid**
Balas, bombas, bajas	Bombs and bullets— take cover
Los vabosos no me podrían matar.	Those fools couldn't kill me. I was a tough kid.
Yo era un bicho belicoso.	

—Psycho

Pablo Neruda he's not, but having experienced the worst the war had to offer, Psycho was certainly savvy about the causes of the conflict in his country. "The poor got tired of being paid shit, so they decided to give it back," he told me succinctly. Frustrated watching their children starve, angry at receiving substandard living wages, and fed up with unsanitary living conditions and government repression, some of these impoverished people decided to take up arms in protest. Psycho's comment reflects a common historical refrain of poor peasants, who, having been exploited for decades by their bosses and repressed by the military, decide to beat their plowshares into machetes. In its postcolonial history, El Salvador has had many rebellions, but the revolts of 1833 and 1932 stand out.

Todos	**All of Us**
Todos nacimos medio muertos	All of us were born half-dead
en 1932	in 1932
sobrevivimos pero medio vivos	we survived but half-alive
cada uno con una cuenta	each with an entire account
de treinta mil muertos enteros	of 30,000 dead
que se puso a engordar sus intereses	that bloated its interests
sus réditos	its income
y que hoy alcanza para untar de muerte	and that today has managed to smear with death
a los que siguen naciendo	those that continue
medio muertos	being born half-dead
medio vivos…	half-alive…
Todos juntos	All together
tenemos más muerte que ellos	we have more death than they
(los asesinos) pero todos juntos	(the assassins) but all together
tenemos más vida que ellos…	we have more life than they…

—Roque Dalton[9]

The first major peasant uprising in El Salvador was in 1833, when an Indian named Anastasio Aquino organized workers in the indigo factories to rebel against the government and landowners.[10] The Salvadoran army quickly defeated the rebels, captured Aquino, decapitated him and nailed his head to a stake in the center of a city park. A hundred years later, in 1932, peasants in the rural part of western El Salvador rose up against the government. The uprising was poorly planned, very disorganized, and chaotically carried out by a few hundred peasants armed with machetes and crude rifles. Indicative of the peasants' lack of sophistication, word got out about the revolt and the day before it was launched, a city newspaper in San Salvador, the capital, announced its time and location.[11]

The military put down the rebellion within weeks, and thousands of indigenous peasants were massacred by firing squad. As a result of this rebellion, the Salvadoran military and government set up a security apparatus to maintain public safety. Among these security forces, the National Guard, the National Police, and the Treasury Police—who the U.S. embassy staff nicknamed the "grim reapers"—were most responsible for the repression that followed.[12] These security forces were involved in numerous human rights abuses, such as "disappearances," torture, and murder. In addition to the security forces, the government also created a large paramilitary force, called ORDEN, to "keep order" in the countryside. Their job was to spy on their neighbors, report any suspicious activity such as criticizing the government, and finger people for assassination.

The goal of these paramilitary thugs was to instill terror in the general population. Because members of ORDEN did not wear uniforms, no one knew which of their neighbors were spies, or *orejas*, the Spanish word for "ears." Many Salvadorans became suspicious and hypervigilant because anyone could be an *ear*, or government spy ready to report them. Among those suspected of being an ear was Psycho's uncle. Some thought his disappearance was due to drunkenness. "My uncle didn't come home one night," said Psycho. "My grandmother thought he'd tied one on [got drunk], fallen down a ditch and broke his neck." After a week, the neighbors suspected that he might have gotten into a fight with one of his neighbors about gambling debts, or that the military mistook him for a Communist and was shot. A few weeks later, they got their answer. His corpse was discovered with one of his ears cut off. "That's the way they treat spies in El Salvador," said Psycho.

> ...The Colonel returned with a sack used to bring groceries home. He spilled many human ears on the table. They were like dried peach halves. There is no other way to say this. He took one of them in his hands, shook it in our faces, dropped it into a water glass. It came alive there. I am tired of fooling around he said. As for the rights of anyone,

tell your people they can go fuck themselves. He swept the ears to the
floor with his arm and held the last of his wine in the air.

—Carolyn Forche[13]

The Salvadoran military considered anyone who protested to be what
they called a *subversivo* (subversive), including labor union members
who participated in strikes for better wages or working conditions.
Trouble's father fled to the United States after receiving a death threat
for participating in a strike against the factory where he worked. Police
broke up the strike and beat up the workers, including Trouble's father.
In El Salvador, this response of the government to protest was typical.
In the late 1970s and early 1980s, mass organizations of teache rs, trade
unionists, peasants, and professionals, known as *las masas*, led large
demonstrations and strikes, and occupied some factories to demand
fair wages and an end to military repression. The military responded
by violently breaking up the strikes, torturing and "disappearing" union
leaders, and shooting demonstrators. The largest demonstration in the
history of El Salvador occurred in the capital, San Salvador, on the anniversary of La Matanza, January 22, 1980. Approximately 200,000 people
marched in protest of government policies. Snipers from the military
stationed themselves on rooftops above the marchers and opened fire
on the demonstrators, killing at least twenty.[14]

In Salvador, Death

> In Salvador, death still patrols.
> The blood of dead peasants
> has not dried, time does not dry it,
> rain does not erase it from the roads.
> …a bloody flavor soaks the land,
> the bread and wine in Salvador.
>
> —*Pablo Neruda*

In response to this repression, the Farabundo Marti National Liberation
Front (FMLN) guerrillas launched a "final offensive," which began the
twelve-year civil war. Despite U.S. involvement in the civil war, hun-
dreds of Salvadorans were being tortured, killed or "disappeared"
each month.[15] Many of these disappearances and extrajudicial killings
were planned by high-ranking military officers and carried out by the

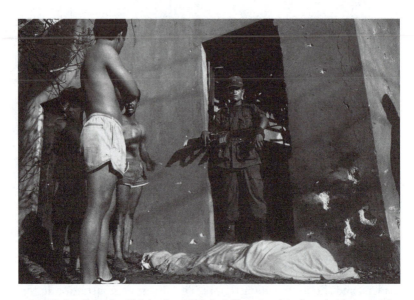

FIGURE **2.2 San Salvador, El Salvador, 1989.** A civilian casualty of combat between the Salvadoran government army (standing over body) and urban commandos of the FMLN (Farabundo Marti National Liberation Front) insurgency. Copyright © Donna DeCesare, 1989.

Salvadoran death squads, off-duty security officers who painted their faces black, called themselves *La Mano Blanca*, the White Hand, or the *Maximiliano Hernandez Martínez Brigade*, and went out at night to terrorize people suspected of being subversive. These death squads would resurface in 1998, only a few years after the end of the war, to deal with the growing gang problem in El Salvador.[16]

Terror in the Streets and at Home

The activities of these security forces and the death squads, combined with the fighting between the Salvadoran military and the FMLN guerrillas, produced a large body count. Human corpses were a common sight in El Salvador, which anesthetized citizens to the daily violence and death that they saw on television or on their way to school or work. The fighting and the appearances of dead bodies were most pronounced in the countryside, places like Santa Maria, Usulután, where Sniper was born and raised. Sniper took his gang nickname to suggest that he was an accurate shooter, which he was not. Short, skinny, dark skinned, with a broad face and almond eyes, Sniper had indigenous roots, and his fellow homeboys often teased him, calling him *El Indio*. Sniper despised this term because of the intense racism against Salvadoran Indians.

Sniper had grown up poor in El Salvador. When his parents went to work, picking coffee beans, Sniper stayed home with his five other siblings. His family's living conditions were rustic. He did not own a pair of shoes, and almost every meal consisted of beans and tortillas with a little salt. His family's one-room house had dirt floors, which his mother swept daily. Because they lived in a combat zone, Sniper was forced to flee from several skirmishes between the military and the guerrillas.

"One day, me and my brothers took our dog to a meadow to pick some *pepetos* [a tropical fruit]," he told me. "I climbed up a tree to get some when, all of a sudden, there was a lot of soldiers and guerrillas shooting at each other. We were caught between them. The military started dropping bombs, and my brothers yelled, 'Hurry up, we gotta get out of here!' So I climbed down and ran. When we got home, we found some shrapnel had hit our dog, but he survived. So we changed his name to Lucky."

Sniper often discovered the dead bodies of soldiers or civilians on the dirt roads or in the fields near his home. On one occasion, Sniper went with his brothers into the hillside to search for coffee beans to sell at the market. "We found some and were filling our sacks when we came across a dead body. It was already stinking badly and had worms coming out. We went to the nearest town to tell someone and they came and got the body and buried it." Sniper's poem indicates his jaundiced view of life.

Nacido para matar	Born to Kill
Quién dice que somos	Who says that we are
nacidos para matar?	born to kill?
Los cadaveres nos dicen	The corpses tell us
que somos nacidos	that we are born
para morir.	to die.

Dead bodies were also a common sight on the streets of El Salvador's capital, San Salvador, where Sniper's friend, Lil' Silent, grew up. Lil' Silent used the diminutive "Lil'" in his nickname because an older

FIGURE 2.3 El Mozote, El Salvador 1989. El Mozote was the scene of one of the worst human rights abuses in the Americas in 1981 when the army massacred a village, killing an estimated 1000 men, women, and children. Years later the evidence of the massacre was visible in the ruins of the village. Copyright © Donna DeCesare, 1989.

gang member from his clique had already claimed the name Silent. According to gang etiquette, Lil' Silent could have dropped the "Lil'" in his moniker when his namesake was killed by an enemy gang member, but as a sign of respect to this fallen homeboy, he chose to keep it. However, Lil' Silent was anything but little. Thick and muscular, he had a large, imposing figure, which contrasted with his shy demeanor. He was an introvert and quite guarded. True to his nickname, Lil' Silent rarely spoke. He did not like to talk about his past because he said the memories of his childhood were too painful.

Despite this, I was able to get Lil' Silent to open up a bit. I asked him about growing up in El Salvador and if he could tell me how many dead bodies he had seen. After a pause, he estimated that he had seen approximately 200 human corpses, *tirados* as he put it. "They were tossed on the ground, with their thumbs tied behind their backs, and left to rot." Having seen so many corpses lying in the city streets, Lil' Silent just wanted to forget the past. "It hurts to remember," he told me. "Seeing all those dead bodies traumatized me as a kid. It gave me nightmares."

Lil' Silent was not the only homeboy who was bothered by nightmares. Trouble told me he couldn't shake the sight of those grisly, disfigured human corpses. "The bodies were sometimes cut up or missing heads," he said. Images of these corpses would sometimes appear in his dreams, an obvious cause of anxiety. Trouble told me, "The military would take trucks full of corpses to the countryside and dump them into a ravine. As a kid, it affected me. I couldn't get those images out of my head." Initially, the psychological trauma of seeing these dead bodies scared Trouble and haunted his dreams. However, over time and geographical distance, he became desensitized to this type of violence.

Another type of violence, which was much more direct and forceful, also traumatized these children. Perhaps the worst psychological trauma these Salvadoran youth experienced was a fear much closer to home. All of the hard-core gang members I interviewed had experienced some form of harsh discipline from their parents.

> My father was an alcoholic. One day he hit me in the nose and broke it. I was just a kid.
>
> — Joker

Joker's response to this harsh discipline was succinct. "If I ever saw my father again, I'd put two bullets in his head," he said. In El Salvador, at that time, it was common for parents to use strict autocratic rule to keep their sons in line. Sniper said that his father punished him for any small infraction, like coming home an hour late from school. "My father made me crawl on my knees on dry corn," Sniper said. "And if I didn't get good grades, he'd beat me with a belt, or make me crawl on dried kernels of corn or bottle caps until my knees bleed. Sometimes he'd make me hold a heavy board across my shoulders to weigh me down so I would feel more pain." Not surprisingly, Sniper felt angry and resentful toward his father.

In contrast, Trouble was more ambivalent in his feelings toward his biological father. "Sometimes he was pretty mean," said Trouble. "One time he put me down a well hole and left me there for hours. But I realize that he had his reasons for punishing me." Despite this rationalization, Trouble felt no great warmth toward his father. "I don't hate my father," he said. "But I don't ever want to see him again." This type of strict discipline did not come only from fathers. "My mom was just as good with a belt," said Trouble.

Lil' Silent was the only one among these hard-core homeboys who never knew his biological father, and for this reason he had no feelings whatsoever for his father. Rhetorically he asked me, "How can you hate someone you never met?" Those who knew their fathers had little respect for their disciplinary methods. The overzealous punishment of these fathers set the table for these young boys' later life as gang members. As James Gilligan, psychiatrist and former director of mental health for the Massachusetts prison system, points out, "Violence, like charity, begins at home. The use of violence as a means of resolving conflict between persons, groups, and nations is a strategy we learn first at home. All of our basic problem-solving, problem-exacerbating, and problem-creating strategies, for living and dying, are learned first at home."[17]

For these MS gangsters, their fathers served them well as negative role models by teaching them that discipline is maintained by violence. But in addition to this harsh discipline, these youth were further traumatized by the violence of dislocation.

Family Ruptures

La Familia	**Family**
El más lindo regalo de Díos,	The most beautiful gift from God,
dichosos los hombres que la posean,	fortunate are those who have one
porque hay aquellos que no.	because there are those who don't.
	—Lil' Silent

As a direct result of the civil war, most of these Salvadoran immigrant youth experienced some form of family displacement. Like Trouble, Psycho had grown up in a zone of conflict. His home in Chalatenango was controlled by the FMLN during the war. Because the Salvadoran army made frequent sweeps into the area where his family lived, he and his mother and siblings were often forced to flee their home from aerial strafing and bombing. "There was constant shooting and bombs

FIGURE 2.4 El Salvador, 1988. Salvadoran peasant refugees traveling by bus to escape the conflict. Copyright © Donna DeCesare, 1988.

blowing up," he told me. "We got under the beds when the shooting started." Psycho said the army forcibly moved his family and everyone in their village to a relocation camp. He said the conditions there were dirty and hot, and there was little food or water. This trauma of relocation was compounded later when Psycho was separated from his mother and siblings, who left him behind in El Salvador when they migrated to the United States.

Family dislocation and a lengthy separation from family members was the norm for these hard-core MS gangsters. Joker was six years old when his mother migrated to the United States to find work, leaving him and his older brother to live with their grandmother. Joker would not see his mother again for seven years. "It was tough when she left," he said. With her departure, Joker grew more detached. "After my mother left," he said, "I became more and more aware of the shit that was going down. Nothing was the same after that. I didn't know what to expect and I didn't care."

Similarly, Sniper's mother left El Salvador when he was five, and he did not see her for seven years. Sniper told me that his father separated from his mother just a few months before she left for the United States.

"My father abandoned my mother," he said. "He didn't say anything, no good-bye or nothing. He just left, and never came back." Because he had no father to turn to during his lengthy separation from his mother, he said he was moved about from one family member to another. "First, I lived with my grandmother, and then with my aunt. And then with my older sister." Rationalizing her decision, Sniper said, "My mother came to the United States to try to make a better life."

Like Sniper, Lil' Silent experienced a long separation from his mother. He was thirteen when she sent for him, after five years apart. She was not his biological mother, but a neighbor woman who had adopted him as a baby when his mother fled the country. "I don't know who my real mother is," he said, "That's just the way it is." Despite his stoicism, Lil' Silent struggled with the experience of never having known his biological mother. Although his adoptive mother took good care of him, after a couple of years she also moved to the United States, handing him over to another neighbor-friend. Indicative of the shame he felt, Lil' Silent never told his fellow homeboys that he was an orphan. When asked if he ever missed knowing his mother, Lil' Silent reiterated what he'd said about not knowing his father, "How can you miss what you never had?"

Trouble had the longest separation from his parents. He and his older brother lived with his aunt for eight years before his parents were able to bring them to the States. Prior to this strange, uncomfortable reunion, however, these Salvadoran youth had to undergo the painful process of being smuggled from one country to another, thousands of miles away, and suffering, among other things, the pain of being uprooted.

Crossing Borders

I almost died in Mexico. I lay in a hospital bed for several days, sweating, dehydrated, running a fever of 103. I had an IV sticking out of my arm and I thought to myself, "Shit, after all this hassle, I'm gonna die here in some fucking I-don't-know-where, Guanajuato."

— Joker

You don't know where they're taking you. You don't know if you're going across the desert or through a river or over a mountain. You don't know if you'll get caught. You don't know if they're taking you to a remote area to kill you or whatever.

— Trouble

FIGURE 2.5 Chalatenango, El Salvador, 1984. An ink drawing of a peasant girl holding her baby brother in a refugee relocation camp. The artist is an MS gang member serving a long sentence in Pelican Bay State Prison. Copyright © T. W. Ward, 2011.

For Trouble and the other homeboys, the emotional trauma of leaving El Salvador was severely compounded by the difficult journey to the United States. *El camino duro*, as the immigrants call it, the hard road, is 3,227 miles long and can be quite dangerous. There are many ways of illegally crossing the borders between El Salvador, Guatemala, Mexico, and the United States—plane, train, boat, bus or car—but for most *illegales*, or undocumented immigrants, some part of the journey is usually made on foot. Many Salvadorans who cross illegally over these borders pay a *coyote* or human smuggler to help them. *Coyotes* refer to their immigrant transports as *conejos* (rabbits) or *pollos* (chicken), a metaphor that reflects their vulnerability to exploitation.

The financial, physical, and emotional costs of being smuggled from El Salvador to the United States are high. A coyote will charge according to his (or her) skills, the mode of transportation, whether he has to procure false documents, and how far he has to transport his rabbits. Half of his fee is usually collected before the trip and the other half upon delivery of his cargo. The cost for a short trip, from one side of the border to the other, for these Salvadoran youth ranged from $200—what Lil' Silent's mother paid to have him transported in raft with oversized truck tire tubs across the Rio Grande—to $3,000, what Joker's mother paid the coyote to provide Joker with a false visa and send him from San Salvador to Los Angeles, alone, by airplane.

For Joker, this was his second attempt at coming to the United States. As indicated in the quote above, his first trip was fraught with difficulties. As in most things, one gets what one pays for. Joker bragged that his flight to Los Angeles was on United Airlines and not TACA, the less expensive Salvadoran airline, whose passengers faced more scrutiny from immigration officials. He credits this difference with the difference between being captured and successfully making the trip. Regardless, his voyage was filled with trepidation.

> During the flight, I was so nervous I read the Bible. The coyote's sister was supposed to pick me up at the airport. He told me she would be wearing a red t-shirt and a 49ers baseball cap. I was only 13 years old, so she was going to have to sign a paper to take custody of me. When the plane arrived, the immigration officer asked me, "Who's going to pick you up?" "My aunt," I said. Then from a distance I saw a woman who fit the description, and shouted out to her, "Heeey!!" We

pretended to know each other and I gave her a big hug. And she said, *"Ahh, m'hijo, aaii, qué hermoso!"*[18]

—Joker

Like Joker, Psycho's trip was successful on the second attempt. After failing once, Psycho's mother paid a coyote $1,000 to bring him across the U.S. border in the large trunk of an old white Cadillac. The cost of failure is not lost on these homeboys. Sniper estimates that his mother lost about $2,000 when he was detained in Mexico and sent back to El Salvador. He considers himself lucky that his second trip was a success. For Trouble, the third time was his charm. On the first two trips, he was detained by the Mexican police in Tijuana and Puebla and deported home, thereby forfeiting the $1,500 and $1,000 advances his parents had paid the coyote. Ironically, he considers the second trip a qualified success because, unlike the first, "I was captured sooner, and we lost less money."

To avoid capture, a good coyote knows the safest routes to travel and whom to bribe. It is almost impossible to make the trip successfully without paying bribes, or what are commonly called *mordidas*, which is the Spanish word for "bites." These bribes or bites are usually paid to police and immigration officials. Joker is certain he would not have made it the United States without paying a bribe. "Grease their palms and they'll set you free," he told me. Coyotes are greedy and to avoid paying bribes to the Mexican police, some of them try to cut corners, taking their rabbits on back roads or, better yet, no roads at all. The coyote that led the group on Sniper's first trip took him and his compatriots over mountains on foot, which added over three weeks to their journey.

"It was rainy and cold in the mountains" said Sniper. "I was sick, so a woman in our group slept beside me to keep me warm. It was tough, I got scratched and bruised from going over those mountains." In addition, the coyote got lost.

> We had to drink water from the river and eat whatever we could find—herbs or sugar cane. I hadn't eaten real food for five days. I had a bad headache, so someone gave me an aspirin. And that gave me a stomach infection. We finally found the highway and the woman we were supposed to meet. She told us she thought we had died on the road.

—Sniper

The group of undocumented immigrants with which Lil' Silent traveled also got lost, trying to navigate a river channel at night by boat. "There were two little rafts, with five of us crammed into each," he told me. "We spent all night on the water, with a strong wind blowing us about. It was too dark to see anything, but we had to bail water out of the raft with cups. During the night, the other raft got separated from us, and we never saw them again. We were lucky to make it out alive." Not all undocumented Salvadoran immigrants are so lucky. In May of 1981, a coyote leading a group of undocumented immigrants, many Salvadorans among them, got lost in the desert near Yuma, Arizona, and fourteen people died of overexposure.[19] In 1987, eighteen people were found dead in a railroad boxcar near the border in West Texas, and in May of 2003, eighteen more were found dead in a trailer at a remote truck stop near Victoria, Texas.[20] No one knows the exact number of immigrants who have died trying to get to the United States, drowning in perilous rivers, or perishing in the remote mountains of Mexico and Guatemala. According to Trouble, one young Mexican woman was never added to the statistics. Although she perished in a boxcar of the train in which Trouble rode, her death was never reported to the authorities.

> She suffocated and died of heat exhaustion. When people die in the heat, they don't shout or cry out. The heat makes you sleepy. You fall asleep, and you never wake up. The heat is slow suffering. We almost died in that boxcar, which was tightly packed with about seventy people. There was no air and we were suffocating. The coyote put me next to a small hole in the train where the wood was broken so that I could breathe. No one had water, and the food ran out. We were dying of thirst. It was like a prison cell. For two days we were locked in that car with her corpse, until the train finally stopped and they let us out.
>
> —Trouble

The roads and highways of these countries are physically less demanding than the mountains, rivers, and rails, but on these routes immigrants are much more likely to get caught by the police. Those who do not have the money for a *mordida* can expect to risk detention, deportation, or worse. Trouble said he had seen many people beaten by the Mexican police when they are caught. Before he was deported, the police beat him when he swore at them for taking the immigrants' money.

To prevent capture, coyotes avoid the usual places where the immigration police stop buses to check documents, but, as Sniper can attest, accidents happen. "We were supposed to take several buses through Mexico," he said, "Each time we would get near an immigration stop, the coyote would get us out of the bus and we'd walk through fields or over hills. That was the plan, but things rarely go as planned. The coyote missed a stop. The police got on the bus and yelled, 'Papers! Papers!' And I knew I was caught."

The police asked Sniper for his documents, and when he said he had none, they asked him for a $100 bribe. He was only fourteen years old and wasn't carrying any money, so they took him off the bus and put him in jail. Sniper derided the corrupt police and their town, called La Ventosa. The place was named for its strong winds, but, as Sniper was quick to point out, *ventosa* is also slang for "passing gas." "I spent fifteen days in jail there," he told me, "I was stuck in a cell with *la pura raza mala* (bad guys), rapists, bank robbers and murderers. Was I scared? Hell yeah, I was scared. I was just a kid."

Although Trouble did not suffer such a fate, he told me of seeing others persecuted. A Mexican official eyed a young woman in his group and took her away. "The man said he'd take care of her," Trouble said. "But who knows what happened to that girl? It's really fucked up. Her story will never get told." These trips caused Trouble nightmares. "I got up during the night and was sleepwalking," he said. "My brother told me that it was because of the trauma, the bad memories. He woke up and saw me opening the door of the hotel room. He got up and put me back to bed." Trouble was not alone in suffering nightmares from the trauma of the trip. Joker told me that after he arrived in Los Angeles, he dreamed he was drowning in a cold river. "It was taking me down. It was dark and I couldn't breathe."

Given their need to avoid detection, these Salvadoran immigrant youth adapted quickly to their new surroundings. One of the first things they learned to change was the way they talked. "The *federales* [Mexican police] can identify a Salvadoran as soon as he opens his mouth," Joker told me. "Our accent is different, and we use different words, like *cipote* or *bicho* for children. And those sons-of-bitches [Mexicans] talk rapid-fire, like [demonstrating in staccato-style], '*Qué-hondas-huey-qué-no-sé qué-qué-no-sé-cúando-qué-no-manches-huey-hijo-de-la-gran-chingada!*'[21] We don't talk as fast, and the *federales* finger us as soon as we say a few words." Given this limitation, Joker said, he learned to keep his mouth shut.

Some of these immigrant kids were genuinely surprised by the generosity of some Mexicans, who helped them in various ways—e.g., giving them food or a place to sleep or warning them when the police were nearby. Sniper told me of a good-hearted Mexican woman who took him to a hospital when he was sick and running a fever. "If not for her," he said, "I might have died." Sniper made friends with a woman in his traveling group, who helped him after they were captured. "After we were deported from Mexico to Guatemala," he said, "I told her my situation—that I had no way to get back to El Salvador. She paid for my hotel room and the bus trip back home."

In contrast, some Mexicans were totally unsympathetic toward the plight of these Salvadoran immigrants. As Trouble told me, "They don't want us on their soil." According to Trouble, these Mexicans act as *orejas*—or spies—and tell the police where the illegal immigrants are hiding. He considered these Mexicans to be *rats* with *mal corazón*—a bad heart. The anger he directed at these traitors was compounded by his *depression* and disappointment at being caught.

> It's sad when they catch you. First, they put you in jail. Then they put you on a bus to take you back, and you have to start all over again. The day I was sent back, there were sixty other people being deported. You can't help but cry when you see all these people who have sold their animals, their furniture, their TVs, everything they owned in El Salvador in order to come to the States, and then, shit! They get deported.
>
> —Trouble

Paradoxically, some of these homeboys like Psycho felt relieved to be captured, because it meant the end to the constant stress of hiding.

> I was glad when *la migra* [immigration police] caught us. We wouldn't have to hide anymore. I was tired of running from the law. The coyote had stuffed us into the trunk of a car to get us across the border. After he closed the lid, it was dark and hot, and there was not much air to breathe—kind of like a coffin, except there's five of you packed in. I was glad they caught us. I got to go home. I didn't want to come to the U.S. in the first place.
>
> —Psycho

Psycho told me that no one asked him whether or not he wanted to come to the United States because, as he said, "I was just a kid." This was also true for other homeboys, each of whom was a first-generation immigrant. Their unwillingness to uproot from their home and illegally immigrate would forever cloud these boys' thinking and feelings about their status in the United States. They told me that they would have skipped the long, dangerous trip and stayed in El Salvador, despite the difficulties imposed by the civil war. They were reluctant to dig up roots because El Salvador was their homeland, and they had developed strong emotional bonds with their (surrogate) caretakers.

Despite the painful memories of their homeland, these homeboys held fond feelings for their country and its beauty. And if given a choice, they say they would have traded the uncertainties of life in the United States for the hardships of El Salvador. As reluctant immigrants, they did not consider the United States a land of promise. They had never heard of Horatio Alger, the fictional immigrant boy who, through hard work, "pulled himself up by his own bootstraps" and became immensely successful in banking. These Salvadoran immigrant youth held no great expectations for their adopted country, and they would soon realize that their country of adoption had little use for them.

Notes

1. Cf. reports, 1984, Lawyers Committee for International Human Rights and Americas Watch, *El Salvador's Other Victims: The War on the Displaced,* New York, April 1984, Bureau for Latin America and the Caribbean and Agency for International Development, *Displaced Persons in El Salvador: An Assessment,* Washington DC, March.
2. Barry, T., and Preusch, D. 1984. *The Central American Fact Book.* New York: Grove Press; McClintock, Michael. 1985. *The American Connection: State Terror and Popular Resistance in El Salvador.* London: Zed Press.
3. Rodriguez, Francisco. 1993. This is an account of a young boy who witnessed his family being slaughtered by machete. See also Diaz, Tom, 2009, p. 27.
4. Cornmeal pancake, fried on a grill with *loroco* [herb—flowers and leaves of a cactus], beans, cheese, and/or *chorizo* [fried pig] inside.
5. Nakagawa, Tsuyoshi. 1975. *El Salvador: This Beautiful World,* vol. 54. Tokyo: Kodansha International Ltd.
6. Dalton, Roque. 1984b. *El Salvador: Monografía.* Puebla, Mexico: Universidad Autónoma de Puebla; 1988 [2010] *Las Historias Prohibidas del Pulgarcito,* 13th ed. San Salvador: UCA Editores.

7. 1982. *Flower from the Volcano*, p. 44. This is my English translation of the poem.

8. Alas, H. 1982. *El Salvador: Por qué la insurrección?* El Secretariado Permanente de la Comision para la Defensa de los Derechos Humanos en Centroamerica, San Jose, Costa Rica; Russell, P. *El Salvador in Crisis*, 1984. Austin, TX: Colorado River Press.

9. 1988 [2010]. *Las Historias Prohibidas del Pulgarcito*, 13th ed. San Salvador: UCA Editores, pp. 124–25.

10. Russell, P. *El Salvador in Crisis*. 1984. Austin, TX: Colorado River Press.

11. Cf. Bailey, J., et al. 1978. *El Salvdor de 1840 a 1935*. San Salvador: UCA Editores; Sanchez, Alvaro. *La Politica en El Salvador en las Ultimas Seis Decadas 1930–1989*, self-published paperback book; Gould, Jeffrey, and Santiago, Aldo Lauria. 2008. "Mataron justos por pecadores": Las massacres contrarevolucionarias [As sinners they were rightly killed: The counter-revolutionary massacres], Trasmallo, vol. 3. San Salvador, www.museo.com.sv; Alas, H. 1982. *El Salvador: Por qué la insurrección?* El Secretariado Permanente de la Comision para la Defensa de los Derechos Humanos en Centroamerica. San Jose, Costa Rica; White, Christopher. 2009. *The History of El Salvador*. Greenwood Press; Ching, Eric K. 2007. *Las Masas, la Matanza y el Martinato en El Salvador: Ensayos sobre 1932*. Universidad Centroamericana.

12. Bonner, Raymond. 1984. *Weakness and Deceit: US Policy and El Salvador*. Times Books.

13. From the prose poem, "The Colonel," in *The Country Between Us*. New York: Harper & Row, Publishers, 1981, p. 16.

14. Cf. Alas, H. 1982. *El Salvador: Por qué la insurrección?* El Secretariado Permanente de la Comision para la Defensa de los Derechos Humanos en Centroamerica. San Jose, Costa Rica; Russell, P. 1984. *El Salvador in Crisis*. Austin, TX: Colorado River Press.

15. Cf. *In Contempt of Congress: The Reagan Record of Deceit and Illegality on Central America*, The Central America Crisis Monitoring Team. Washington, DC: Institute for Policy Studies, 1985; Martínez, Ana Guadalupe. 2008, *Las Cárceles Clandestinas* [Clandestine Prisons]. San Salvador: UCA Editores. Note: "Disappeared" means being captured, often tortured, and killed, but one's body is never recovered. Disappearences were a common tactic of the "dirty wars" of Chile, Argentina, Guatemala, and El Salvador.

16. Cf., Carbonero, Nathalie Villarroel. 2004. *Sentencia de Muerte: Ex-pandilleros bajo amenaza* [*Death Sentence: Ex-gang members under threat*], vertice@elsalvador.com, May 12; Cerón, Nicolás. 2006. "Sombra

Negra" amenaza a extorsionistas y pandilleros, *Redacción Diario Co Latino,* September 1; Cruz, J. M., and Portillo, N. 1998. *Solidaridad y violencia en las pandillas del gran San Salvador. Más allá de la vida loca.* San Salvador: UCA Editores; Dalton, Juan José. 1995. Vigilante groups help step-up the violence, *InterPress Service* (IPS), 27 April; DeCesare, D. 1998. The children of war: Street gangs in El Salvador. *NACLA* 32 (1), July; *Orionce.net.* 2009. "La Resurrección de la Sombra Negra" ["The Resurrection of the Black Shadow"], October 26.

17. *On Violence,* 1996 p. 5.
18. *Oh, my son, wow, how handsome you are!*
19. Spelling. 1982. *Escape.* Those who survived were forced to share a plastic jug of their collective urine, which after a couple of turns recycling through their bladders, turned a thick acrid brown—and still they fought over it.
20. Gold and Ellingwood, 2003.
21. Rough translation: "What's up, dude, I don't know what, I don't know when, don't fuck up, dude, son of a bitch." Manchar means to stain, or soil; for example, a family's reptutation. The reflexive form of the verb means to get dirty or become soiled.

....

CHAPTER 3

Hard Times— Welcome to America

After a difficult journey to the United States, these Salvadoran immigrant youth faced a number of different problems adapting to a new, strange environment. Among these were being undocumented, dealing with culture shock, trying to learn a new language, and being picked on by bullies at school and in their neighborhoods. But the first problem they had to confront was the difficulty of family reunification. Having been separated for so many years from their primary caretakers, with feelings of having been abandoned in El Salvador, it is not surprising that their family reunions were not causes of celebration. None of these immigrant youth felt their parents warmly embraced them with open arms. For this reason, and others, it would take these youth many years to emotionally reconnect with their parents, and rebuild the frayed bonds of trust.

Family Reunion—Mending the Bonds of Trust

> For six years I was separated from my mother. When I saw her again it was very strange. I didn't know this person. Who is she? What does she like? What *doesn't* she like? One has to get to know her all over again.
>
> —Sniper

Like Sniper, each of these Salvadoran immigrant youth faced the daunting task of trying to mend the bonds of trust with their parents. Reflecting the difficulty of this task, in the quote above, Sniper says, "*One* has to get to know," using the singular impersonal instead of the first person singular (I). This psychological distancing device indicates how awkward Sniper felt. Who was this person who was calling herself his mother? Although she was an adult who held claim to the title, it had been such a long time since she had fulfilled the role of mother that some degree of estrangement was inevitable.

It was almost impossible for Sniper to make a positive emotional connection with this woman whom he hadn't seen for most of the formative years of his life. Because Sniper suppressed this feeling of betrayal, as most of his compatriots did, he was not fully aware of its impacts on his behavior. One result of Sniper's subconscious feeling of abandonment was his distaste for *authority*, which was represented in his mother, who had neglected him, and his alcoholic father, who had abused him. Sniper's mother did nothing to dispel a negative impression of Salvadoran men, denigrating them as role models. Her experience with Sniper's father had given her a jaundiced view of them, and she more than once she had told her son, "They're all *cabrones* (bastards)."

Given his negative view of authority, Sniper responded to his reunion with his mother as might be expected. He rebelled against her wishes. Although each of these young immigrant boys responded to their family reunions differently, most shared with Sniper a distaste for authority. Like Sniper, however, few of these homeboys were fully conscious of their feelings of abandonment. Some suppressed them out of a fear of being a burden to others, while others suppressed them from a vague feeling of guilt they felt for their ingratitude. Like his fellows, Sniper wasn't completely ungrateful for being brought to America, but he resented never having been asked what he thought or felt about moving from his homeland. Although he was grateful for the sacrifices his mother made to bring him to the United States, what stuck with him was the fact that his feelings about having been uprooted were never acknowledged.

Joker understood why his mother never asked him how he felt about the move. "You don't ask children what they want, or how they think or feel," he told me, "because moving to another country is a decision that can only be made by an adult." This rationalization, however, did little to assuage the pain of relocation. Separation and uprooting made these youth feel unsafe. And because the emotional development of children is intimately connected with the safety and nurturance provided by their environment, these youth were emotionally stunted and ready to react violently.

Children universally attach themselves intensely to their caregivers. This is a survival mechanism necessary to provide the needs that a child is unable to satisfy alone.... Traumatized children have trouble modulating aggression. They tend to act destructively against others or themselves.[1]

Adding to these immigrant youths' feelings of resentment about being abandoned and then brought to the United States against their will, many resented the fact that they were just supposed to take it, without complaint. In Spanish, the word for this is *aguantar*, to suffer in silence, or grin and bear it. This is a major feature of many Latino cultures, including Salvadoran. When he came to the United States, Sniper felt supremely alienated, distrusted authority figures, and resented the fact that his feelings were never considered. After such a long separation, and with these feelings of resentment, it is not surprising that it would take Sniper many years to rebuild some kind of bond of trust with his mother.

Unfortunately, Sniper's mother, like most of these homeboys' caretakers, did not have the necessary free time to adequately rebuild this bond of trust. Working long hours—cleaning office buildings or working in sweatshops—did not afford these Salvadoran parents the luxury of spending a lot of time with their children. In addition, one must consider the attitude of Salvadorans towards their offspring. Some part of this attitude is conveyed when they refer to them as *bichos*. A "bicho" is a bug, and the expression has both positive and negative connotations. Bicho can mean as "cute" as a bug, or it can mean as "ugly" as a cockroach. On the negative side, this attitude reflects a lack of patience with their children and is exhibited in their harsh discipline, which, as these youth could attest, can include severe physical beatings that do little to build emotional bonds of trust.

It is no coincidence that *trust* was one of the highest commodities for these immigrant youth, because it was missing from their childhoods. The Spanish word for trust is *confianza*, but it is not something you "do," it is something you "have," and it can be taken away. "When I came to the United States and met my mom, I had to get to know her all over again," Joker told me. "I didn't have *confianza* in her." Joker was flooded with ambivalent feelings about this reunion, a strange mix of joy, profound sadness, repressed anger, and confused numbness. "I didn't know what to feel," he said succinctly. Because they spent so little time together in their tiny one-bedroom apartment, it was difficult for Joker to rebuild trust in his mother. "My mom wasn't home much," he said. Like other undocumented immigrants, Joker's mother worked long hours cleaning office buildings and was not home to bond with her son. He explained:

> She worked in a garment factory, twelve hours a day, six days a week. Because she was without papers [undocumented], at the end of each work cycle, she got laid off and she'd have to start searching for a new job. Sometimes, she would get lucky and the same factory would hire her back again, but other times not. It was tough on her, looking for work, working hard when she got it, then coming home tired to cook and clean. She was gone most of the day. Sometimes at night I'd fall asleep on the couch, watching television.

This situation added to Joker's ambivalence about reuniting with his mother. "When I saw her again, it was really strange," he said, echoing the words of Sniper. "I grew up without her. I didn't know this woman, and now, after all these years, I was going to live with her. What was I going to say? How was I supposed to act?" Partly as a response to this situation, Joker began to hang out with homeboys he had met at school. Because he lacked his mother's supervision, Joker was able to spend a lot of time with them and form an emotional bond, which eventually led to his joining the gang.

The absence of adult supervision was a common theme for all of these hard-core gang members. Like Joker, Psycho lacked strict adult supervision. Although he was only fifteen, Psycho would sometimes stay away from home for several nights a week. Much to his delight, when he returned home, his mother did not protest his absence. "My mother didn't say anything when I came back," Psycho told me. "She didn't care where I went or for how long. She was just glad I was back." Sniper also lacked adult supervision. Sniper's mother worked long hours cleaning hospitals and clinics. "Most of the time I was in the apartment alone," said Sniper. "I would watch television, but after a while that got boring. So I went out into the street and that's where I met the homeboys."

Trouble also went largely unsupervised. His parents worked long hours, for little pay, sewing labels in a garment factory or washing dishes in a restaurant. Trouble's parents were devout Pentecostals, so each night after work and on weekends they went to church services that Trouble said could last three hours or more. "They'd try to drag me along to church," he said. "But I ditched because it was so boring. I couldn't stand all that singing and praising the Lord." Trouble rebelled against his parents' efforts to discipline him and spent more and more time away from home. His parents told me that they worried about the mischief he might be getting himself into, but they were unsure how to handle the situation. Their efforts to keep him in check seemed futile, so they decided to be lenient, not wanting to kick him out to the street.

Compounding this problem, Trouble and the other immigrant youth experienced a double *generation gap* between themselves and their parents. The first gap, of course, was that shared by all teenagers and their parents: the large gap of time and experience that colors and shapes their tastes, their attitudes, and their views of the world. In addition, like his cohort, Trouble shared a large gap in *culture* between himself and his parents. This gap is represented in their language, their form of dress, the music they listen to, their mannerisms, and their sense of identity. These immigrant youth learned to speak English much better than their parents, which gave them a distinct advantage in this new environment. However, as first-generation immigrants, coming to this country as "illegal" adolescents, this gap also meant that these youth had to form a new national identity, a conflicted, hybrid one, as undocumented Salvadoran-Americans.

Because of the generational gaps and the gap in time of separation, it was extremely difficult for these youth to emotionally reconnect with their caretakers. Among the gangsters, Lil' Silent saw the least of his caretaker. His mother worked six days a week as a live-in maid for a doctor in Beverly Hills. On Sunday, the only day they spent together, Lil' Silent's mother prepared him enough meals to last the week. "I didn't get to see her much," he told me. "She was always working." Like his compatriots, Lil' Silent said it felt strange to be reunited with this woman who he barely knew. "I didn't remember her from my childhood, so it felt strange to be living with her now."

This situation took a severe turn for the worse when his mother took in a boyfriend, whom Lil' Silent described as a raging alcoholic from Mexico. This man took an instant dislike to Lil' Silent and began verbally abusing him, accusing him of being a juvenile delinquent. "He cussed me out all the time," said Lil' Silent. "So I stayed away as much as

I could." Finally, when he put a gun to Lil' Silent's head at 2 o'clock one morning, Lil' Silent fled to the streets, where he was eventually adopted into the gang. The gang gave him an excuse, if he needed it, not to go to school. But at this point in his life, Lil' Silent didn't need an excuse not to go to school. He had little incentive to attend school, because, like his fellow homeboys, his experiences of school were nothing but trouble.

Tongue-Tied and Bullied

> We fought all the time, at lunch, during recess, after school, before school, sometimes even during school. That's all we did was fight.
>
> —Sniper

For these Salvadoran immigrant youth, school was not a safe haven or a place of learning, but a place of alienation and discrimination. At school, they did not fit in and had no feeling of belonging to a particular group. Part of this difficulty was the result of cultural differences. "The Chicanos dress different and talk different from us Salvadorans," Trouble told me. "They looked at us Salvadoran kids like we were low and dirty, you know, *wetbacks*. They made fun of the way we spoke. Mexicans use "tu," whereas we use "vos." So they made fun of us." Joker told me he had never heard English before coming to the States, and he hated getting teased for his lack of English.

> When I got here, I heard these kids on the bus speaking a strange language and I asked my mom, "What are they speaking?" She told me it was English, and then I asked, "How did they learn it?" My mom said, 'They grew up speaking it.' Then I thought, "Oh shit, *I'm* going to have to learn that!"

Joker was unprepared to speak English when he started high school three months later. "Without English, school was tough," he said. "My sister taught me some words, but I didn't know shit. I couldn't understand the teacher or the other students. A *vato*[2] in the class translated for me sometimes, but I didn't learn much that year." Not surprisingly, Joker found school incredibly boring. "I spent all day doing nothing," he said. "I took ESL (English as a Second Language) classes and talked with other Latino kids at school. There were so many Spanish-speaking people, we didn't care about learning English." Because it seemed illogical, Joker objected to English as a means of communication.

> You don't say the words the way they're spelled. There's no way to know how a word is supposed to be said. Spanish is easy: you put a "p" and "a" together, you get "*pa*," which means *father*. You add an "l" and an "o," you get "*palo*," which means *stick*. "*Tu pa te pega con su palo*", right?[3]

Although Joker said he wanted to learn English, at first he didn't fare too well. "It was embarrassing," he said. "I made a lot of mistakes and the teachers didn't understand what I was trying to say." Worst of all was the teasing from the other kids when Joker made mistakes. "They made fun of me," he said. In self-defense, he quickly learned English swear words so he could cuss out his tormentors. After two years of ESL classes in high school, Joker had still learned very little English. "But they kept passing me," he said. However, the bullies at school did not limit their teasing to the way these Salvadoran immigrant kids talked. They also teased them for the way they dressed.

Growing up in El Salvador, most of these youth had to dress in school uniforms, and all the uniforms tended to look the same. They wore button-down, short-sleeved dress shirts, and the pants on the boys fit snug, not baggy. So when these Salvadoran youth showed up to school dressed like that, they were teased by other kids, wearing their $100 sneakers and low-hanging Levi's and big t-shirts, or jerseys from football teams. Often the teasing played on their masculinity. Sniper said he was often asked, "How can you wear those tight-ass pants?" or "Are you a mama's boy?"

In addition to this teasing, the ethnic diversity in their new schools greatly surprised many of these Salvadoran immigrant youth. From the moment Joker stepped on campus, he realized he was different from the other students. "It was strange seeing black or white kids," he said. "But, if you look at a kid wrong, he says, "Hey, what's up?" They got mad at me and called me all kinds of names. They would call me *spic* or *wetback* and tell me to go home. I had to learn the ropes fast." Joker had never experienced racial discrimination in El Salvador, where nearly everyone is *mestizo*, of mixed Indian and Spanish ancestry. Now he had to defend himself against the racial epithets of bullies. "I wasn't going to just sit there and take it," said Joker. "So, I got into lots of fights—*lots* and *lots* of fights."

Joker's fellow homeboys experienced similar fates at school. Although he did not welcome conflict, Sniper said it was almost impossible to escape fighting with other students at school. "After school, I had to run home to avoid kids who wanted to beat me up," he told me. "They also used to come looking for me at lunchtime." Finally, Sniper decided it was better to fight than run, and this eventually led to his joining a gang. In contrast to Sniper, Trouble and Psycho were eager to fight at school. It gave them an excuse to express their anger and an opportunity to hone their fighting skills. Among them all, Trouble enjoyed fighting the most. What this constant fighting taught these Salvadoran youth was that there is strength in numbers. Outnumbered by the bullies picking on them at school, some of these Salvadoran immigrant youth sought protection by joining a street gang. Ironically, some of them joined the very gangs that represented those bullies who had previously beaten them. Beginning in the early 1980s, before MS was a viable option, many of these Salvadorans joined one of many other Latino street gangs in Los Angeles, including 18th Street, the Harpys, the Crazys, and the Playboys.

For most of these Salvadoran youth, school was the first place where they encountered gang members and developed friendships with some of them. Making friends with gang members is a normal precursor to joining a street gang, but contrary to popular opinion, research indicates that many of the gang members' friends never join a gang.[4] Sniper's first and best friend at school was a boy named Juan, who called himself Johnny. "Johnny came up to me at school and asked where I was from," said Sniper. "I told him I was from El Salvador, and he said, 'That makes us friends. Hang out with me so that nothing will happen to you. If there's a fight, I'll watch your back and you won't get hurt.'"

When Sniper found out that Johnny was in a gang, he started to consider joining. Johnny showed Sniper the ropes and taught him about the enemy gangs in the neighborhood. Ironically, joining Johnny's street gang only meant increased fighting for Sniper, for which he was eventually expelled from school. "I'm not sure if I finished the 10th or 11th grade," he told me. "I got kicked out and couldn't go back." Like Sniper, all of these gang members fought at school, which resulted in many of them getting transferred to another school in enemy territory

FIGURE 3.1 San Salvador, El Salvador, 1993. Gang initiation of Mara Salvatrucha gang members. The gang spread in El Salvador once the United States began deporting gang members from Los Angeles. Copyright © Donna DeCesare,1994.

or permanently expelled. A few, like Lil' Silent, dropped out and never went back. This fighting at school served as a reason to join a gang and prepared them well for gang fights later. Once they decided they wanted to join MS, if the other members of the clique agreed, they had to be properly initiated. And the proper initiation for MS was what they called *la Gloria Brincada*.

La Gloria Brincada—Welcome to the Barrio

> I got home late, after partying all night. I went to the bathroom to take a piss and saw my face in the mirror. It was a mess. My lower lip was bleeding and swollen. My cheek and jaw were sore. I tried to think of an excuse to tell my mom for the bruises I knew I'd have by morning. The pain in my face was nothing, though, compared to the tremendous throbbing on the side of my head. It felt like someone had put my head in a vice and pounded my ear with a hammer. I thought to myself, "What the fuck have you done now?!"
>
> —Joker

In this quote, Joker describes the aftermath of his initiation into the gang. The ceremony is commonly called a *jump in*, but MS gang members liked to refer to it as *la Gloria Brincada*. This ritual is the most typical form of initiation into a street gang, when there is any initiation at all. It consists of a physical beating by one's fellow members, which lasts for a prescribed amount of time.[5] For Mara Salvatrucha, the initiation lasts thirteen seconds and typically involves three to five people to do the beating. However, one gang member said he was beaten by seven.[6] The term *brincada*, from the Spanish word "brincar," means "to jump." The homeboys modified this term with "la Gloria" to signify *ascension*. The idea behind the phrase is that the initiate is ascending to the status of a full-fledged member of their street gang, which is glorious.

In the delusional minds of these young gang members, their gang rules the world, or at least some significant part of it. For MS gang members, the glorious *jump in* signals a drastic shift in identity from a wannabe[7] to a street gangster, or from a plebian commoner to a holy warrior. As Joker explained to me, whereas the wannabe is a *no-count*,[8] the gangster keeps a careful tally of his fellow homies who have been beaten, shot, or killed in battles with the enemy and seeks revenge. Whereas the wannabe wishes for respect, the gangster demands it. Whereas the wannabe "takes it" from bullies, the gangster is supposed to dish it out. In the gangster ideology, the wannabe sits on his hands, while the gangster grabs whatever he wants, whenever he wants it. It was with this hedonistic concept of gangster that Joker decided to join MS. In order to give some sense of this gang initiation, I provide a brief description of Joker's initiation. This description is taken from one of two *jump ins* that I witnessed during fieldwork.

It was a warm summer night, and the gang members were hanging out in a parking lot behind an apartment building. Carlos had told several of the homeboys that he had decided to join the gang. They had held a meeting of the clique, where it was agreed by the majority that he was acceptable. He knew tonight would be the night for his initiation, but he wasn't sure just how it would play out. Without warning, Psycho turned to Carlos and punched him squarely in the chest, knocking him to the ground. Taking this as a signal, Lil' Silent and Sniper joined in, viciously kicking him in the head, back, and buttocks. Instinctively, Carlos pulled his legs into the fetal position and covered his head with his arms.

Trouble grabbed Sniper by the arm and yelled out, "Watcha, hold up. Let him get up and fight like a man!" The homeboys stepped back long enough to let Carlos stand up, but as soon as he got to his feet they jumped in again, pummeling him with rapid blows. Carlos fought back, throwing his arms wildly, flailing like a broken windmill, and landing a few blows to his attackers. Off to the side, Trouble was counting slowly, "Sies... siete... ocho," seconds that seemed to drag out like minutes. With his teeth clenched tightly, Carlos ducked and dodged like a boxer in a futile attempt to avoid the onslaught, but he was hemmed in and taking a good beating. "Déle déle! Give it to him!" yelled the other homeboys, Shadow and Puppet, as they moved toward the fighter's circle, ready to pounce in the remote chance that Carlos might get the upper hand.

Meanwhile, Trouble kept counting, "Diez... once... doce..." until he reached thirteen. He paused and then shouted out, "Ya estuvo! That's it. Stop!" Two of the young men backed off, but Sniper struck another blow. Trouble grabbed Sniper's arm and pulled him away from Carlos, admonishing him, "Cabrón, that's enough!"[9] Carlos scowled at Sniper, but the tension was broken by the laughter of the other vatos, or gang members, whose faces of serious concentration had now melted into joyful merriment. "Vaya! Way to go, Carlos!" they said as they approached, giving him the gang handshake: palms slapping together, fists one on top of the other, and a punch of the knuckles with the index and pinkie fingers spread out in the sign of the devil, the typical greeting for MS gangsters. "Felicidades, homes! Now you're one of us," said Sniper, vigorously patting Carlos on the back to make sure he harbored no hard feelings for the late blow. Then, proudly pounding his own chest with his fist, he loudly declared, "I'm Sniper. ¿Y vos?" A grin spread slowly across Carlos's face as he answered, "You can call me Joker." Trouble, a carnal[10] to Carlos, approached him and gave him a big hug. "Welcome to the barrio, Joker. Mara Salvatrucha forever!"

After his initiation, Joker's homeboys threw a big party to honor him and celebrate the occasion. At the time, Joker felt on top of the world, invincible. But early the next morning, when he returned home to his apartment, drunk and battered, Joker began to have serious doubts. He stumbled into the bathroom, trying not to make noise and wake up his mother or aunt, who had a long workday ahead of them. When he turned on the light, the image Joker saw in the mirror startled him. His face was much more banged-up than he had expected, and for the first time he began to reflect on his decision to join the gang. Suddenly, he was infected with a plague of doubts. "What the fuck have you done now?!" Joker thought to himself. But after a moment of self-recrimination, Joker returned to the stubborn fact that whether he liked it or not, he was now a full-fledged member of la Mara Salvatrucha, and he had better play the part.

By joining the gang, he felt he had killed off his old identity as Carlos and replaced it with the gangster status of a *Joker*. What lead Carlos to join the gang? Did he feel pressured to join, or was it a completely voluntary decision? What aspect of his personality and disposition made him a likely candidate for joining? What parts of his past and his present circumstances compelled Carlos to become a hard-core member of the gang? In order to understand the complexity of factors that led up to his decision to join MS, let's look at the anatomy of his decision.

The Anatomy of a Decision

Like most important decisions, the decision to join a street gang is multi-determined, based on a complex combination of emotional and practical considerations involving psychological, social, and cultural factors. What surprised me most about Carlos and these other youths' decisions to join MS was the fact that they were often not carefully thought out or based on a careful cost-benefit analysis. On reflection, this shouldn't have been a surprise. The actions of teenagers, whether male or female, can be quite capricious and unreasonable. Although there are many practical or logical reasons why youth choose to join a street gang, including their needs for protection, status, and belonging, the fact is that their decisions are heavily influenced by their adolescent frustrations.

Adolescence is a maturational stage in human development that is typified by conflicting thoughts and feelings, spurred by raging hormones. In addition, adolescents lack the brain development to make good decisions. The area of the brain responsible for decision-making is the pre-frontal cortex, which in some males is not fully developed until age twenty-five.[11] As a result, youth are handicapped at the start. An immature brain partly explains why these Salvadoran immigrant youth decided to join a street gang, but it doesn't consider their experiences of their hostile environments and their need for protection.

Some youth join street gangs out of fear for their personal safety, while others join out of a need to belong to a group of like-minded individuals or to satisfy their appetites for power, prestige, money, or sex. All of these physical needs and desires are emotionally charged. The gang's hedonistic, rule-breaking ideology fitted these immigrant youth's stereotype of a desirable group, one that embraced them with open arms.[12] While each of their reasons for joining the gang had a strong emotional component, the context for their thoughts and feelings was their harsh environments. Given these harsh environments and a strong emotional connection to gang members, it is no surprise that some of these youth chose to join the gang. Despite all the rational reasons for joining, many of these youth put little thought into making this important decision.

> I didn't really think about it too much. I started dressing like a cholo, acting like a cholo, drinking like a cholo, and then one day, I just decided to become a cholo. We went to a ditching party at the beach, and I decided right then and there to get jumped in. I don't know why I decided then. It seemed like the right thing to do at the time.
>
> —Sniper

Like Sniper, Joker's decision to join the gang and participate in gang-like behavior was not well thought out. For him it was a gradual incorporation into the gang that started as a fashion statement. He said he loved the gangster *look*: the khaki, super-sized baggy pants—good for hiding guns or stolen merchandise—the plaid long-sleeved shirt, buttoned to the neck to hide one's tattoos, and the Nike Cortez sneakers, good for making a quick getaway. Joker had already shaved his head to make his shiny brown-skinned crown look menacing, and these clothes completed the look. "I didn't dress like a cholo at home," he said. "I didn't want my mother to know. So I would take my cholo clothes to school and change there." Joker liked the way this gangster appearance made him feel, both cool and tough. However, although fashion played a role in his decision, it was only one of many reasons why he chose to become an MS gang member.

Alcohol, drugs, and cigarettes also played parts in his decision. Joker was attracted to the idea of being able to drink and smoke, and he knew he could drink and smoke as much as he wanted once he joined the gang. Liquor was almost always a part of hanging out, what the homies

FIGURE **3.2 Los Angeles, CA, 1993. Trigger poses holding the first teddy bear he has owned. Copyright © Donna DeCesare, 1993.**

call *kickin' it*. And drugs were widely available to those who wanted them. In addition to alcohol and drugs, Joker was attracted to the idea of owning a gun. Like most teenage boys, firearms fascinated him, and he knew that by joining this gang he would get easy access to them.

> I liked the way the guns looked and the feeling I got when I was hold-ing one. When you have a gun in your hand, you feel very powerful and people pay attention. With a gun in your hand, you have power to end someone's life. You can make him give you whatever you want, whatever he's got.

In addition to this sense of power being an MS gangster gave him, per-sonal safety also played a part in Joker's decision to join. At the time, he figured he wouldn't get *punked out* if he were *packing*—i.e., bullies would no longer pick on him if he were a member of a notorious street gang carrying a loaded weapon. Joker told me that anyone can buy a gun on the black market or steal one, but it is much easier to get a gun if you are in a gang. "And better yet," he added, with a menacing grin, "being in a gang gave me an excuse to use it." Intimately tied to his concern for safety, the excitement engendered by firearms provided Joker a powerful incentive to take the risks involved with being a hard-core gang member, including the risks of death, disability, or life behind bars. Like his fellow gangsters, Joker looked forward to opportunities to hunt down enemy gang members, but even this was not a sufficient motive for him to join the gang.

In addition to the excitement and danger of death inherent in fighting gang enemies, joining a gang provided Joker the milder forms of excitement of friendships and parties. "I liked to kick back with homeboys and party," he told me. Because he shared many interests with his *compas*,[13] Joker felt he *belonged* to this particular group of misfits. "We clicked," he said. Joker shared his homeboys' ribald sense of humor, their Salvadoran culture and accent, their sense of alienation, and their desire to break rules. His new friends were generous in sharing their alcohol and drugs with him. And once Joker joined the gang, his opportunities to attend parties increased geometrically. Protection, excitement, solidarity, camaraderie, and constant partying were compelling reasons for Joker to join the gang, but they, too, formed only part of his decision to join this street gang.

Dating was another significant reason why Joker decided to join MS. A couple of days after he was jumped into MS, I interviewed Joker about his reasons for joining the gang. When he told me that he joined the gang to get a girl, I didn't believe him at first. "You did it for *a girl*?!" I asked incredulously. "Yeah, there's this cute girl in my class," he answered, "She is so beautiful. She has long black hair, big shapely hips, a nice fat ass, and really big tits!" he said, gesticulating enthusiastically. Because this young woman was a *hood rat*,[14] Joker correctly calculated that joining the gang would give him an opportunity to date her. However, post-conquest, Joker eventually lost interest in his new girlfriend. "There so many other girls to choose from," he said later, rationalizing his decision to dump her. The gang satisfied Joker adolescent desire for dating and sexual relations, but despite his claim, getting the girl or girls was not the tipping point in his decision to join MS.

Among the many reasons he gave for joining MS, street socialization was a factor that Joker neglected to mention, because it was something that he took for granted. He lived in a gang-infested neighborhood, where the ideology or code of the streets predominates. For some of these impressionable, disenfranchised immigrant youth, street gangs have a positive connotation. From this defiant or deviant perspective, gangs are not only powerful, they are also honorable or even heroic. African-American and Chicano youth or poor young immigrants from El Salvador, Vietnam, or Samoa who grow up in these barrios of Los Angeles are attracted to street gangs because of a glorified notion of the "gangster." Joker told me a gangster is someone who defies the law, someone who "takes no shit," and who lives by his own rules. He said that a gangster goes where he wants to, and he takes whatever he wants, whenever he wants it. For Joker, becoming a hard-core MS gangster meant becoming liberated or freed to do whatever he wanted. It also meant being rewarded for his deviant behavior, which increased his reputation and the reputation of his gang. In sum, Joker considered a gangster as his own law and disorder.

This hedonistic impulse of hard-core street gangsters, like Joker, finds its forbearers in the nineteenth-century bandits of the Wild West, such as Jesse James or Billy the Kid, and in the gangsters of the 1920s and 1930s, such as Bonnie and Clyde or Al Capone. These legendary gangsters formed bands of criminals, like The Wild Bunch or the Hole in the Wall Gang, who lived hard, fast lives. They set the standard for later gangsters who also took risks for fame and fortune. Although Joker knew little about this history, the sentiment behind his participation in the gang was the same. One has to break rules in order to get what you want.

Ostensibly, a gangster has a code of honor, but this is contingent on attitudes and opportunities. Some street gangsters do not let loyalty to their tribe get in the way of personal gain. In order to create a better life for himself, a gangster must learn how to successfully buck the system by breaking rules. For Joker, becoming a gangster meant that he could break rules, and he fully expected that this would bring him wealth, power, and status. The extent to which members of street gangs achieve these goals is debatable. But the fact that these youth, like Joker, see joining a street gang as an opportunity for fame and fortune is enough to convince them to join and actively participate.

Many people, believing what they see on TV news reports, think that gang membership is the result of inheritance or family tradition—a misperception that is also perpetuated by the police and newspapers.[15] Although many youth who become street gang members have relatives who are in gangs—and having parents or siblings who are members of a street gang significantly increases one's risk for joining—very few children of gang members are born into traditional or multi-generational gangs. When MS started, none of the original members had parents or relatives that were gang members. The founders of the gang—and there were many—were first-generation immigrants and first-generation gang members. None of these immigrant youth had parents who were gang members, and none of their parents approved of street gangs. Joker was no exception to this rule. His mother was not a gang member, and she thought that street gangs were disgusting. Joker was the first and only member of his family who joined a gang.

What I consider the *tipping point* for Joker's decision to join MS was his desire for status and a surrogate family, one that accepted him for who he was at that particular place and time. The street gang became his adoptive family, even though it was more dysfunctional than the one he left behind. He created his criminal identity by imitating his peers and his elders. Although Joker's decision to join the gang was capricious and spontaneous, it was made within the context of all of these risk factors, including safety, status, sex, and successful adaptation to a hostile environment. This illustrates the complexity of the risks for joining a street gang.[16] Joker had his many personal motives for joining MS, but they were situated within a social context. His decision to join the gang was also influenced by biological factors, including brain development and changing hormones. As an adolescent immigrant, Joker was motivated to join MS because of the way it made him *feel*. It made him feel important, like someone who counts. The gang also gave Joker a feeling of belonging to a group of like-minded individuals.

Contrary to the stereotypical view, some of the older, wiser members of the gang tried to dissuade Carlos from joining. These veterans of MS told him, "Don't be an idiot, stay in school!" Because Carlos was a good student, they had greater expectations for him. More importantly, however, they considered him a soccer player with great potential. Despite their admonitions, however, Joker would not be dissuaded from joining MS. Like his fellow homeboys, Joker had been primed for gang life, having witnessed and become desensitized to the extreme violence of the civil war in his homeland. Joker was also a good candidate to become a hard-core gang member because he had endured the harsh discipline and emotional neglect of his father and survived the rupture and dislocation of his family. Carlos had been uprooted from his home in El Salvador and plopped down into a violent barrio of Los Angeles. He faced new pressures in his "adoptive" country, including the harassment of hostile neighborhood gang members and a new school where his fellow students teased him in a foreign tongue.

Like his fellow gang members, Joker wanted to belong to a group that that supported him. Many of these rebellious adolescents considered their gang as the only group who accepted them fully for who they were, despite their flaws. The gang also provided them protection. As Joker said, "When the shit hits the fan, who has your back?" For Joker and his fellow gang members, the gang was the group that was there for them when they needed it the most. Many gang members suffer from a deficit of beliefs and a deficit of opportunities. The deficit of beliefs are those doubts that one can "make it" in the world and be "successful." All of these MS gang members wanted a good life, however they conceived it. Generally speaking, gang members feel a lack of comfort and believe that the gang can ameliorate this deficit. For these undocumented Salvadoran immigrant youth, there were not many positive options available. Given this deficit of options, Joker and a few of his fellow immigrant youth decided to seek comfort in a street gang.

Materialistically speaking, comfort for a gang member can be a set of wheels, a girl on each shoulder, a toke of reefer, a cold Corona, a nice set of threads, or a Gat in his giddy-up (a gun tucked into his pants). From a psychological perspective, comfort for a gang member is much like comfort is for the rest of us—the feeling of "counting" and being cared for. Whether for materialistic or emotional needs, a small minority of youth decides to join a street gang. Usually, it is a case of both needing a meaningful emotional connection *and* wanting all of the material goods available. In addition, some adolescents join a street gang to escape a dangerous environment at home, at school, or in the neighborhood. The decision to join a gang only makes sense to those who believe that their gang will protect them and keep them from psychological or bodily harm. It only makes sense to those who believe that their gang will provide them with wealth or elevated status or that their gang is the perfect social club for dating. It only makes sense to those who believe that their gang deeply cares about their welfare. At some level of expectation, one or more of these beliefs compels these impressionable youth to join a street gang.

Given the complexity of the decision to join a street gang, it is not surprising that there are no good predictors for who will join or for outcomes. My fieldwork with these Salvadoran gang members revealed that the complexity of the interaction of these risk factors made prediction impossible. Risk factors are descriptive, post hoc phenomena. They can serve as warning signs for the statistical probability of someone joining a gang, but they cannot definitively predict who is going to join or the length of time or the nature of their participation. Nor can these risk factors predict outcomes for active gang members.

Despite this limitation, it is still useful to know what typically motivates youths like Joker to join a street gang. Based on my research, I divide the these root causes for joining a street gang into six main problems areas, each representing a different level of analysis: (1) *personality*, or psychological disposition; (2) *puberty*, or biological maturation; (3) *parenting*, or family dynamics, caretaking, and discipline; (4) *poverty*, or relative economic and ecological deprivation, for example, poor schools or poor neighborhoods; (5) *prejudice*, or discrimination; and (6) *peers*, which are pro-social or deviant. These problems areas can be conceptualized as concentric circles enveloping an individual, a metaphorical map of an individual's physical reality and his or her state of mind, which is governed by reason and emotion. A diagram of these factors would represent all of an individual's interactions in the past and present, as well as his or her future expectations.

A youth's decision to join a street gang is heavily influenced by what he or she anticipates as possible outcomes. Because context is a significant factor in youths' decisions to join a street gang, it should be represented as an overlay that covers these other aspects. Context clouds the thoughts and feelings of these adolescents, confronted with the opportunity or pressure to join a gang. These problem areas are interactive and interdependent, and they change over place and time. The decision to join a gang is a highly personal one, but youths' pasts, their parents, their environments, and especially their peers heavily influence their decision to join a gang.

The Salvadoran youths that joined MS were children of poor, undocumented immigrants. Some of these youths were motivated by a need to escape painful conditions, such as physical beatings. They were also motivated by a desire for material goods, such as money, drugs, cars, and guns. In addition, they were motivated by a search for sex and excitement or the status and respect that come with being a "gangster." All of the hard-core MS gang members that made up this study were motivated by a combination of all these factors. Although their decisions were also influenced by their fatalistic attitudes, rebellious dispositions, and frustrations with the status quo, joining the gang was heavily influenced by their desire to escape from misery or suffering.

Escape from Misery

Kids join gangs to get away from an abusive home. 87 percent of juveniles incarcerated in California for murder were victimized physically or sexually in the home.[17]

Sharing miserable pasts was one of the bonds that emotionally linked these Salvadoran youths and created a sense of solidarity. Psycho did not complain about his past but instead channeled his pain and frustration into an aggressive, take-no-prisoners attitude toward his gangster life. Although he never mentioned suicidal intentions, his actions demonstrated a self-destructive bent. For Psycho, joining MS was his way to escape from his misery. Misery is both a physical condition and a state of mind. It includes a feeling of loss, as well as a severe lack of contentment or tranquility. Psycho was somewhat depressed as a result of his perceived poverty and squalor, and he felt a lack of spiritual connection to people or a place. Discrimination only added to his feelings of sadness and anger.

Psycho's feeling of misery began at an early age. He never knew his father, who had been killed by the military when he was two years old, and because of his constant bouncing between relatives during his childhood, he had developed no strong emotional attachments to his kinfolk. The brutality he witnessed in El Salvador during the civil war had made him cynical. As an unwilling immigrant to the States, he was discontented with his new surroundings. For these reasons, he was suspicious, aggressive and had an exceedingly short fuse. His attitude toward life was extremely fatalistic. When he joined MS, Psycho told me that nothing mattered to him. "What the fuck," he said, "What do I have to lose?" Given this feeling of emptiness, Psycho felt he had everything to gain and nothing to lose by becoming a gang member. When he joined MS, Psycho decided to go all out. Other MS gang members told me that Psycho was crazier than most, and he sometimes took unnecessary risks, like walking through an enemy's turf at night, alone.

In contrast, Lil' Silent was not an extreme risk-taker. He joined the gang to escape an abusive relationship at home. As described earlier, when his mother's alcoholic boyfriend put a gun to Lil' Silent's head, he immediately left the apartment and began sleeping in the park or in metal dumpsters at night. For the next two weeks he was homeless. He scavenged for food and shelter until local MS gang members unofficially adopted him, giving him a place to sleep and food to eat. "They took me in," said Lil' Silent, "I had no place else to go." This rescue was reason enough for Lil' Silent to join the gang. He felt he owed them his life, and they also gave him friendship and a sense of caring and belonging.

Among the many miseries that Sniper was escaping were prejudice and discrimination. As a short, dark-skinned immigrant, with Indian facial features, he experienced an enormous amount of racism, particularly from his peers at school. In addition to being teased about his appearance, Sniper was sometimes beaten by the school bullies, who were Mexican or Mexican-American gang members. When they started stealing Sniper's lunch money and his backpack, he decided to seek help. "I needed backup," he told me. "And my homies gave it to me." MS not only provided Sniper with immediate protection, it instilled in him a sense of masculine pride. As a hard-core member of this respected gang, Sniper gained a macho gangster identity, which was an antidote to the stigmatizing degradations of racism. While all of these hard-core Salvadoran gang members were motivated by a need to escape their misery, they were also drawn into the gang because of their desires for status, pleasure, camaraderie, and excitement, or an escape from boredom.

Jales, Jainas, and Ranflas

There is nothing boring about jales, jainas, and ranflas. For male gang members, few things are as exciting as a *jale* (drive-by shooting), a beautiful *jaina* (girlfriend), and a *ranfla* (car). Of these attractions to the gang life, girlfriends tend to be overlooked as risk factors. Like Joker, Sniper was powerfully motivated to join MS in order to explore his libidinous lust. At school, he noticed that the prettiest girls were attracted to gang members. "The hottest jainas hung out with the homeboys," Sniper said. "There was one in particular that I wanted to date. So, I joined the gang to get the girl." But like Joker, Sniper soon lost interest in his conquest. This aspect of street gangs as dating services, or "sex clubs," can be found in the autobiographical literature on gangs.[18] As Sniper and Joker's cases illustrate, dating and sexual relations can be compelling motives for some youth to join a street gang.

Although Trouble was even more of a "player" or womanizer than his fellow homeboys, he said he joined the gang for excitement and status. He was also attracted to the gang for financial gain. He had grown up extremely poor in El Salvador, and seeing the low-paying jobs his parents held in the United States., he rejected the idea of following in their footsteps. Trouble saw the gang as an economic opportunity, which would provide him with easy, albeit illegal, ways of making money. After he joined the gang, he was able to extort "rent" from drug dealers and street vendors in the neighborhood. He also made money by robbing people on the street of their money, purses, or jewelry, and stealing cars and selling the parts. In addition to this economic incentive, the gang gave Trouble access to drugs, which, infrequently, he sold at a handsome profit. In addition, he loved the danger of being a hardcore gangster, which gave him opportunities to test his fighting skills. For him, there was nothing more exciting than the deadly battles with enemy gang members. Fighting provided him not only an escape from the misery of being picked on by school bullies, it also provided him a major form of entertainment.

There are two other factors regarding the decision to join a gang that deserve mentioning. The first concerns the amount of information a novice has about the gang's activities, including the incumbent dangers, before he or she decides to join. This raises the question of how accurate the youths' assessment of risk is and to what extent they miscalculate the risks of involvement. Gang members, like other people, are fairly bad at calculating risk. As the gang members told me, most gang initiates have a fairly good idea of what they're getting into because they have lived in the neighborhood a sufficient amount of time, and they have watched and learned from active gang members. "They already know what's going on," said Sniper. "They know they can be killed and they don't really care." Despite this fatalistic attitude, the people making the calculations of risk are adolescents, who are not mature enough to know what it means to die. To have a general idea of what is involved in gang activity bares only a slight resemblance to actual experience of participation and the sometimes dire consequences of their actions. Many older members told me that although they knew about the risks, they were somewhat naïve when they joined the gang. After years of gangbanging, many of these ex-members repeated some version of the mantra, "If I had known what I was getting into, I never would have done it."

The second point rarely gets mentioned in discussions about joining street gangs. This is the fact that some active gang members, especially *veteranos* (or OGs, original gangsters), who have experienced the negative effects of gang participation, try to steer kids away from gangs. For example, several of the older gang members of his clique told Joker that it was stupid for him to join their gang and tried to prevent him from joining. Because he was an excellent student athlete, they told him he should stay in school, and several times they refused to jump him in. But Joker was hardheaded and ambitious, and he pestered the homeboys until they finally let him join. In another illustrative case, Trouble's older brother tried to keep him out of the gang. "My brother told me, 'I'm gonna kick your ass if you join,'" said Trouble. "But I knew some pretty cool homeboys, and they jumped me in, anyway." To avoid conflict, Trouble asked his fellow gang members not to tell his brother. "I kept it a secret for about four months," he said. "It was pretty funny. I was writing my *placaso* all over the alleys and in the streets. One time, my brother asked me, 'Who's this Trouble from Southside?' And I said, 'I don't know, but he gets around.'" Eventually, Trouble's ruse was exposed.

> My brother got shot in the leg. And one of the homeboys said, "Trouble will take you to the hospital." Then, when I got in the car to drive him, he didn't want to believe it. "You're Trouble?" I was afraid he was going to beat me up, but he said, "Nah. You got jumped in, what can I do?" It was too late. That was it.

Despite these disincentives and warnings from older gang members, some hardheaded, rebellious youth, like Trouble, still decide to join a gang. All of the MS gang members that I got to know well shared the risk factors of poverty, family dysfunction, culture shock, discrimination, and physical attack. In addition to these risk factors, they suffered many years of separation from their families, and their reunions in the United States were extremely difficult. It was hard for these immigrant youths to bond with parents who they consciously or subconsciously felt had abandoned them. Those who had fathers or stepfathers found them distant, overworked, or abusive. Home was not a refuge for them, and neither was school. Without a place where they felt safe or wanted, and with no sense of belonging, these young kids quickly escaped to the city streets, which also proved no safe haven. Life on the streets merely posed a different set of challenges. In each new setting, these immigrant youth learned what all animals know instinctively—that life is first and foremost about survival.

Having undergone the traumas and uncertainties of the civil war in El Salvador, being uprooted, and moving to a new country, where they did not speak the language and did not know the customs, these boys and girls became hypersensitive to the issues of security and protection. They had experienced and become desensitized to the powerful effects of violence and death in their homeland. They learned to identify both with the victims and the perpetrators of violence, and thus were ripe to resort to violence when confronted by yet another harsh environment. In the barrio streets of Los Angeles, they found one sufficiently harsh. They quickly learned that to survive on the barrio streets of Los Angeles, one needs protection. It is not hard to see why some of these vulnerable immigrant youth, socialized from an early age to violence, might turn to a street gang for solace and safety. In their minds, the gang would provide them the status, solace and security they so desperately sought. And they couldn't have been more wrong.

Notes

1. Van der Kolk, 1987, pp.14, 16.
2. Vato can be translated as "dude," "guy," or fellow barrio warrior.
3. Translation: "Your father hits you with his stick."
4. Cf. Klein, 1995; Spergel, 1995. To understand what separates these gang members from their fellow Salvadoran immigrant youth who decided not to join the gang, see "Anatomy of a Decision," later in this chapter.
5. Cf. Huff, 1996; Sanchez-Jankowski, 1991; Rodriguez, 1993; Shakur, 1993; Sikes, 1997.
6. This "tough" gang member said when they started his brincada, they put three homeboys on him. But because he was getting the upper hand, they added another two, and then another two (which makes seven). Other gang members who were present at his initiation corroborated his story.

7. This is someone who "wants to be" a gang member but has not joined the gang, and may never join the gang. A wannabe is anyone who looks or "acts" gangster, and likes the gangster status, but is unwilling to take the risk of joining.

8. This means that if s/he dies or is beaten or exploited, he or she does not "count"—i.e., merit retaliation by the gang members.

9. Cabrón means bastard or cuckold, or (in Chile) a pimp.

10. A blood brother or best friend.

11. Diamond, Adele. 2002. Normal development of prefrontal cortex from birth to young adulthood: Cognitive functions, anatomy, and biochemistry. In Stuss, Donald T., and Knight, Robert T. (eds.), *Principles of Frontal Lobe Function*. New York: Oxford University Press, pp. 466–503.

12. And closed fists.

13. Spanish slang for "good friends"; from *compañeros*.

14. A "hood rat" is a girl who is attracted to gang members and hangs out with them.

15. Cf. Moore, 1991, p. 49.

16. Cf. Howell, 1998; Huff, 1996; Maxon and Whitlock, 2002; Thornberry et al, 2006; and Miller, 2006.

17. Al Valdez, quoted in Fuchs et al. 2007.

18. Cf. Rodriguez, 1993; Sanchez, 2000.

CHAPTER 4

....

From Prey to Predators—
The Origins and
Transformation of MS

Where did our gang come from? Well, there was this soccer match between a Mexican and a Salvadoran soccer team, and two of the players got into an argument and started throwing punches. The other players immediately joined the fight, including some Mexican cholos [gang members] who had been watching the game. Because the Salvadorans were outnumbered, they got beat up. So these guys decided to form their own gang for protection, and they named it after that soccer team, which was called Mara Salvatrucha.

—Sniper

This story of the origin of MS is illustrative of the inadequacies of oral history. Sniper's version of his gang's birth as the result of a soccer war represents one of the two most prominent myths about the origin of MS. Older members of the gang had told Sniper this story, but he wasn't there to witness it. It made sense to Sniper that some of his fellow Salvadoran youth, provoked by bullies, would organize themselves into a street gang for self-defense. In 1993, when I began this research, I asked MS gang members about the origin of their gang, and many of them told me some version of this story of the soccer fight. Several of these gang members said this fight occurred in the summer of 1982, in Lincoln Park, a large city park in East Los Angeles. No one knew for certain why the fight started, but they suspected that it had something to do with overly aggressive play or nationalistic pride. They knew from their own experience that Mexicans were racist against them and used ethnic differences as an excuse to pick on them. To these Salvadoran immigrant youth it seemed reasonable that a fistfight could escalate into a brawl and that this would be sufficient cause to form a street gang. Regardless of whether or not this soccer fight actually took place as they reported, it was not the origin of their gang.

The second major myth of the gang's origins has been perpetrated by law enforcement officials. Their version of the story bears even less resemblance to the truth of how MS got started than that of these misinformed gang members. For example, according to Al Valdez, of the National Alliance of Gang Investigators Associations,[1] the Mara Salvatrucha gang is a "South American Import" [sic], formed in the late 1980s by a coalition of Salvadoran refugees in the United States, some of whom had ties to a violent street gang in El Salvador, called La Mara, and others who were guerilla combatants from the Farabundo Marti National Liberation Front, "adept at using explosives, firearms, and booby traps." In response to attacks from neighborhood Hispanic gangs in Los Angeles, these immigrants from El Salvador formed their own gang, whose membership, according to Valdez, "continues to be fed by refugees from groups like FMNL [sic]."

This version is riddled with errors. First, El Salvador is not in South America but Central America, which is part of the North American continent. Second, MS was not an import but was started in Los Angeles by Salvadoran immigrant youth. These youths did not bring the gang subculture with them but learned it in the barrios of southern California. Furthermore, there is no evidence of a gang in El Salvador called La Mara. And lastly, although a few MS members were former combatants with the FMLN, as many gang members were former soldiers within the Salvadoran military. A few of these soldiers were trained in the School of the Americas in the United States and brought to the gang their knowledge of counterinsurgency tactics. Valdez gives the false impression that MS is the offspring of indigenous Salvadoran gang members and former combatants from the guerrilla forces of the Farabundo Marti National Liberation Front.[2] This misconception is also proposed by another gang investigators' organization, calling itself Know Gangs, which claims that MS started in El Salvador from a group of former guerilla soldiers who called themselves Salvatruchas, or Salvadoran gangsters.[3]

As products of oral history, both the gang members' and law enforcement's versions of the origin of MS are flawed by misinformation.

Whereas the soccer war version was based on rumors spread by its own members, the law enforcement version of the origin of MS takes half-truths or complete fabrications and wildly exaggerates them. The story of the soccer fight had acquired the status of an origin myth within the gang, and its veracity was enshrined through repetition. On the other hand, the law enforcement version of events was propagated through police conferences and the Internet and became established fact to another sector of society. None of the MS veterans or original gangsters I interviewed had belonged to any gang in El Salvador, much less a fictitious gang called La Mara. And although a few MS gang members had been FMLN combatants or soldiers in the military, the vast majority had no prior experience fighting in the civil war. Out of approximately 150 gang members I interviewed in Los Angeles during the course of fieldwork, only six were former guerrilla combatants. In contrast, seven members I interviewed had previously belonged to the Salvadoran military. The documentary films *Children of War* and *Fruits of War* suggest that within the MS and 18th Street gangs in El Salvador, the numbers of former combatants from both sides of the civil war is much higher. But these youths joined the gangs after the mass deportations of gang members from the United States in the mid-1990s, long after the gang had been formed.

Contrary to the law enforcement view, Mara Salvatrucha did not originate in El Salvador. It was not a guerrilla offshoot, nor was it the product of gang transplants from El Salvador. Salvadoran immigrant youth learned the street gang subculture in the United States and then exported it back to their homeland after they were deported. MS was also not the result of a soccer fight. Although both of these versions have grains of truth—gang formation as a result of violence and discrimination—the roots of MS are deeper and much more complex than either of these stories suggests. Mara Salvatrucha was born in Los Angeles and, as such, constitutes a very small part of a long history of American street gangs. Like many of the earliest street gangs in the United States, MS was the result of discrimination and the victimization of impoverished immigrant youth. Like their past brethren, these Salvadoran immigrant youths suffered the indignities of being outcasts of society. Like their early forbearers, they banded together in their struggle to cope with the harsh conditions of their adoptive country. But what is most interesting about the formation of Mara Salvatrucha is that it did not start out as a violent, predatory organization but as a vehicle for the satisfaction of adolescent hedonistic desires. MS did not start out as a prototypical or traditional street gang. In fact, it started out as a stoner gang that, metaphorically speaking, is a bird of a completely different plumage.

A Devil's Pact—The Mara Salvatrucha Stoners

According to elders of the gang that I interviewed—the *veteranos* or old timers who were around from the start—the real roots of MS date back to the mid- to late 1970s, when a group of longhaired devil worshippers got together and formed a stoner gang, which they called Mara Salvatrucha Stoners, or MSS. The name derives from a popular Spanish street slang term, *Salvatrucha*, which refers to a Salvadoran in the United States who has become "Americanized," acculturated in his dress, speech, or manners. Salvatrucha is a compound word, whose prefix, *Salva* is an abbreviation of Salvadoreño, which identifies their nationality, and its suffix, *trucha*, which is Calo or Mexican-American street slang for "Watch out!" or "Be careful!" The dictionary definition of the Spanish word trucha is *trout*, and the word also means sleight of hand, a trickster, or a con man. However, I doubt the stoners intended any of these additional meanings when they chose the name of their gang.

Mara is a colloquial term in El Salvador for the common people, or the masses. For example, in El Salvador in the past, they might refer to the kids who live in high-class or ritzy neighborhoods by saying— "*Ah, bá, hay pura mara fresa.*" *Fresa* means "pretty boy" or "rich kid," and thus "*mara fresa*" refers to a group of stuck-up rich adolescents. "*Hay mara escandalosa*" is another example that refers to a group of delinquent youth. It wasn't until the late 1990s, with the rapid expansion of gangs in El Salvador, that the term *mara* became synonymous with a street gang. Thus, the name Mara Salvatrucha can be loosely translated as "Watch out for us Salvadoran folk, or gangsters," which is both a warning and a declaration of nationalistic pride. It loosely means, "Don't mess with us."

As a stoner gang, MSS was as different from street gangs as heavy metal music is from gangster rap, the types of music that inform each of these groups, respectively. Stoner gangs are unlike street gangs in their attire, attitudes, activities, and their *raison d'etre*, or reason for being. These stoners did not wear the stereotypical cholo outfit of Nike

Cortez sneakers, knee-high white socks, sleeveless, "wife-beater" t-shirts (V-neck cotton shirts without sleeves) and baggy khaki pants, starched to a fine razor-sharp crease. Instead, they wore Converse tennis shoes—whose logo of a five-pointed star mimics a pentagram—and gave their tight bell-bottomed blue jeans a roughed-up, beaten look by slitting them with razor blades and repeatedly rubbing stones over them, the precursor to stone-washed jeans. They draped their black leather jackets over cotton short-sleeved t-shirts decorated with the pictures of their favorite bands, such as AC/DC, Anthrax, Vampire, Black Sabbath, Slayer, Iron Maiden, Metallica, Motley Crüe, and Twisted Sister. And unlike street cholos with their shaven heads, these stoners let their shaggy, uncombed hair grow long enough to hang down their backs.

MS Stoners were also unlike cholos in their attitudes and activities. They did not try to prove their machismo by starting fights with enemy gang members or by committing crimes, like theft, extortion, drug dealing, or drive-by shootings. The stoners' attitude was reflected in their main activity, which was getting *stoned* on marijuana. Their other main activity was tripping out on the cacophonous beats of ear-splitting, mind-bending heavy metal music. Sometimes to augment this experience, stoners were known to drop a couple of tabs of LSD before a rock concert and then dive into the slam pit (or mosh pit), which is the area in front of the stage where the audience amuses itself by physically slamming into one another. In this respect, stoner gangs are closer to party gangs than traditional street gangs, entrepreneurial gangs, or fighting gangs. In another respect, however, this particular stoner gang was unique—or one of a kind. A few of its members were hard-core Satanists who worshipped the devil and went so far as to practice gruesome animal sacrifices. These Satanists gave MSS its badass reputation for evil.

Although the vast majority of these stoners never participated in these bloody ritual animal sacrifices or gave any thought to becoming Satanists, they banked on their gang's reputation for devil worship, which gave it and them an aura of mystery and terror. Stoners have reportedly killed lambs, pigs, goats, dogs, and cats by cutting out their livers or hearts or severing their heads. They have also been reported to squeeze hamsters to death with their bare hands, or shake them in a box of nails, and then smear the animal's blood over their own bodies. Supposedly, stoners skinned and ate these animals or cut off their fore and hind legs to symbolize the denial of the passion of Christ, whose hands and feet

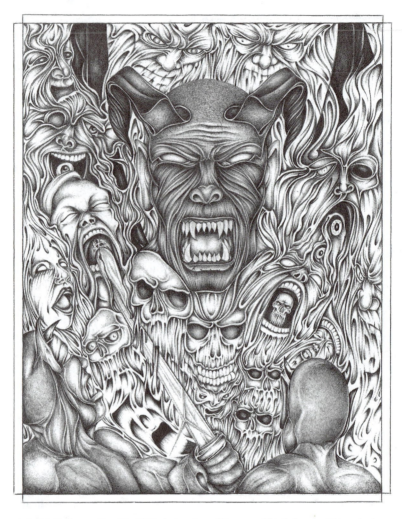

FIGURE 4.1 Crescent City, CA, 2010. A drawing of Satan and his followers. The artist is an MS gang member serving time in the Security Housing Unit, C-9 of Pelican Bay State Prison. Copyright © T. W. Ward, 2011.

carry the stigmata, or the signs of sacrifice.[4] There are also unsubstantiated rumors of stoners sacrificing humans, as in 1990, when four people were ritualistically slaughtered in Salida, California, as part of an initiation rite.[5] Diaries of these cult members recount forced sodomy and beatings for disobedience, bloodletting curses, and secret oaths.

Over the course of research, I met with four of these hard-core Satanists, two of whom had joined the gang in Los Angeles and two in El Salvador. At my request, a gang member I knew well set up my first meeting with one of these MSS members who had a reputation as dedicated worshiper of Satan. The interview with this Satanist took place in a cemetery, but I declined to go at night. For the purpose of masking the identities of these four MSS gang members, I will call this composite character Evil, which is a popular nickname. Evil said he joined MSS as an act of rebellion against his mother, who was a devout Jehovah's Witness. "She would beat me if I didn't learn my Bible lessons," said Evil. "From an early age, I had to go out on street corners and preach the gospel to strangers. I despised the long hours we had to sit in church, so I went the opposite way."

Evil claims he was born with a bit of the devil already inside him because of his Scottish father, whom he never met, but was told had bright red hair. What little Evil knows about Scotland—the history of English invasion and the rape of Scottish women—he learned from the movie *Braveheart*. Like its main character, Evil saw himself as a heroic rebel. He later showed me a black-and-white photograph of himself as a stoner, performing a satanic ritual in a graveyard. In the photo, Evil's long straggly hair conceals his face as he bends over what looks like a woodland campfire. He explained to me,

> This was taken in a graveyard where I performed sacrifices to Satan. Some angels who came to me in a dream told me I was an archangel and should do his bidding. The devil himself visited me once, and told me he would fulfill my wishes if I sacrificed and prayed to him. I know he is extremely powerful, because I've felt it.

Evil said his initiation into MSS was simple. "We went to a cemetery and swore an oath by drinking each other's blood," he said. "We took a knife and cut our hands and then drained our blood into a cup to drink it. We smoked a lot of *mota* [marijuana], and then we cut open a cat." I had no way of corroborating his story, but then again, he didn't appear to be exaggerating. Although Evil told me he is no longer a stoner and has sworn off satanic worship, he still believes he is an archangel with the power to call on Satan for help should he need it. Evil confirmed for me what other older gang members had told me about the low representation of devil worshipers amongst their membership. He said that he was one of only a handful of such dedicated supplicants within MSS.

Evil also told me that his stoner gang's activities were never structured or organized. "Each guy just did what he wanted to do, and what
he thought was cool," he said. Unlike traditional street gangs who see
themselves as protectors of their neighborhoods, stoners see themselves
as destroyers and are known for desecrating graves and tagging graffiti
of their gang name on tombstones.[6] Evil told me that their rituals, which
were usually spontaneous and unplanned, were often influenced by the
lyrics of their favorite heavy metal songs. "Some of us read the Black
Bible, but most of us just made shit up," he said. "Once, when I was tripping on acid, I took a Bible and lit it on fire. I was holding it out like this
[with his arms outstretched], and another homeboy knelt down before
me and started speaking in tongues. We were definitely tripping out!"

Stoners are typically nomadic and nonterritorial, and their members do not conflict with traditional street gang members, who see the
stoners as wimps or sissies because of their dress and the perception that
they do not want to fight.[7] Evil said that although his gang did not fight
with street gangs, they did beat up disco dancers. To place this in context, this was the late 1970s, when disco music was still in fashion. Evil
said that these disco folks were stuck up, and that was reason enough
to beat them up. "They thought they were better than us because they
drove nicer cars, wore better clothes, and had prettier girlfriends,"
he said. "Sometimes they tried to steal our girlfriends, which gave us
another excuse to beat them up."

Hard-core Satanists purportedly take a blood oath of silence, and
other stoners are also highly secretive. As a result, no one knows the
exact number of these stoner gangs or their members. Miller estimated
there were some 5,000 hard-core Satanists in Los Angeles County in
1985, and Trostle states there were at least twenty-seven stoner gangs in
Los Angeles that hung on into the early 1990s.[8] What compounds the
problem of accurately identifying "real" Satanists from their impostors
is the fact that few of the impostors want to admit that they're not really
devil worshippers. According to Evil, the vast majority of the MSS members in Los Angeles were not real Satanists. "Most of them did not take
devil worship seriously," he said, "but I was one of the few who did."

After he was deported to El Salvador, Evil met a Satanist who was
even more hard-core than he. This stoner went by the nickname Diablo.
According to Evil, "This guy was seriously satanic. He had tattoos all
over his body. On his back was a tattoo of a man in a priest's robe with a

goat's head, and his hands flashing the sign of the devil. He also had two crosses tattooed upside-down on his arms." Ozzy, an MS gang member who was later killed in a Salvadoran prison, introduced Evil to this hardcore stoner. He took Evil to visit Diablo where he lived. Evil described it as a dungeon-like room in the blacked-out basement of an abandoned apartment building. "When we got there, this guy took out his altar and started chanting some scary shit," Evil told me. "I was tripping on acid and started getting really paranoid, thinking that I was going to be his next sacrifice. So, I said, 'Fuck this, if I'm going down, I'm gonna take him with me!'" Sensing his anxiety, Ozzy told Evil to chill, and that nothing was going to happen to him. "He does this every night," Ozzy reassured him. The rumor on the street was that because Diablo had a pact with the devil, he was indestructible. He had killed many people and therefore had many enemies who wanted to get revenge, but until now they had had no success. "He was once featured on the TV show *America's Most Wanted*," Evil told me. "The police were looking for him, so he fled the U.S. for El Salvador."

It was under the tutelage of Diablo that Evil delved deeper into the black arts in order to gain more power from the devil. What he learned in the process was that if you play with matches, you could get burned. Evil's first-hand experience of the presence of Satan is what turned him into a devout Evangelical Christian. The incident that caused Evil's spiritual conversion involved what these Satanists considered to be the ultimate ritual sacrifice to the devil. As Evil explained to me,

> One night, me and other two Satanists decided to perform a ritual to prepare for the ultimate sacrifice. According to the ideology of Satanism, the greatest sacrifice one can make to the devil is the killing of an innocent life. The most innocent life, according to Satanists, is that of an unborn baby.

In Catholic ideology, the ideology that dominates Salvadoran culture as a result of colonization, people are born into sin. This means that as soon as a human baby comes out of its mother's womb, it is a sinner. According to this view, an unborn fetus is still pure, and therefore it represents the ultimate sacrifice to those who seriously worship the devil. Evil told me that their plan was to call on Satan to get his permission to kill an unborn baby. Because this was the ultimate form of sacrifice, Evil and his friends believed they would gain enormous power and as a result the satisfaction of all of their hedonistic desires. The target they had lined up was a pregnant teenage girl who was an associate of their gang, what the homeboys often referred to as a *hoodrat*. This girl was often strung out on drugs, so the homeboys thought that it was not going to be difficult for them to get her to a secluded spot in order to kill her and her unborn baby. Evil was well aware that this sacrifice would involve the taking of two lives, but his demented desire for Satanic power clouded his thoughts and feelings.

On the night before this fateful ritual was to be carried out, Evil and his fellow homeboys got drunk and stoned. However, according to Evil, they were not drunk enough or stoned enough to actually cause them to hallucinate. "We hadn't dropped any tabs of acid or smoked PCP," he said. After having chanted the magic incantations, the homeboys felt the presence of a powerful entity, which soon appeared in the corner of the room as a large and ominous black shadow. Evil said there was no question in his mind that Satan had visited them that night. But it was what the Satanists discovered the next day that convinced Evil it was time to reconsider his worship of the devil. "The next morning," he said, "We found a very fine black powder of soot on the floor in the shape of the devil—the kind of fine powder produced from car exhaust." This ominous apparition scared Evil enough that he decided he could not go through with the sacrifice. "It had gotten too serious," he said. Confronted in this direct way with the power of evil, Evil decided it was not for him. In order to atone for his past sins and prevent the permanent loss of his soul, he decided to become an Evangelical Christian. "Now I pray to God for protection," he told me, "Because sometimes I can still feel Satan's presence."

Stories like this of the rituals of these hard-core Satanist stoners circulated through the neighborhoods of Los Angeles in the late 1970s and early 1980s and gave MSS a mystique that the stoner gang cultivated. Later, MS gang members spread *chambres*, or rumors, of ritual human sacrifices that had been investigated by the police. "The other gangs knew we worshipped the devil," said Sniper, "and that we were real crazy, crazy enough to sacrifice people. This gave us a good reputation." The myth of human sacrifice was sufficient to stoke the flames of infamy, even though it had been created by rumors and gossip. By the early 1980s, the Mara Salvatrucha Stoners gang had grown from its original five cliques to twelve. There were at least two things that caused these cliques of MSS to change into cholo-style street gangs. One was incarceration. "When we got locked up, we had to cut our hair," said Evil. "We had no choice, we had to dress like the other inmates. When we got out of jail, some of us kept the cholo style in order to fit in." Pressure from other street gangs also caused MSS to change its identity. "As the gang got bigger, we bumped into other gangs and eventually started fighting with them," said Evil.[9] In addition, the stoner style of dress was going out of fashion, and by the mid-1980s, all of the cliques of MSS had transformed from stoners into cholos. This shift marked the transition from MSS as a stoner or party gang to MS as a traditional style street gang.

Today, little of their stoner past remains. When MSS became MS, it kept its reputation for Satan worship, which gave it an aura of demonic mystery. The gang retained the stoners' hand signal, the index and little finger raised, which is the sign of the devil's horns. MS gang members flashed these devil's horns to friends and foes. This sign of the devil was also used in the traditional handshake of MS gang members, created by smacking one's knuckles together with the two fingers raised. Perhaps most noticeable to the public, this hand sign of the devil was sprayed up on walls as part of their gang's graffiti. Today, it is still prominently featured in the gang's *tags* or graffiti in El Salvador, Honduras, Guatemala, and the United States. This hand sign of the devil has been featured prominently in the media, which helped to perpetuate the gang's notorious international reputation.

At the same time that MSS was transforming into MS in the early 1980s, other Salvadoran immigrant youth were joining other street gangs, like 18th Street, the Rebels, the Crazies, the Playboys, T.M.C., Crazy Riders, Night Riders, Florencia, Lennox, and the Harpies. It was these already existing LA street gangs that pressured a need for Mara Salvatrucha Stoners to change. When they dropped the stoners from their gang name, MS gang members were signaling a change in identity. The transformation of the stoners into a cholo-style street gang started as self-defense against attacks from other street gangs, in prison and on the streets, but it did not stop there. The gang quickly evolved from an organization dedicated to protection into one that was predatory

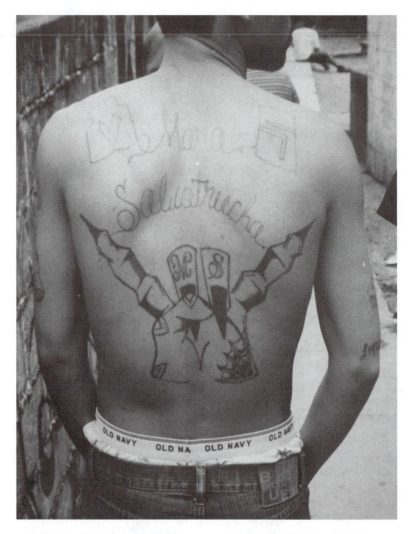

FIGURE 4.2 San Salvador, El Salvador, 2007. A homeboy displays his devil hand sign tattoo. Copyright © T. W. Ward, 2011.

in nature. I suspect that the evolution of this stoner gang into a large, traditional street gang is fairly atypical. Regardless of its uniqueness, this transformation marked a significant change in this particular gang's activities, structure, and function, which directly affected its type of leadership.

The Structure and Leadership of Street Gangs

The stereotype of the street gang as a large, extremely violent and very well-organized criminal organization is an image perpetuated by the media and law enforcement. This image is also conveyed in most gang members' autobiographies and in some gang research. Yablonsky's[10] depiction of street gangs as violent, sociopathic groups provided the dominant, albeit distorted view held by the public and public officials for many years. Extrapolating from a few gangs in New York City at the peak of their violent outbursts in the 1960s,[11] Yablonsky characterized street gangs as very large, highly organized, and driven to acts of extreme violence by what he called "sociopathic" leaders. The few researchers who found the gangs they studied to be well organized have fueled this suspicion that all street gangs are equally highly organized and criminal.[12] For example, Sanchez Jankowski suggests that this high level of organization is a necessary aspect if the gang wishes to survive and prosper.[13]

Reports of super-gangs in Chicago—confederations of local gangs, like the Blackstone Rangers, the Vice Lords, the Disciples, the Latin Kings, and the People and Folks—have also contributed to this stereotype with stories of how the gangs developed commercial enterprises and political affiliations and used violence to control drug markets.[14] Autobiographies by former gang members leave the vague impression that all street gangs are violent, tightly organized, mini-drug cartels or illegal quasi-corporations.[15] With these accounts and the plethora of media images of ultra-violent street gang members, it is understandable that this image of street gangs persists today. Less sensationalistic academic studies that contradict this view tend not to attract as much public attention.

However, as academic research shows, this stereotypical image of street gangs as highly organized fits only a small minority of all gangs in the United States and indicates that most street gangs are highly *disorganized*.[16] Even among street gangs considered to be highly organized, like the Vice Lords, the level of disorganization is exemplified in the lack of knowledge of their gang membership. Fleisher found that even hard-core Vice Lord members, those who knew the highest number of fellow gang members and were known to the highest number, knew *fewer than 10 percent* of the members of their gang.[17] Large street gangs like the Vice Lords are called *traditional*, or sometimes *vertical*, and they usually have several thousand members, are somewhat well organized, and survive for many years.[18] In some cases this means becoming an institutionalized permanent part of its community with several generations of members, who create a gang "tradition."

Traditional gangs consist of several cliques, sets, or subgroups in different locations, each with peer cohorts based on age, including *pee-wees, juniors,* and *veteranos,* or O.G.s, original gangsters, ranging in age from 12 to 42.[19] Many consider these gangs to be well organized because of their size and sustainability. However, the size of the group makes tight organization more difficult, and survival of the gang as a whole is not dependant on organizational coherence, or a clearly defined leadership. Most street gangs are not like these traditional gangs. They are much smaller, less structured, and less cohesive.[20] Academic literature indicates that there are a huge variety of different types of what we call street gangs. Examples of different types include *retreatist* gangs, *party* gangs, *scavenger* or *territorial* gangs, *entrepreneurial,* and *fighting* gangs.[21] However, only a few of the current street gangs in the United States fit one of these types. Klein states that the most common form of street gang is the *autonomous* or *compressed* gang, which is small in size (ten to fifty members), loosely organized, with small territories in schools, housing projects, or city blocks, and is composed primarily of adolescent minority youth.[22] These types of gangs usually spring up for a matter of months (lasting up to several years) and then disappear, never to be heard from again. In contrast, Klein identifies the culprit for the stereotype of street gangs as extremely well organized, the type of street gang that tends to get reified in the minds of the public. It is called a *specialty* gang or *drug* gang.[23] Unlike traditional or autonomous gangs, the specialty gang specializes in a particular crime, such as drug distribution, burglary, or auto theft. Although these specialty gangs represent but a tiny fraction of all street gangs in America—5 to 10 percent— because of media representations, they tend to become the official representatives for all gangs.

As can be seen, each of these different typologies or categories is descriptive of the gang's primary activities or its *raison d'etre.* Among all street gangs in the United States, MS is atypical in its size, distribution, notorious reputation, and its level of violence. As an evolving traditional street gang, MS members were involved in a wide variety of criminal activities that gave the gang its elevated reputation. The gang fed on this reputation for violence, both in terms of the dedication of its hard-core members and in its ability to attract new members. Although only a tiny fraction of its members actively participated in violent crimes, the various members of the numerous cliques of MS throughout the United States borrowed from their gang's reputation for violence in order to gain some sense of status and self-esteem.

MS shows how one particular type of gang (stoner) can change completely into another type of gang (a traditional street gang) in an historical blink of an eyelash. This makes categorization of a particular street gang somewhat tenuous and problematic. All gangs, like MS, change over time. This point was made by Short, who states that the character of any street gang is likely to change with the times and that new types will eventually evolve.[24] The prime distinction within these gang typologies—the extent to which these adolescent groups are involved in serious crime and violence—is greatly influenced by the gang's leadership structure.

Generally speaking, the more hierarchical and formal (clearly defined) a gang's leadership, the more likely the gang is to be well organized. This is important because the more well organized a gang's structure is (think "organized crime"), the more stable and permanent and the more criminal it is likely to be.[25] Given the stereotype of street gangs in public perception, we would expect them, therefore, to have a formal hierarchy and be very well organized. But, as stated above, most street gangs are not so well organized, and they do not have a clearly defined nor clearly obeyed system of leadership. The rebellious natures of these adolescent delinquents make strict obedience to a gang's unwritten rules somewhat problematic.

Like much of gang violence that gets exaggerated in the media, I suspect that there is a tendency of law enforcement to overestimate the level of organization in street gangs and the extent to which they have a clearly defined leadership structure. This makes sense when one considers the need to crack down on gang violence. If gangs are highly organized, then the actions of one member of the gang can prove culpability to the other members of the gang who knew of, planned, or ordered such criminal activity. For this reason, RICO (Racketeering Influenced and Corrupt Organizations) statues have been applied in the United States to street gangs since the late 1980s. RICO statues were originally developed to fight organized crime in America. Prosecutors and law enforcement officials were able to convince the courts that street gangs like MS meet the criteria for organized crime under these statues. While no one would argue that these street gangs are not corrupt organizations, a sober view shows that most of their activities do not fall within the purview of RICO.

The main problem with the popular stereotype of street gangs as highly organized, with a clearly defined leadership structure, is that it ignores the bigger picture, which is much more complex and varied. Street gangs come in all shapes and sizes, and even large, traditional street gangs like MS have a large variety of different types of cliques, or subgroups, each with its own unwritten rules of behavior, each with its own expectations for *puttin' in work*, defined as bringing in income or defending the barrio against enemies. Each of these subgroups also has its own vaguely defined notion of who gets to call the shots. I would argue that it is most useful to think of most street gang members as a subcategory of petty thieves, similar to Irwin's description of *disorganized criminals* engaging in spontaneous, impulsive, and fairly unprofitable ventures.[26] In addition, the vast majority of these gang members never participate in any serious crime or acts of violence.

As always, the devil is in the details. Much depends on which type of gang is under investigation at that particular place and time. For example, a researcher studying a *specialty* gang is going to come up with very different results than one studying what are called *autonomous* gangs.[27] Specialty gangs are much more organized than their counterparts. In a similar vein, some Chinatown gangs tend to be highly organized, while others are not.[28] However, if one seriously considers the big picture, one finds that most street gangs, even many of the cliques or subgroups of the notorious MS gang, are not highly organized and lack a defined form of leadership. Street gangs have no published membership rosters or flow charts, and their organization depends on the loose associations of its individual members whose sense of loyalty and obligation is often quite tenuous. That is not to say that street gangs, like MS, have no leadership structure at all, only to say that the leadership structure of these large, traditional gangs is quite complicated and shifts considerably over place and time.

Who Calls the Shots?

Most street gangs have some sort of *pecking order*, but leadership is highly varied between these gangs. Like other aspects of gang structure, it is hard to make completely accurate generalizations of leadership type. Some gangs have no leaders or "shot callers," while others have many leaders, and still others combine different types of leadership structure within the different cliques or subsets of the gang. In larger traditional street gangs like MS, leadership is often a *group function*, with one or more leaders, or shot callers, at each age level within each clique.[29] This serves the purpose, intentional or not, of distributing leadership throughout the gang rather than concentrating it within a select few of the older members who have clout.[30] One practical reason for this is that it makes it more difficult to destroy or incapacitate the gang's operations if a leader is incapacitated, either by death or imprisonment. Diffusion of gang leadership is also adaptive because all leaders get old, and the vast majority of them eventually retire from the gang life. In order to survive, the gang needs new shot callers, ready to step into leadership roles.

Sanchez Jankowski provides the most detailed analysis of leadership types within street gangs, dividing them into three categories based on how leaders are designated: *vertical, horizontal,* or *influential.*[31] In the vertical model, shot callers are the elder statesmen, and there is a clearly demarcated hierarchy of presidents, vice-presidents, warlords, and sometimes even a treasurer, with assigned roles and responsibilities. This type of leadership fits the stereotypical model of the street gang, although it only represents a tiny fraction of all street gangs. In the horizontal model there are several shot callers, evenly distributed by reputation and age, with a leader in each age grade or gang generation, which are usually about three years apart. The influential model is much more fluid, and shot callers tend to be those with charisma—good fighters, friendly, or smart— those who know how to influence followers.

Leaders of street gangs, like other gang members, defy easy generalizations, but are generally older clique members with a strong reputation within the gang. However, older, wiser, and stronger do not always translate to obedience from younger gang members.[32] What I found in MS was that the group decision-making process was quite complex and differed between different cliques and age grades, over time. As a large gang, leadership within MS could vary considerably according to the different cliques' activities. For example, some hard-core gang members were addicted to "fighting the enemy" and led by example. However, they often had little influence over economic or social affairs within their cliques. Also, leadership shifted over time and place as MS gang members grew older, found work, went to jail, got married, deported, hospitalized, crippled, or killed.

As Klein points out, in most street gangs there is no "typical" gang leader.[33] He gives an example of a gang leader he observed who did not meet the popular stereotype. This leader was quiet, well liked, not a highly visible fighter, and, unlike many of his fellows, had completed his high school education. In addition, Miller makes the point that gang leadership is typically flexible and democratic and that the stereotypical leadership models—the "military command," the "key-personality," and the "collective"—are overgeneralizations that obscure the fact that many gangs incorporate all three of these characteristics in their decisions regarding who to follow.[34] Miller suggests that the fact that street gangs are stereotypically imagined to have centralized authority is probably wishful thinking, as these are more amenable to control through arrest and incarceration.[35] This is metaphorically expressed as chopping the head off the monster in order to kill it off. I found that the leadership structure within MS was extremely complex, with shifting role expectations and considerable variability. However, what informed the vast majority of these MS cliques was their ideal of the *collective*.

Democratic Anarchy—Collective Leadership within MS

> We don't have leaders. Decisions are made by vote, and everyone has a say. We all have our *cora* [pride and anger], and nobody wants to be bossed around. The little homies give respect to the older homeboys, but no one is going to call the shots.
>
> —Sniper

Most street gangs provide a certain degree of independence within its ranks, with fairly flexible rules and roles, as is the case for Mara Salvatrucha. For a respectable gang to survive, however, it requires a core membership of dedicated individuals who are willing to *put in work*. Like other large Latino gangs, by the mid-1980s, Mara Salvatrucha saw itself as a traditional fighting gang. During the 1990s, MS gang members estimated that they had approximately 2,000 to 3,000 active members in Los Angeles. Over the course of research, I documented forty cliques or subsets of MS within Los Angeles County, most of which had already expired. These cliques were named after their street or neighborhood, and most of them were involved in frequent skirmishes with enemy gangs. Some of these cliques were short lived, having few members and lacking the resources to maintain their cliques after members retired or were jailed or deported.

In the United States, MS cliques now exist in almost all cities that have a large Salvadoran or Central American population, including San Diego, San Francisco, Las Vegas, Dallas, Houston, Washington, DC, New York, and Boston.[36] Beyond the U.S. borders, there are scattered MS cliques in Canada and Mexico.[37] At the time of my participant-observation fieldwork in the 1990s, MS gang members estimated that they had approximately 5,000 members in southern California and another 10,000 to 15,000 members in El Salvador. What I found among these various cliques of MS in different states and countries was that leadership with the gang was quite complex, and no one form of leadership applied to all of them.

Like other large gangs, MS has many cliques spread over a large territory, and although there was some variability with regard to how decisions were made, most of these cliques had an influential form of leadership that could be called *democratic anarchy*. By this, I mean that decisions were made by group vote within a particular clique, but often there was disagreement over decisions, leading to numerous fights and, in at least one case, group fission. In this particular case, some members of one MS clique in Los Angeles separated from the main group and formed their own clique, with a new name and identity. This reflects a natural tendency in human groupings: the larger the group, the more likely it is to experience dissention and friction within its ranks, which sometimes leads to fission, or breaking up of the group into smaller units. A democratic form of leadership like that of MS is dysfunctional for a paramilitary group that wants to be well organized.

Decisions about who gets to join the gang, what rules will be enforced, which enemy to attack, and allocation of resources (money, drugs and guns) are made only by the active members of a particular MS clique. Although sometimes there are alliances between different MS cliques, each clique is self-sufficient and makes its own decisions independently from other cliques, unless it is a matter that involves other cliques or the gang as a whole. These decisions are made at clique meetings that are held regularly. At the time of my research, all active members of an MS clique are either expected or required to attend these meetings, which are usually held within the barrio, in a secluded alleyway, parking lot, or nearby park.

Once the gang members have exchanged greetings and gang handshakes, the meeting is called to order. Although there are no official leaders within most MS cliques, some members have more say than others. The person with the most clout is usually called a "shot caller" or *primera palabra* (first word). The shot caller calls the meeting to order and sets the agenda. For most cliques, there is also a *segunda palabra*, or second word, the person who has secondary clout. Generally speaking, this does not mean that a shot caller can order another gang member to commit a crime or some act of violence, although this happens on occasion. Because MS prides itself on its defiant sensibility, the gang's ideology reinforces the idea of democratic anarchy. This means that dedicated gangsters are supposed to volunteer for active duty. There is often pressure on younger members to step up so that they can prove their worth and loyalty. However, according to the gang's unwritten rules, a shot caller cannot order another member to do a drive-by shooting because it violates the democratic spirit of the gang. In addition, as Joker pointed out, ordering a hit would implicate the shot caller in the crime, and gang members wanted to avoid complicity.

In these clique meetings, those whose words carry the most weight are generally the ones with the most *respect*. The qualities that accrue this level of respect include:

1. How much that person has "*put in work*," defined as the number of times he or she has fought the enemy—and has the scars to prove it— and brought in resources through robberies, drug dealing, or extortion
2. How much time that person has been active in the gang
3. How many times and how long that person has been *torcido*, or imprisoned
4. The extent to which that person has "heart," or courage, and is a good fighter
5. That person's social skills—how effective he or she is in gaining rapport with and support from fellow gang members

This begs the question to what extent the hard-core MS gangsters I studied were leaders or shot callers of their various cliques. Among my core sample, Trouble, Joker, and Psycho had a lot of clout within their cliques, but for very different reasons. Trouble led by example, as he was always eager to engage in a fight with an enemy gang member, and for a long time he stayed active in committing robberies. He had served time in jail and prison for armed robbery and attempted murder, which only added to his status within his gang. For these reasons, his word carried some clout in gang meetings. Joker, on the other hand, only fought when necessary or if he was drunk. He gained his status with his clique through his generosity and good humor, and the good will he showed to his fellow gang members. Because he was willing to *put in work* for his gang, Joker was well respected within his clique and had as much say in its activities as Trouble did in his. Like Trouble, Joker had spent some time in jail for attempted murder, for which he accrued credit within the gang. Although his word carried weight, Joker was not as highly invested in becoming a leader of his clique as Trouble.

In contrast, Psycho wanted to become a shot caller of his clique. The fact that he was a co-founder of his particular MS clique was reason enough for him to want to be its leader. However, among his fellow clique members, he was considered "a loose cannon," someone to be feared as well as respected. Perhaps because of this level of fear, many of his fellow gang members did not fully trust Psycho to be the best leader of their clique, and as a result his wishes were not always followed. Among the sample, Lil' Silent had the least clout within his clique. This was not because he was not willing to fight or *put in work*, but because he had neither the personality nor the desire to lead. Lil' Silent was an introvert and soft-spoken. As discussed earlier, he joined the gang as an escape from an extremely abusive relationship at home. The gang was his family, but he had neither the desire nor the inclination to try to direct the actions of his fellow gang members. And lastly, Sniper had neither the rapport nor the clout in his clique to influence major decisions. He claimed somewhat unconvincingly that he was never interested in calling the shots at gang meetings, where all the important decisions are made.

Regarding the question of leadership, what can be learned from these particular members of MS? We learn that leadership within the various cliques of MS in Los Angeles was diffused and was based on a complex set of factors. Each of these gang members had some say in the structure and function of their cliques, but some of them were more motivated than others to call the shots. What overrode the desires of some of these hard-core members' desires to lead their cliques was the gang's ideology of *democratic anarchy*. As many MS gang members often told me, they prided themselves on not taking orders from anybody. This defiant attitude toward authority posed problems for MS in terms of getting all of its various members to go along with the plan, whatever that plan might be. MS gang members confirmed my perception that their gang was plagued by dissention within its ranks. Over time, the gang developed the reputation within the street gang subculture in southern California as a group that likes to fight, but all too often these fights were internal. Those with clout, the so-called shot callers, tried to instill some sense of order within their cliques, but they were often overruled by the unruly masses.

One way that order was instilled in its members was through punishment, or what they call *corte*. If a member does something bad, something that violates an unwritten rule of the gang, he or she is going to get beaten. Before the beating occurs, however, a meeting must be called. Although anarchic, their system is still somewhat democratic. My impressionistic view is that at least a third of all clique meetings dealt with the problem of keeping members in line and doing what they were supposed to do. Among the things they were *not* supposed to do was fight with each other. But all too often, different members of different MS cliques clashed, and fighting would ensue.

When such fighting has the potential to escalate into all-out warfare, which happened on occasion, a larger group meeting between representatives of various cliques is called. These types of meetings are extremely rare, but they happen. In these larger meetings, the particular issue was talked out until a settlement was reached. In some rare cases, they agreed to disagree, which usually led to more intragang fighting. One such disagreement erupted between two large MS cliques in Los Angeles. One of the cliques was committing robberies within the others' neighborhood, which was a violation of one of the unwritten rules of the gang. The rule was that you do not rob within your own barrio or those of other MS cliques, because it alienates one's neighbors and attracts the attention of the police. In this case, a meeting was called to put an end to these robberies, and the perpetrators reluctantly agreed to stop. However, because of the belligerence of a few of the members of this MS clique, which, at that time, had about 100 active members, the robberies started up again later. This eventually led to a feud between these two cliques (see Chapter Six). It is conflicts like this one that delineate the gang's unwritten rules and taboos.

Gang Taboos

Never let your barrio down. Gotta be *down* for your barrio. If you don't *throw down*, you're gonna get thrown down. If you fuck up, you're gonna get *fucked up*.

—Psycho

A *taboo* is a forbidden act or object. The term, which originally referred to things or actions with negative magical properties, derives from the Polynesian word *tabu*.[38] Taboos are illustrative because they describe the core fears of any individual, group, or organization. From my research, I found that like paramilitary units and secret societies, MS had two main taboos regarding fear and betrayal. The first is to *show no fear*, and it has the corollary of *never backing down*. The second states that one should *never "rat out,"* or inform on, one's own group or any of its members.[39] Both of these core taboos—backing down and ratting out—deal with the extremely sensitive issue of betrayal.

Most gang members, especially young men with a certain history or experience, have no difficulty avoiding the first taboo, having been socialized from an early age to be, or at least pretend to be, stoic, strong and willing to fight. It is easy to see why showing fear would be taboo within the gang. It reveals a weakness, which, in turn, encourages disrespect and possible attack. In the animal world, predators such as dogs or baboons can sense fear in their prey. The corollary of showing no fear is never backing down, what the gang members call either *punking out*, or, in Spanish, *chavaliarse*, which can be loosely translated as girlish behavior or becoming a *sissy*. Because MS considers itself a fighting gang, all of its members, including females, must be willing to fight "like a man."

Showing fear will disqualify someone from being eligible to join the gang. Trouble said, "We want to know if he's willing to fight. You can't be afraid to fight, even if you're going to get your ass kicked. You can't show fear and be a part of our gang." Once one is admitted into the gang, one should never back down, no matter how badly he or she is outnumbered. However, if there is no one to witness one's cowardice or "good sense"—security being the better part of valor—the tendency of some gang members is to run for safety. If their own gang members find out, however, they will be punished. Psycho and Trouble had a method for testing this in new recruits of their cliques. They asked several homeboys from another MS clique, unknown to the newcomer, to drive up to their hangout and ask the new recruit, "Where you from?" If he did not claim his barrio loudly, "Mara Salvatrucha!", or tried to run, Psycho and Trouble would pop out the back seat of the car and give him a good beating to remind him of an important unwritten rule of their gang. As Trouble said, "Never let your barrio down, homes!"

Like backing down, the second taboo, ratting out, is violated more often than most gang members would like to admit. "Some guys rat out their homeboys because they are afraid," said Joker. "If two homeboys do a drive-by, and then one of them gets caught and tells the police the other guy did it, he's a traitor, a rat. He doesn't want to go to jail, so he rats to the police and then moves to another state or back to his country." MS gang members, like Joker, claimed that they took this violation seriously. "If we catch him, we will take care of him." By taking care, Joker means the person will be severely beaten, stabbed, or even killed. The gangs' term for ratting is *echar rata*—literally, to "throw rat." Joker told me of two MS gang members that had been "taken out" (killed) for ratting on another homeboy regarding a drive-by shooting, though his story could not be independently verified. According to the tough street gang ideology, the only proper response to someone who rats out is a death sentence. For example, in September of 2010, Chano, or Criminal, a member of the 204th Street gang, testified that he and other gang members took turns stabbing a suspected snitch eighty times in a cramped garage.[40] The most famous (or infamous) case within MS of the stabbing of a "rat" was Brenda Paz, which I discuss in the next chapter.

Ratting out one's own gang member is a form of betrayal similar to setting up a gang member to be shot by an enemy gang or leaving one's gang in order to join another street gang. Like other large gangs, MS did not take kindly to its members changing affiliations. There were two uncorroborated reports of MS gang members being severely punished for leaving the gang to join another. According to these reports, one culprit was stabbed several times, hospitalizing him for months, and the other was shot to death while he was sitting on the porch step in front of his apartment. No gang likes to admit that some of its members change affiliations or, worse, that some of its members rat out on fellow members. However, despite the threat of severe punishment, many gang members inform on fellow members in order to avoid a long prison sentence. Said Trouble, exasperatedly, "Lately, there are so many people throwing rat that no one knows who's betraying the gang."

In addition to these two taboos, some MS gang members identified rape as a third taboo, because it puts girls in their barrio at risk, alienates neighbors, and invites police investigations. During my research, one MS clique punished one of its members for raping several girls in their barrio. After it was brought to their attention, a meeting was called, where it was decided that the punishment for rape would be a stabbing. Ignoring this warning, the homeboy raped another girl, so the clique held another meeting, which was attended by Joker and Lil' Silent. Joker volunteered to carry out the punishment. He asked Lil' Silent for a knife, but Lil' Silent had forgotten to bring one. Improvising, Joker assigned four homeboys to severely beat the rapist for five minutes. It should be noted that not all MS members agreed with the designation of rape as a taboo. Sniper, for example, said that rape was a murky issue, difficult to properly identify. As he said, "Some *hoodrats* have sex with a guy, then regret it and claim they were raped. How are you going to know who's telling the truth?" Generally speaking, most of these gang members treated hoodrats as third class residents, or no counts. Sniper said his clique did nothing about rape accusations unless the victim was a member or a girlfriend of a member of their MS clique. It should also be noted that different cliques have different rules, and these rules change over time. Some MS gang members do not see rape as a crime worthy of punishment.

A possible fourth taboo is the taboo of members' trying to leave the gang too early. According to MS gang members, "too early" means before a member has *paid his dues*. In MS, as in many other large street gangs, once a person joins the gang, he or she is not supposed to leave the gang until dues have been paid. Paying one's dues means either spending sufficient time—loosely defined by some MS members as approximately three to four years—as an active member of the clique, or participating in a sufficient number of gang activities, particularly fighting enemy gang members and bringing in resources, like money and guns. According to the gang's ideology, a member who wants to leave before he or she has paid dues must be beaten out of the gang or stabbed. As one might imagine, however, this is extremely rare, because MS gang members who want to leave the gang are smart enough not to say so explicitly, or ask fellow members for permission. Rather, they move somewhere outside the barrio or take up another activity such as getting work, starting a family, or going back to school.

A lesser taboo within the gang relates to the need of its members for respect. Most MS gang members said that their members should always show *respect* to their fellow members. According to this unwritten rule, showing disrespect for a fellow gang member is also showing disrespect to the gang. Needless to say, given their defiant personalities, this minor taboo was violated all the time. Mainly as a result of their need for self-respect and to prove their *cora* or courage, these MS gang members fought with fellow members quite frequently. If the fight was internal, meaning within the same clique or subgroup, a meeting of its active members was called in order to try to settle the dispute. At these clique-level meetings, the dispute was usually settled by letting the two disputants fight with fists, or what the gang members referred to as *throwing down*. Knives, bottles, bats or guns are not allowed. After the fight is over, regardless of who "wins," the matter is settled and disputants are not supposed to let the argument carry over. As Joker put it: "If one of my homies wants to throw down with me, fine. But afterward, it has to stop there, no matter who won or lost. If we continue to fight over and over again, we're gonna get courted."

In MS, there were other infractions that required a beating. As mentioned previously, most MS cliques forbid burglary and robbery in one's own neighborhood. In addition, fighting anyone in the neighborhood who is not an enemy gang member was also generally frowned upon, if not strictly enforced. Trouble got courted for this. "I got into a fight with a Chinese guy in the street," he told me. "He was talking shit, so I went back and hit him once in the face. When he fell down I took his wallet. My homies found out and gave me a hell of a beating." Like rape and robbery in one's own barrio, fighting non–gang members brings police presence and aggravates one's neighbors, which makes life more difficult for the gang members.

Violating another taboo within MS always met with a severe beating. MS, like most street gangs, does not condone the killing of babies, whether or not it's intentional. The media and some law enforcement officials are ignorant of this taboo within the gang. I read a sworn deposition of an LAPD officer for a murder trial in Ventura involving MS gang members, in which the officer claimed that gang members get more respect within their gangs for the murder of babies. There are two reasons why this is not true. First, the vast majority of gang members see babies as innocent, and killing them is a violation of their morals. Second, and perhaps more importantly, killing a baby is going to bring "a lot of heat" (police investigations), and diminishes the individual's and the gang's reputation. According to MS rules, when babies become collateral damage in their gang battles with enemies, the perpetrator must always expect either a severe beating or stabbing.

In addition to these taboos and unwritten rules, in the 1980s and the early 1990s most MS cliques in Los Angeles had unwritten rules about certain types of drug use. For example, in all cliques it was acceptable to drink heavily and smoke marijuana frequently, as long as these vices did not interfere with the "business" of the gang, which was protecting the barrio and fighting the enemy. Smoking crack cocaine, however, was initially forbidden within MS. This unwritten rule gradually changed over time as the newcomers to MS, defiant young gangsters, expressed their desires "to do whatever the fuck we want," as one gang member told me. Some of these new members were extremely belligerent and forced a change in the rules, thereby allowing gang members to smoke *piedra* or crack cocaine. This eventually led to a new rule: anyone who smokes too much crack will be kicked out of the gang. Joker, who joined his clique in the early 1990s, almost got kicked out of his clique for his heavy use of crack. The reason that MS forbid its active members from using heavy drugs like crack or heroin was because it jeopardizes the gang's activities and renders the addict highly irresponsible. Sniper did not smoke *piedra* nearly as much as Joker, but like Joker, he learned that it sometimes led to unintended negative consequences. Sniper told me he got hyped up on crack one time and lost a gun that had been loaned to him for a hit on an enemy gang. Sniper had broken two unwritten rules—i.e., don't get too high on crack and don't lose a valuable resource. These infractions meant he had to be severely punished by his fellow gang members in a beating that they call corte.

Other unwritten rules of the gang were much less strictly enforced. For example, many MS cliques had two unwritten rules regarding girlfriends, neither of which was strictly enforced. The first stated that there was to be no flirting with a fellow homeboy's girlfriend, and the second prohibited dating a *homegirl* (or female gang member) from an enemy gang. Regarding the first rule, Joker said, "That rule was bullshit. If a homeboy can't keep his *jaina* (girlfriend) in check, that's his problem! She has the right to choose who she wants to fuck, *es pedo de ella*—that's her business." And with respect to the second, Trouble confirmed the rule but admitted that it was violated all the time. "Our clique had that rule," he said, "but homeboys, including me, broke it all the time! When it comes to jainas, there ain't walls high enough to keep a homeboy out." I discuss this rule violation in greater detail in the next chapter.

Another unwritten rule of the gang was quite sexist, as it applied to only homegirls. Like the rule against dating the enemy, this rule was also not strictly enforced. According to this rule, homegirls were expected to be responsible for their children. "If they aren't," said Trouble, "They will get courted out. If you get courted out, everybody in your own clique beats you up. Everybody. And there's no time limit to the beating." Punishment or what gang members call *corte* is meted out at the meetings of the clique. There are no definite rules regarding the severity or length of the beating, but generally speaking, the worse the infraction, the worse the beating. "Unless we're courting him out," said Psycho, "we don't want to hospitalize him. It's too much of a hassle to drive him to the emergency room, and people are going to start asking questions about how he got hurt."

Given the belligerent attitudes of most of these MS gang members and their disdain for authority, it was extremely difficult if not impossible to enforce all the rules. And because the rules are unwritten, there was a great deal of flexibility regarding enforcement. Some gang members, especially newcomers, claimed ignorance of a rule they had broken. However, this tactic rarely kept punishment in check. Each clique decided what rules it was going to enforce and the appropriate punishment for an infraction. As previously stated, the unwritten rules of MS changed over time and place. Some were ignored and subsequently died out (e.g., personal use of certain drugs), and new rules were created to deal with current problems (e.g., do not rape girls within one's own barrio). Each clique makes up new rules as particular problems arise, and each generation within a clique has a slightly different attitude toward the importance of certain rules. Let us now turn to a completely different aspect of gang life, one that gets short shrift in media depictions—the extent to which gang life is extremely boring.

A Day in the Life—The Anatomy of Boredom

Shirtless, wearing only a pair of baggy boxers, Lil' Silent woke up at noon to the low, incessant rumble of barking—Ruff! Ruff! Ruff! Ruff!—from the neighbor's dog, Spike, a medium-sized, muscular pit bull. This is the favorite breed for gang members and others who want protection. Lil' Silent had grown accustomed to the noise of this dog, which almost blended in with the sounds of the busy traffic on his street. He shifted his position on the couch in the living room where he was sleeping and sleepily eyed the clock on the kitchen wall. He noticed that the other homeboys had already left the apartment, which gave him the excuse—if he needed it—to catch a few more winks. He yawned, stretched, and sank back into the couch.

It was too early to start his day, having stayed up until 3 a.m. drinking and smoking with his homies in the parking lot next to the local 7-Eleven convenience store. At quarter past one, a fly, which entered from the open kitchen window, buzzed near enough to Lil' Silent's ear to annoy him awake again. He got up and went to the bathroom to take a leak and then splashed some water onto his face. Carrying the hand towel with him into Joker's room, he tossed it on the bed. Lil' Silent opened a drawer of the dresser that he shared with the others and pulled out a clean t-shirt with a Led Zeppelin logo and a pair of baggy blue jeans. He lazily pulled them on before shuffling into the kitchen to look for something to eat.

He opened the refrigerator— one of those old white round models with the thick metal handles that click shut, the kind whose small freezer compartment door won't shut because of the ice buildup. He scanned the leftovers: carne asada, rice, beans, plantains, and yucca in Styrofoam containers; a partially eaten hamburger and some cold fries in a paper bag; unwrapped stale tortillas on a dinner plate; two clear plastic bags—one with tomatoes and the other with green onions; three bottles of Corona; a half-empty liter of generic cola; and a pitcher of lemonade with two lemon slices floating on top. He chose the cola and drank it straight from the bottle and then walked to the cupboard and took out a package of Pop-Tarts®, which he microwaved. Lil' Silent walked back into the living room and picked up the remote. He turned on the television, and sat down at the small round card table that served as their dining room and watched a talk show while he ate his breakfast. More time passes, an hour, maybe less, when Lupe, Joker's girlfriend, and her cousin Tina came home from their part-time jobs at a local market, where they stock shelves and bag customers' purchases. They were carrying heavy bags of groceries, but Lil' Silent ignored them and continued watching TV.

"Where's Joker?" asked Lupe. Lil' Silent did not hear her, so she asked again, "Where's Joker?" "I don't know," said Lil' Silent, without looking at her. Tina piped in, snidely saying, "He's probably out looking for trouble," clearly intending the double entendre. Lil' Silent turned up the volume on the TV, trying to drown out their voices. Lupe asked him to please turn the TV down, but instead he turned it off, pulled on his sneakers, got up, and walked past the girls without a word. As he made his way out, Lil' Silent grabbed his pack of Marlboro cigarettes from the kitchen counter, turned and walked out the door. Lil' Silent walked quickly down the two flights of stairs, as if he had somewhere to go, but he stopped abruptly on the top step outside. He looked left and then right, and then took out a cigarette and sat down to smoke. A few minutes later, an old Latino man, a neighbor wearing a fedora, walked slowly by with the help of a cane. This man looked up at Lil' Silent and greeted him, "Hola, Edgardo. Qué tal? Comó estás? How are you?" The old man refused to call him by his gang name, which bothers Lil' Silent not at all.

"Bién, y usted?" he answers. "Pues, por aquí todavía," says the old man, "Still here." He knows better than to try to engage Edgar in long conversation, so he smiles and gestures good-bye. Lil' Silent acknowledges the gesture with a slight nod of his head. He watches the old man slowly walk all the way down the block until he turns the corner, and then lights another cigarette and watches the cars and other passersby. Time passed slowly until Trouble arrived in his souped-up Honda Civic with Joker in tow. Eager for something to do, Lil' Silent hopped in the back of the car and they drove to a small parking lot behind an apartment building, one of the hangouts of their clique.

Psycho was already there to greet them. He was sitting on two cases of Corona beer stacked up between some large green plastic bins—LA's version of garbage cans—and the parked cars. As the homeboys approached, Psycho raised a bottle of Corona to his mouth and popped its cap between his teeth. He offered it to Trouble, who acknowledged the gesture with a slight nod of his head. Psycho passed out beers to the other homeboys, as they found their places on crates and broken down metal chairs. "Homes," Joker asks Psycho, "Where's that underage *jaina* I saw you with last week?" "How the fuck should I know?" Psycho responds, "I'm not her babysitter." "You could be," says Joker, laughing, "You're old enough to play the part." Psycho gives him a dirty look, but says nothing.

From Prey to Predators—The Origins and Transformation of MS   103

Trouble turned the talk to the Galaxy, LA's professional soccer team, and Cobi Jones, one of its stars, who had been unable to prevent its latest losing streak. The minutes crawled into hours, and having polished off most of one of the cases of beer, Trouble went inside the apartment to get a set of dominoes. The homies set up a long flat board on top of some boxes, and the four of them played dominoes for a couple hours, betting dimes, quarters, and occasionally dollar bills. After Joker and Lil' Silent each had lost about five dollars gambling, they decided to get a bite to eat at the local taco stand and then cruise for girls. Although they were valiantly fighting tedium, tedium was clearly winning the battle.

Few people who have not experienced gang life realize just how boring it can be. Given gang members' seemingly unbounded need for stimulation, it is no wonder that they seek solace in friends and booze. One of the best kept secrets of gang life is the huge gaps in time between things happening, whether it is a party, a gang meeting, committing a crime, or putting in work fighting the enemy. With no school and no job to go to, there was little else for these homies to do but hang out and try to kill time. The mind-numbing boredom of killing time is what gang members call *kicking back*. Subtract the beer, gambling, and the occasional *coco-puff* (a cigarette laced with crack cocaine), and you've got a sewing circle without the tapestry, but just as much gossip. Most people—overly influenced by the media—think that gang members are constantly on the prowl, stealing stereos or shooting up the neighborhood. But *kicking back* or hanging out is what they do most of the time. Malcolm Klein succinctly makes this point:

> …with the occasional exception of a boisterous meeting, a fight, an exciting rumor, [gangbanging] is a *very dull life*. For the most part, gang members do very little—sleep, get up late, hang around, brag a lot, eat again, drink, hang around some more. It's a boring life.[41]

Were it not for the occasional fight or shoot-out, gang life would be unmitigated tedium. Obviously, the media are not going to report this, because it is not newsworthy. But they are not the only culprits in popularizing the image of gang members as ruthless street fighters or cold-blooded killers. Police and the gang members themselves do nothing to dispel this image because doing so would diminish the status of "gangsters" and the cops who fight to keep them off the streets. My research with MS gang members confirmed what Klein claims about gang members in general: they spend most of their time hanging out. However, gang members do not gain a reputation or respect by just hanging out. They get their bad reputations from what the gang members call "banging" and "slanging."

Banging and Slanging

"Banging" refers to committing crimes and fighting the enemy. "Slanging" means selling illegal drugs. Crime and violence distinguish streets gangs from other youth groups, but they hardly encapsulate the gang experience holistically. Continued focus solely on these two issues serves to reinforce gang stereotypes and distorts the picture of what it really means to be a gang member. Although the payoffs of crime and the excitement of violence are central attractions of the gang life, many youth join gangs not only for protection but also for the camaraderie of the group and the freedom to do nothing at all. Part of the reason street gangs attract youth is because there is a great deal of "play" involved, in terms of fun and excitement. This is why many gang members refer to gangbanging as the "fast life."

What was most exciting for most of these MS gangsters, in addition to fighting the enemy, was robbing citizens of their groceries, their money, their jewelry, or their cars. Keeping in mind that there is considerable variability between cliques and individual gang members regarding the amount of time spent in each of these activities, generally speaking, a list of the top twenty things MS gang members do, from most frequent to least, would look like this.

1. Hanging out, socializing on street corners, alleyways, in front of apartment buildings or in strip malls.
2. Sleeping at home or a friend's place or looking for a place to sleep.
3. Eating a meal at home or at a friend's place or a fast-food restaurant.
4. Watching television or movies or playing video games
5. Drinking beer or other alcoholic beverage at a hangout or at home.
6. Smoking dope (marijuana) or *primos* (crack-laced marijuana) or *coco-puffs* (crack-laced cigarettes).

7. Partying, which includes drinking alcohol, taking drugs, dancing, cruising for girls, hitting on girls and "scoring" (fondling, fellatio, or sexual intercourse).
8. Picnicking in the park, at a backyard BBQ, or taking a trip to a public beach or lake.
9. Attending gang meetings.
10. Fist fights with fellow clique members, often in an inebriated state.
11. Working part-time jobs.
12. Getting kicked out of school for fighting.
13. Committing one of a wide variety of crimes:

  a. Tagging gang graffiti on walls of public buildings.
  b. Stealing food and alcohol.
  c. Burglarizing cars (for auto parts or stereos) or, less likely, homes (for money, jewelry, guns, or any other valuables).
  d. Robbery, including armed robbery (for money, jewelry, cell phones, watches, and Walkman stereos).
  e. Extorting money from drug dealers, gambling dens, or shopkeepers.
  f. Dealing drugs.
  g. Stealing cars.
  h. Pimping prostitutes (very rare).
  i. Arson or other serious vandalism (extremely rare).
  j. Contracting to commit murder (also extremely rare).[42]

14. Spending time in jail, going to court, visiting probation officers.
15. Fighting with enemy gang members with their fists, bats, chains, knives, or guns (including nonlethal drive-by shootings).
16. Being hospitalized and undergoing physical therapy.
17. Visiting fellow gang members in the hospital or jail.
18. Fighting with family members, neighbors, or nongang friends.
19. Attending a funeral of a fellow gang member.
20. Committing a gang-related homicide (*drive-bys* or *walk-ups*) or suicide.

It should be noted that the activity in which these MS gang members spend the least amount of time—drive-by shootings—is the one that gets the most attention and is reified in the minds of the public as the characteristic activity of all gang members. Although the deaths of fellow members give gang members the opportunity to practice their epideictic rhetoric, most gang members do not die in gang warfare.[43] Most street gang members, even hard-core members, do not participate in drive-by shootings against enemy gang members. And of these shootings, most do not result in fatalities. Granted, this is little solace to those non–gang members who have been wounded or killed in the crossfire. My point is not to trivialize the impact of these tragic shootings but to place them within the holistic context of gang life. These gang shootings are infrequent, if extremely dangerous and sometimes deadly.

As stated above, gang members spend most of their time hanging out. Activities that fall under the rubric of "banging," or *gangbanging*, include marking turf with graffiti, "representing" the gang, protecting the barrio, bringing in valuable resources, and fighting enemy gang members. How much time a gang member spends engaged in these activities depends on whether he or she is a peripheral, core, or hard-core member of the gang. Hard-core gang members are much more involved in crimes and violence because of their desire to get respect and make a reputation for their gang. However, even hard-core MS members spend more time tagging and committing petty crimes than committing serious crimes like armed robbery and drive-by shootings. Gang members tag their gang name and their gang *placasos*, or gang nicknames, on the walls of their neighborhoods to mark their territory. This is to let people know who controls the area and to try to keep out enemy gang members.[44]

MS gang members in Los Angeles claimed that they tagged wherever they wanted, but I noticed that some cliques initially avoided tagging on individuals' property (houses and apartment buildings) so they would not alienate their neighbors. "The neighbors knew that we were helping them," said Trouble. "They told us what walls we could tag on. They didn't want us to mark up their buildings, so we only put up our tags in other places." Tagging, or what the gang members called *plaquiando*, on homes would have violated the gang's self-expressed duty to protect the neighborhood. However, the most compelling reason they refrained was because it would have alienated neighbors. Originally a defensive gang, MS did not prey on people within its neighborhoods, and gang members took pride in defending their barrios. Gang members told me they protected their areas from robbers, thieves, enemy gang members, and unsanctioned drug dealers.

We were never going to rob in our own backyard. We weren't going to shoot up the streets or break into cars on our streets. We wanted to protect our barrio. We didn't want to make enemies of the neighbors. So, instead of calling the police on us, they would warn us about the police. 'Hey, here comes the cops! Watch out!' they'd tell us.

—Joker

Trouble told me his homeboys defended the barrio by keeping watch. "I remember one time around 3 a.m., when we were upstairs in a *destroyer* [an apartment where drugs and guns are stashed]. We saw a car drive slowly down the street, like they were looking for something. The car turned around at the end of the block and drove by again and stopped. Some black guys got out of the car and were trying to break into a car. We got a .22 rifle and shot at them and scared them away." This incident shows that in its early days, MS saw itself as a barrio defender. But over time, and with new members joining their ranks, MS began to lose control over its defiant younger gang members. This often led to conflict within cliques, and some gang members were punished for robbing within their own barrio.

When MSS turned itself into a traditional cholo-style street gang, its members took cues from other gangs as to what constituted *gangbanging*. What gives a traditional street gang its reputation is the degree to which its members commit crimes and violence. MS has received so much public attention because of the litany of crimes and violence its members have carried out since the early 1980s. Crimes committed by MS gang members run the gamut from auto theft; burglary; armed robbery; assaulting rivals; carrying concealed weapons in school; using, selling, and stealing drugs; assaulting victims, witnesses, and police, as well as their fellow members; participating in drive-by shootings and homicide; arson; kidnapping; and rape.[45]

In the gang literature, these crimes are often categorized as either *instrumental* (functional) or *expressive*, which are not mutually exclusive categories. Gang members commit crimes instrumentally in order to survive, earn a profit, and gain a reputation, for themselves and their collective. These crimes are also committed as an expression of rebellion against status frustrations—e.g., low SES (socioeconomic status), low self-esteem—as well as anger at parents, peers, and society for perceived or actual abuse, neglect, and/or discrimination. Like other gang members, MS gangsters also committed crimes for the thrill of breaking rules and the pleasures gained from a sense of personal power that is used to control others and instill fear.[46] Crime is both a survival mechanism and a reaction to poverty, lack of prestige, and a sense of powerlessness. It is also a way of satisfying greed, a shortcut to success for those willing to break the rules.

Regarding the other stereotypical activity of street gangs, *slanging*, or selling drugs varies as much as *banging* between different gang members and different cliques of the gang. In the popular imagination, drug sales and use are synonymous with gang life. Although some research supports this assumption, a couple of important points need to be made.[47] First, generally speaking, members of street gangs do not control the drug trade in terms of its production or distribution. Gang members tend to be middlemen who acquire drugs from professional drug traffickers and sell them on the streets, sometimes at considerable profit. Second, despite law enforcement and media claims to the contrary, the vast majority of street gangs do not exist to sell drugs, and drug sales do not represent an organized, collective gang activity.[48] For many gang members, drug sales are a means to an end rather than an end in itself. Without other opportunities to make money, some gang members turn to selling drugs. Most gang members, however, do not sell any drugs. Competition for drug sales and profits is always high, and many gang members do not feel sufficiently motivated to fight for drug distribution rights and benefits. And most street dealers of drugs do not make it rich.[49]

None of the MS gang members I interviewed said they joined their gang primarily or solely to make money from drug sales. They considered the profits from drug sales as easy money, one of the fringe benefits of being a gang member. Of the seventy-three MS gang members I formally interviewed about dealing drugs, only thirteen, or approximately 18 percent, said they sold drugs on a regular basis. From my observations, MS gang members who are engaged in *slanging* sell a wide variety of drugs. The most common drugs sold by MS members were crack cocaine and marijuana, followed by powdered cocaine, prescription pills, PCP, LSD, and heroin. Although I knew a few MS gang members who made considerable profits from dealing, they were more likely to make money by taxing the non–gang member dealers within their turf. However, the vast majority of MS gang members did not deal drugs on a full-time basis. And those MS gang members who dealt part-time did not make nearly enough money to satisfy their desires for safety and comfort.

Taxing drug dealers in their neighborhoods was a profitable venture for several MS cliques and involved lesser risks than selling the drugs themselves, specifically robbery and arrest. Robbery or stealing are other ways that gang members make a living that fall within the category of gangbanging. In addition to carjacking (which is rare) and robbing people of their cash, MS gang members usually stole items that were easy to sell on the black market. These include stereos, car parts, cell phones, and jewelry. Cars are stolen either to strip and sell their parts or to use for an armed robbery or drive-by shooting—with the benefit that if the license is traced, they won't get caught. Prostitution was practiced in a few neighborhoods, especially near downtown Los Angeles, but I knew of no cases in which gang members controlled such activities. One gang member bragged about renting out one of his girl-friends to an acquaintance. However, when I checked out his story, I found that the young woman had been duped into this sexual favor—her boyfriend got her drunk and charged another homeboy a nominal fee to sleep with her. This incident is just one example of the ways in which male gang members exploit young women who associate with gangs. Female gang members face different risks from girlfriends who are not members of the gang. For them, being a homegirl means living on the margins of masculinity, which is the subject of the next chapter.

Notes

1. NAGIA, 2000, nagia.com.
2. In Spanish, the acronym FMLN means Frente Farabundo Marti para la Liberación Nacional.
3. knowgangs.com. For another inaccurate account of MS, which calls them "cop killers," cf. Domash, Shelly. 2005. America's most dangerous gang. *Police Magazine*, March 16.
4. Trostle, 1992, p. 142.
5. Stapley, 2003.
6. Trostle, 1992. Other common stoner graffiti are the number 666, upside-down crosses, or backward handwriting, which symbolizes the triumph of evil over goodness, like the graffito !Selur Bubezleeb (Beelzebub rules!).
7. Trostle, 1992.
8. Cited in Trostle, 1992, p. 70.

9. MSS was not the first stoner gang to change its affiliation. According to Trostle (1992), other stoner gangs allied themselves with street gangs for protection or were incorporated into a street gang en masse as a separate clique.
10. *The Violent Street Gang*, 1971.
11. Klein calls this a "temporary anomaly" (1995, p. 57).
12. Bloch and Niederhoffer, 1958; Keiser, 1969.
13. 1991.
14. Cf. Short, 1996, p. 224; Dawley, 1992; Olivero, 1991.
15. Shakur, 1990; Sanchez, 2001.
16. Klein, 1995; Short, 1996; Huff, 2002, 2006; Egley Jr., et al. 2006.
17. 2002, p. 210. See also Dawley, 1992; Keiser, 1964.
18. Klein, 1995; Moore, 1991.
19. Sanchez Jankowski, 1991. Grouping based on age is called "age-graded."
20. Klein, 2004.
21. Cloward and Ohlin, 1960; Fagan, 1989; Taylor, 1990; Thrasher, 1927; Fagan, 1989; Hagedorn, 1998; Padilla, 1992; Short and Strodtbeck, 1965.
22. 1995, 2004. These groups are generally not involved in serious crimes of violence.
23. 2004, p. 68.
24. 1968.
25. Decker, Bynum, and Weisel, 2004.
26. 1972, p. 122.
27. Decker, Bynum, and Weisel, 2004, p. 253.
28. Chin, 1998.
29. It also serves as a source for group *fission*, or the splitting of a larger group into smaller parts. Cf. discussion below.
30. Klein, 1995.
31. 1991.
32. Klein, 1995.
33. 1995, p. 62.
34. 1981.
35. 2001.
36. *Mara Salvatrucha Street Gang: An International Criminal Enterprise with Roots in El Salvador's Civil War*, March 2005, Report prepared by Alvi J. Castro, Supervisory Immigration Enforcement Agent, Immigration and Customs Enforcement / Department of Homeland Security.
37. I.e., Vancouver, Toronto, and the southern state of Chiapas in Mexico.
38. Common etymology traces taboo to the Tongan word *tapu* or the Fijian word *tabu* meaning "under prohibition," "not allowed," or "forbidden."

Cf. Cook, James. 1821. *The Three Voyages of Captain James Cook Round the World*, London: A&E Spottiswoode; Robert Arthur, *You Will Die: The Burden of Modern Taboos*, Suburra Publishing, 2008.

39. I.e., accuse a fellow member of one's gang of any crime or act of violence.
40. Kim, Victoria. 2010. Violent slaying retold in court. *Los Angeles Times*, September 10, p. AA1.
41. Klein, 1995, p. 11 (emphasis added).
42. I was present at a local hangout when a middle-aged Latino woman asked some MS gangsters to put a hit on her husband. They agreed to do the hit for $5,000, half of which was demanded up front. After this woman paid the front money and left, the homies laughed at her, calling her disparaging names. The joke was on her, for they had no intention of carrying out this assassination.
43. Epideictic rhetoric includes funeral orations and obituaries.
44. Cf. Phillips, Susan A. 1999. *Wallbangin'—Graffiti and Gangs in L.A.*, University of Chicago Press.
45. Mara Salvatrucha Street Gang: An International Criminal Enterprise with Roots in El Salvador's Civil War, March 2005. Report prepared by Alvi J. Castro, Supervisory Immigration Enforcement Agent, Immigration and Customs Enforcement / Department of Homeland Security.
46. Katz, 1999.
47. Fagan, 1998; Huff, 1998.
48. Klein, 1995; Decker and Van Winkle, 2006.
49. Levitt and Dubner. 2005. *Freakonomics: A Rogue Economist Explores the Hidden Side of Everything*, William Marrow.

....

CHAPTER 5

"Girls" in Gangs—On the Margins of Masculinity

If you want to be respected by the homeboys you have to act like them. You have to do what they do. You have to be *down* for the barrio and *take no shit.*

—Loquita, *MS homegirl*

You got your *rucas* and your *jainas* and you got your *homegirls*. Rucas and jainas are good for sex. But homegirls are different. They're just like us. They pay their dues and they get their props.

—Sniper, *MS homeboy*

...Shygirl settled down into the front seat like an old woman. Her leg was asleep, she explained, the one that was hit during a drive-by. The bullet remained lodged in her thigh, a souvenir. "I can't run that fast. It's worse when it gets cold, 'cause the bullet gets cold."

—Sikes[1]

I was sitting in my beat up Toyota 4Runner, driving two MS homegirls to a dance club, and listening to one of them tell me how one of their fellow gang members, Lonely, had recently died. Angel, sitting shotgun, was trying to tell me that an enemy gang member had murdered her homegirl Lonely, but she was having difficulty pronouncing the word "murder." "How do you say it?" she asked me. "It's murrrr-der," I said, stressing the first "r" sound missing from her pronunciation. "Mad-der? Mud-der? Mod-der?" she said in her heavily accented English. Angel had told me of her frustration and embarrassment in mispronouncing "murder" during conversations with her fellow gang members. "Some of the homies speak real good English," she told me. "But when I tried to say it the other day, they made fun of me." I tried to help Angel with her pronunciation. After what seemed like an eternity but was probably less than five minutes, I gave up and suggested she use the word "homicide" instead. "What's that?" she asked me. "It's another word for murder," I answered. Angel thought for a minute and then asked, "How would you say, like, 'Did he homicide him?'" "Unfortunately, you can't use homicide as a verb," I answered. After a pregnant pause, Loquita, Angel's friend and fellow homegirl, who had been sitting quietly in the back seat, said, "You can just say, 'He killed him.'"

At that time, in the early days of fieldwork, it seemed more than a bit surreal to me to be teaching this MS homegirl the proper pronunciation of the word murder. But it wasn't strange to Angel, who was, by then, well acquainted with death. Although only sixteen years old, Angel had already attended five funerals for fellow gang members, and now she was preparing to attend another two. With her ear-to-ear smile and cherubic, smooth round face, Angel's nickname suited her. She had the complexion and broad features of her mestizo ancestors, but unlike her forbearers, Angel wore heavy make-up, large earrings, dark fingernail polish, and a frou-frou hairstyle. Like her fellow homegirls, she wore the typical dress of a gangster—baggy blue jeans with a loose, oversized jersey, and jet-black sneakers. A stocky 5 foot 2 inches tall, Angel was a ball of frenetic energy. She spoke rapidly as she told me of Lonely's death by an enemy assassin.

"Some *chavala*[2] from *feighteen*[3] shot Lonely and Guilty on their way to Pollo Loco," she said. Lonely was a member of Angel's clique, and Guilty was her boyfriend. Pollo Loco was one of the local strip mall hangouts of their clique. About five blocks from this destination, Guilty stopped his car at a red light. According to Angel, this is where "a *chavala* walked up and capped them." Guilty got a bullet in the head and another in his chest and died almost instantly. Lonely was hit three times in the chest and arm and died on her way to the hospital.

This story illustrates a sad fact about the subculture of street gangs—that women are much more likely to be its victims than the perpetrators of violence. According to Moore, females in gangs suffer more long-term harm from gang membership than males.[4] Despite media reports on hyperviolent homegirls, research suggests that their increased participation in gangs is attributable to females' increasing economic marginalization and that females' positions and opportunities within street gangs have not changed significantly over time.[5] Research has also found that females are more likely than males to be exploited and victimized by fellow gang members or through gang-related activities.[6] Although a great deal of variation has been found in the involvement of females in gangs, qualitative and ethnographic research confirms high rates of both offending and victimization.[7]

Lonely's death sent Angel into a self-destructive, drug-riddled phase of her life. "It left a hole in my heart," she told me, "Lonely was my big sister." Angel was depressed to hear of Lonely's death, but she was not shocked by the news. When she recounted this story, Angel's voice had a tone of acceptance of the inevitability of death. Like many of her compatriots, she had grown up in El Salvador during the civil war and was therefore somewhat numbed to seeing dead bodies. This process of desensitization toward violence and death began in El Salvador, where she lived until she was thirteen years old, but it found its fruition in the gang barrios of Los Angeles. Although street socialization prepared Angel for the rigors of gang life, she was nonetheless deeply impacted by the death of her mentor, friend, and confidant. The irony of Angel's predicament was that she never intended to become a member of la Mara Salvatrucha, or any other street gang for that matter. In fact, prior to her association with gang members in Los Angeles, she found street gangs repugnant.

Angel's Decision to Join MS

When she came to the United States, Angel knew little about street gangs, and so she never gave any thought to joining one. In 1990, when Angel was thirteen, her mother sent her to Los Angeles partly to better Angel's life, partly to better her own. During the civil war, Salvadoran families who could afford it sent their young daughters to the United States to get jobs as seamstresses or domestics. These young women, usually between the ages of thirteen and twenty-five, were expected to live frugally and to send money home in the form of remittances. It would be difficult to overestimate the significance of this phenomenon given the degree to which El Salvador's economy was dependant on transfers of money sent from the United States. Remittance dollars they sent home to El Salvador during the war surpassed the annual U.S. aid budget and continued to outperform El Salvador's coffee exports as a source of foreign exchange.[8]

When Angel's mother sent her to the United States, she did so with the expectation that Angel would get a job to help the family. What she didn't know was that the little slip of paper on which she had written her sister's address in Los Angeles was erroneous. When the coyote tried to deliver Angel to her aunt's apartment, they found that the address did not exist. Angel was relieved when a girl in her group, with whom she had bonded during the trip because of their similar ages, offered to put her up at her place until she could find her aunt. Angel went to live with this girl, her mother, and her four brothers and sisters in a cramped one-bedroom apartment. Within a few weeks, a lady from Guatemala who lived next door found her a job in a jewelry store and helped Angel get a fake I.D. and a work permit. Despite her youth, Angel was able to pass as employable. After about six weeks of work, Angel received an invitation to move into this neighbor lady's apartment and share a room with her teenage daughter. Angel got along quite well with this woman, whom she called "auntie," and her daughter, whom she called "cousin." Angel has fond memories of this short period in her life. "My auntie was nice to me," she told me. "She treated me like her own daughter."

A few months later, Angel's real aunt had tracked her down and went to collect her. But Angel did not like this new living arrangement. Because her aunt worked as a babysitter and was gone for days, Angel felt lonely and missed the company of her fictive kin. Angel continued working at the jewelry store, contributing to her aunt's expenses, and sending the rest of her wages to her mother in El Salvador. Given her isolation, Angel dreamed of an alternate life with her father. "I never met him," said Angel, "But I couldn't help but wonder about him." Angel projected onto her father the possibility of a better life.

What fueled Angel's warm feelings toward her biological father was the knowledge that he had tried to locate her when she was just a baby girl. "I know that my father looked for me when I was little," Angel told me. "But my mother's folks didn't like him, so they wouldn't tell him where my mom was at." Angel overhead some family gossip that her father had moved to New York City, and she began to harbor the idea of moving there to live with him. However, this would prove extremely difficult because Angel didn't even know his real name. When Angel asked her mother, she brushed off the question. "She told me she didn't know his real name," said Angel, "only the name he used on his fake I.D. And it was like—'Oh, what's his name'— *Salvador Muñoz Calderon*, or something like that." Thus hindered, Angel temporarily gave up the idea of getting in touch with her father. It wasn't until many years later, after having experienced the disappointments of the gang life, that she would act on this impulse.

Angel's work permit expired a year later. As an unemployed worker, her attention shifted to education. Angel said she told her aunt she wanted to go back to school, but her aunt was incredulous. "'You really want to go to school?' she asked me. 'Yeah,' I answered, 'I want to learn English,'" said Angel. Angel was pleased when her aunt finally consented, and she was grateful for the opportunity to learn something useful. Despite her limited English skills, she excelled in most of her subjects, unaware that school would become her gateway into the gang life. In one of her classes, she met Loquita, an MS homegirl who became her best friend. "We were tight," said Angel. "Inseparable, like sisters." Loquita, like Angel, was Salvadoran, and they shared many of the same interests. However, when Angel's aunt found out that her niece had befriended a gang member, she threw a fit.

"My aunt accused me of being a bad girl," said Angel. "She thought I was in the gang, but I wasn't. She'd be gone for the whole week, and when she got home, she would scold me, saying, 'Yeah, I know you go out with *her* [meaning Loquita], and I know you go out with *guys,* too. You know what, some of these days they gonna shoot you. They gonna do *something* to you. And I don't want that to happen to you.'" Despite her aunt's concern for her safety, this accusation stung Angel, who protested her innocence vehemently.

And I'm like, "Nooooooo." At the time I didn't know *nothing* about gangs. I was a *New Waver*. I used to wear my hair, like—you know— *real short*, like a New Waver. But my aunt didn't know that. She didn't know how gangsters dress.

To back up her argument, Angel showed her aunt her report card, which had only A's and B's. Unconvinced, her aunt decided to separate Angel from the dangers of the gang by sending her back home to her mother. "She even buy me the ticket," Angel told me. "But I refused to go." Her aunt interpreted this willful rebellion as further proof that her niece was already a member of the gang. "She used to keep saying that I was against her," said Angel. "But I wasn't. And that used to get me *maaad.*" Angel said she got more support from her friends in the gang than she did from her aunt. "When I got an A in math, which was a hard subject for me, the homies threw me a big party to celebrate," she said. "They even bought me a cake! But when I told my aunt about my A, she told me, 'Go wash the dishes.'"

Unwilling to return to El Salvador, and feeling unwelcome and unsupported by her aunt, Angel decided, with help from a counselor from her school, to move into a homeless shelter. Angel referred to this shelter as *placement*. Appropriately, the name for this shelter for homeless youth was Angel's Flight. "It's a place for kids whose parents don't want them in the house anymore," Angel said. "Runaways and kids like that." After a little less than a month at this shelter, Angel moved in with three women from Central America. One of these women was a friend of Angel's social worker or school counselor—Angel used these terms interchangeably—and agreed to have Angel come live with her in Hollywood. "These women were real nice to me," said Angel. "They used to feed me and send me to school and everything. And they didn't charge me nothing." Unfortunately, after only a few months this arrangement ended abruptly when one of the women got married and moved back to Guatemala and another had to go to El Salvador to arrange her legal documents. Because the third woman couldn't afford the rent, Angel was forced to move again.

Angel moved in with a friend from school and her mother, who lived nearby. At first, Angel got along with this girl, but then she started having problems with her. Most of this had to do with the fact that this girl was a member of the T. J. Locos gang. "I moved out from there because we didn't get along," said Angel. "Because, you know, I didn't like gangs. I used to tell her, '*Maaan*, look at you. You're in this and that. Some of these days they're going to shoot you.'" The irony that she was echoing the very words of her aunt was lost on Angel. This homegirl ignored Angel's admonitions. "She wouldn't listen to me," said Angel. "She used to go to her neighborhood and she didn't tell me, you know. And her mom used to call me and ask me where her daughter was, and I used to tell her, 'Oh, she went to the liquor store, or she went to do this or that.' I didn't want to lie but I didn't want to rat her out."

Eventually the situation became intolerable for Angel. "We were always fighting," she said. "And I don't like that. So, after a couple of months, I moved out." No doubt, by this time Angel must have felt like a bouncing ball. Now, Angel felt she had nowhere to go except to the streets. Weighing her limited options, Angel decided to move in with

Figure **5.1 Trippy's Tattoo, Los Angeles, 1997. A master tattoo artist from the Mara Salvatrucha tattoos a homegirl's back. Copyright © Donna DeCesare, 1997.**

Loquita, her best friend from school. It was this move that sealed Angel's fate in terms of becoming a gang member. Although it was not inevitable, within six months Angel had followed Loquita into her gang.

Angel said she chose to get jumped into Mara Salvatrucha because she did not want to be perceived as merely a ruca, jaina, or hoodrat—a girl for sex. In order not to get this reputation, when Angel joined the gang she avoided sleeping around with the homeboys. Because she had neither the desire nor temperament, Angel did not become a hard-core member of MS. She participated in no *jales* (drive-by shootings), no robberies, and no extortions. Only reluctantly did she get into a few fist-fights when it was necessary to back up her homegirls. Her gang career was spent hanging out, getting high, and sharing food and shelter with her fellow homies. The fact that Angel joined MS more for social or familial reasons than a need for status or excitement meant that she was predisposed to be a peripheral member of the gang, one who stays at the margins.

Although she attended clique meetings, hung out with her fellow gang members, and occasionally sold drugs, Angel was not considered hard-core. She was not committing serious crimes of violence and she was not active in the internecine battles for power within her gang. For Angel, MS was a surrogate family, people who are supposed to provide for you and give you shelter. Angel wanted to belong to a group of like-minded individuals, people who cared for her.

> Everything that was happening to me at that time was depressing. I think this is what pushed me to join the gang. It wasn't that I liked the gang. No. But it was this that pushed me [into the gang]. My financial situation. Shit. I was depressed. Really depressed. And all that, you know, it pushed me to get into la Mara Salvatrucha.

In addition to the camaraderie she felt with the gang members, by joining the gang Angel felt more secure economically. "As a gang member," she said, "I always had some walking-around money, even if it was only five bucks in my pocket. And if I didn't have any money to eat or for something, my homies would help me out. You know, *por eso*, I didn't suffer. My homies were *firme*, you know, nice to me. Some of them, they go, 'Have you eat already? You wanta eat? Let's go to this place.' Some of them are like that. But some others, they don't care." Although MS did not have a strict rule that you have to help out a fellow gang member, there was a general ethic that you should. Especially among her home-girls, Angel felt a sense of sharing and caring.

"In my clique we used to get money and stay in a hotel," said Angel. "It always had to be girls, just girls. No guys. And we'd just get a room and stay there. And sometimes the guys would get mad and say, 'How come we can't go?' And we're like, 'No. We're girls. You have to respect us.' We wanted to have respect too." For Angel, respect meant being given the opportunity to enjoy the company of her sisters, unencumbered and unmolested by her brothers in the gang.

Although Angel avoided dating her fellow homeboys for a time, eventually she succumbed to the temptation. However, her choice for a boyfriend was not the best. Despite his nickname, Angel started going out with Tricky. "Loquita warned me about the guys," said Angel. "She told me, 'When guys are around girls they're all dogs with only one thing on their minds.' She didn't have to tell me what that was." Soon after Angel started dating Tricky, he was arrested for illegal weapons possession. When she later found out about his sexual peccadilloes, Angel wrote him off. She stopped writing him letters and visiting him in jail. With Tricky out of the picture, and having become tired of the gang life, particularly burying her fellow homies, Angel's mind began to wander back to thoughts of her father, the one she had never met.

"I really wanted to meet him," Angel said. "'Cuz I didn't want to be in the gang no more. I wanted out." Although Angel managed to locate her father's relatives who lived in Los Angeles, at first they did not want to give Angel her father's name and phone number. "It took me a long time to get the number out of them," Angel said. "Finally, I got the number and I called him. He said he was coming to Downey to visit his brother." This might have been great news were it not for the fact that Angel's father refused to make the minimal physical effort of a side trip to visit his biological daughter. This further depressed Angel. "He wouldn't come to my house and see me," she said, holding back tears. "So I had to go to Downey." Their meeting was anything but warm or convivial.

> The most me and him had a conversation was like ten minutes. From there, he totally ignored me and talked to my brother. Because my big brother grew up with him, my father liked him best. He could have asked me, "What's going on with your life?" But he didn't even care. So, I was like, "forget him."

Despite this sting of rejection, Angel called her father and left messages. "He never called me back," she said. Soon after, her father's phone was disconnected, and her letters were returned unopened. "I really didn't have no feelings for it," she said, as if trying to convince herself of the fact. "He's never been around so I really don't care." As if to put a lie to this sentiment, she quickly added, "My wish for him was that he was dead. That's my wish for him." Like Angel, many female gang members join their gangs as a form of rebellion against rejection or limited opportunities. And like Angel, many of them are runaways.

Rebels and Runaways

> Homegirls are either rebels or runaways, or both.
>
> —Loquita

Most of the early studies of gangs ignored females completely, made a passing reference to them, or focused solely on their psychological dysfunctions and social maladjustment.[9] Stereotypical images of female gang members were produced because male researchers conducted these studies by interviewing male gang members about their attitudes toward their female counterparts. Most male gang members, whether Latino, African-American, Asian, or white, have sexist attitudes toward women.[10] In these early, androcentric studies, female gang members were described as either *tomboys* or *sex objects* whose primary function was to serve male members as girlfriends, providers of sexual services, mules to carry weapons and/or drugs, temptresses to lure enemy gang members into a trap, or spies to gain vital information from enemies.[11]

These stereotypes prevailed until researchers began to directly study females in gangs in the late 1970s. Females' roles in gangs were found to be much more complex and nuanced than these early studies suggested. Although young women played some of these stereotypical roles, their gang activity was marked by varying degrees of independence from and subservience to male gang members.[12] These studies indicated that females join street gangs for basically the same reasons that males join: for independence, protection, respect, money, clothes, fun, access to alcohol and drugs, affiliation, friendship, sex, to protect turf, to maintain a family tradition, to escape problems in the family and/or at school, and as rebellion against racism and discrimination.[13]

Campbell's study of Hispanic gangs in the New York area paints a familiar picture for female gang members.[14] The homegirls she studied joined gangs because they felt they had few alternatives and were not happy about the prospects of domestic servitude. Their backgrounds are an all too familiar picture of the urban underclass. Many had come from households headed by single women on welfare, and most had dropped out of school and had few marketable skills. Although the men in their lives were not supporting them emotionally or economically, they were still trying to call the shots. And given the triple handicaps of ethnicity, class, and gender, the future prospects of these women were bleak. According to Campbell, 94 percent would have children and 84 percent of them would have to raise their children without a husband and thus would have to depend on welfare.[15]

Research indicates that many female gang members are runaways from dysfunctional families. Many of Fishman's sample of Vice Queens, an African-American female auxiliary gang to the Vice Kings of Chicago, were runaways, who spent most of their time hanging out on the streets with the guys, consuming alcohol, engaging in sex, and occasionally committing petty crimes such as prostitution and shoplifting or getting into fights with other groups of young women.[16] Fishman characterizes these females as the sexual playthings of the males, who get them pregnant but do not want to marry them. These young women learned to defend themselves against abusive men and out of necessity had become independent, assertive, and willing to take risks. Having adapted to their environment, they demonstrated a greater flexibility of roles than their male counterparts.[17] In contrast, Lauderback, Hansen, and Waldorf studied an African-American female gang in San Francisco, whose members, all under twenty-five years old, had remained independent of male gangs and supported themselves and their young children through sales of crack cocaine.[18] Abandoned and abused by men, these women bemoaned the circumstances that led them to sell drugs and wished they had alternatives, but they held out little hope for change in the future.

Campbell found that, like males, females join the gang to escape the boredom and harshness of their impoverished lives.[19] The gang represented economic opportunity and freedom from the restrictions of the traditional female subservient domestic roles of housewife and mother. The gang served as only a temporary escape from poverty and marginalization, but it offered a degree of independence and solidarity with their sisters. Street-oriented families, who are more permissive with their daughters and provide them with opportunities and role models for delinquent behavior, are more likely to produce female gang members.[20] Moore found a self-selection process in gang participation that revolved around gender.[21] Because it was more acceptable for young men to be "out on the streets," they were more likely to come from conventional working-class families, whereas young women tended to come from underclass and/or abusive families and were more likely to have alcoholic or heroin-using parents. Three quarters of these young women had run away from home at least once. Unlike the male gang members, more than a third of the females had had family members make sexual advances toward them.

The literature suggests that there are three main differences between females and males in their reasons for joining a street gang: (1) females are somewhat more likely than males to join gangs for affiliation, and males for excitement; (2) females are more likely than males to come from backgrounds of domestic violence and sexual abuse; and (3) females tend to join gangs at an earlier age, eleven to thirteen years old, than males, thirteen to fifteen years old, and tend to leave gangs earlier.[22] A fourth possible distinction is their method of initiation.

Sexing In—"The Easy Way"

> Most of the homeboys are big liars. They'll say anything to get you in bed. One homeboy told me that if I had sex with him, he'd get me into the gang. I knew he was lying.
>
> — Angel

> If you got a all girls crew, they think you're "soft" and in the streets if you soft, it's all over....It's wild, but fellas really hate seeing girls getting off. Now, some fellas respect the power of girls, but most just want us in the sack.
>
> —Taylor[23]

Getting "sexed into" a street gang is one of the most misunderstood aspects of female participation in gangs. According to the media stereotype, having sexual relations with male gang members is a common way for homegirls to get initiated.[24] Although a very few gangs allow its female members to get sexed in, the vast majority do not allow this practice because it denigrates women and makes their gangs look weak. Another reason that most gangs do not allow females to get sexed in, as Psycho explained to me, was because afterward the girl could say it was rape, and it would be her word against the others. For these reasons, most females become members of street gangs similar to the way males become members, by hanging out and becoming assimilated into the gang or getting jumped in.

Whereas a few gangs allow females to be sexed into their gang, it goes without saying that males never can. The simple reason for this is because male gang members do not see having sexual relations with women as a form of sacrifice. "It's too easy," said Trouble, cynically, "and too many guys would choose it." This sexual form of gang initiation for young women has been called *throwing the dice* or *pulling a train*. Throwing the dice means that a young woman tosses two dice and then must have sexual relations with that number of male gang members, with a maximum of twelve. Pulling a train means the same thing, but with no minimum or maximum number of homeboys. Male gang members from MS that I interviewed told me that a girl could never get sexed into their gang—what they called "the easy way." But some of them admitted that they weren't beyond playing tricks on some girls. "Sometimes the girls were too scared to get jumped in," said Psycho. "So they just opened their legs. When a girl would ask about getting sexed in, she would say, 'If I prefer to do sex, how many guys am I gonna get?' We'd say, 'Oh, let me see...' And all the homeboys would say, 'Hey, over here! I'll go.' No, we'd give them a choice. 'Okay, you're gonna get four. Pick the ones you want.' But this was just a trick to get them to sleep with us. Afterward, we'd laugh at them and call them sluts."

Trouble rationalized his participation in such rituals of deception, saying that some girls just want to have sex. "I remember this one girl, man," he said. "She was a freak, I guess. She used to love sex a lot. Everybody, I mean everybody fucked her. Every day in a motel, where one guy was living, three guys would come in and she would fuck them all. Then more guys would show up and fuck her. She must have slept with twenty guys. I guess she must have loved having sex."[25] Gang members are highly disparaging and equally suspicious of "loose" girls like this, with a large sexual appetite. "The guys see how the girls are," said Sniper. "They're with one guy, and then the next minute they're with another. There are some girls that just like to party with different guys in different gangs. Obviously, this causes problems, and the guys don't want those girls in their gang."

Gang members do not want these females in their gang because it often causes fighting between homeboys. MS had an unwritten rule that one is not supposed to date more than one gang member at one time, a rule that was violated quite frequently. Although this rule applied more strictly to females than males, some of the homeboys felt that dating more than one person at a time was problematic. "I didn't like that," said Sniper. "Playing around with a lot of homegirls, you get into trouble. If a homegirl you're dating goes out with another homeboy, that's when fights begin." Sniper had first-person experience of this.

> That happened to me. I got out of jail and I got together with a homegirl. I found out later that she had another homeboy in jail. When he got out of jail he came looking for me. But I didn't know she was with

him before. She didn't tell me. He said I took his girlfriend. But I didn't know anything about it. If she was going out with me it was because she wanted to, not because I was trying to take someone else's girl. If I had known, I would have respected him and not gone out with her. When he came to find me, I explained the situation to him and he said, "The same thing is going to happen to you." And it did. I was with her for three months and then got locked up. And she got with another guy. It's not only the guys who choose. The girls pick the guys a lot of times.

Trouble divided girls who associate with gang members into two types, roughly equivalent to the terms *jainas* and *homegirls*, above. "There are two types of girls," he said. "There are girls who like sex and crazy girls. Crazy girls get jumped in like the homeboys." According to Trouble, only crazy girls were respected members of MS. Psycho agreed that a homegirl who wants to become a respected member of MS must be *jumped in*, beaten up to show their toughness and dedication. Joker said that before the homegirl was jumped in, "They would hang around with us. We would see how they are and stuff. They had to be good fighters. We had homegirls that were short, like 5 feet 2 inches, but they were *mean*, man. They could throw down with the best of us." Sniper echoed this sentiment. "We had some homegirls who were down for the barrio," he said. "Yeah. I had several girls right here that I jumped in. Shorty, Flaca, Giggles, Baby Doll, and Larga, they all got jumped in. They was good girls 'cuz they could get down with anybody, even if they were bigger than her, even a man."

Female gang members were present in most of the MS cliques I studied. I was told of only one all-female MS clique, an auxiliary with about twenty members. It was called *Chicas Locas* or Crazy Girls, and according to the homeboys, it lasted only a couple of years in the late 1990s before it disbanded as a result of internal conflicts. The numbers of female members varied greatly over time and between MS cliques, with some cliques having as many as twenty active members out of a total membership of 100, and others having as few a three or four females out of approximately fifty members. At various points in time, some cliques had very few, if any, active members. How this compares to other street gangs is debatable. Studies have found that the percentage of females in mixed-gender street gang ranges greatly from 5 to

75 percent, with a reasonable estimate ranging from one third to one fourth of all gang members.[26]

Although females are well represented within street gangs, law enforcement tends to neglect them. This is primarily because there is a bias within law enforcement that female gang members are not as violent or criminally oriented as their male counterparts. This bias is accurate to the extent that homegirls like Angel represent female gang members. But if one considers the hard-core homegirls, like Loquita, this bias overlooks female gang members who are active in crime and violence. Law enforcement officials are not the only ones who tend to disregard the efforts and the amount respect that some female members garner within their gangs. Within large street gangs, like MS, there is a tendency for the male gang members to disrespect their female counterparts. Nothing encapsulates this negative attitude of young men as well as their motto *trust no bitch*.

"Trust No Bitch"—Spies, Snitches, Traitors, and Rats

Trust no bitch.

—Gang *tattoo* on the upper arm of Joker

Women are snakes. They're gossips. They rat out. They screw around with other vatos and they insult your clique.

—Trouble

As these quotes indicate, many male gang members have little trust in their female counterparts. The pervasive myth within MS was that most females are unreliable. Angel, like her fellow homegirls, had to fight this stereotype against females as rats, or traitors. In addition to accusations of infidelity, some homeboys said that girlfriends betrayed their boyfriends in the gang by telling enemy gang members where to find them or even setting them up by bringing their boyfriends into enemy territory. Whether or not this was true, many male gang members felt that most females could not be trusted with gang secrets, such as information regarding criminal and violent activities.[27] Part of this suspicion was based on rumor, but another part was based on experience. Trouble said, "Before, in my barrio[28] there were *un chingo de* (a bunch of) homegirls. But of all the girls, there were four or five who were rats—*moras que eran ratas*. When the homeboys wanted to do a jale, they got scared and they snitched on the homeboys. They ratted us out to *la jura* (the police)."

Trouble claimed that when the police arrested these weak homegirls, they would buckle under pressure. "The police made them scared so that they would tell them what's up," he said, "and the girls snitched." Stories like this reinforced the stereotype of females as rats or snitches. As a result, a few of the homeboys, like Joker, got "Trust no Bitch" tattooed on their upper arms or chests. The tattoos I saw on MS and 18th Street gang members were written in Chinese characters, presumably because they looked "cool." When I asked Joker about his tattoo, he said proudly, "It's Chinese for *trust no bitch*." I asked Joker if he read Chinese characters. "No," he said, frowning. "Why?" Teasing him, I asked, "How do you know it doesn't say, 'I am a bitch'?" Wanting to avoid a punch in the face, I quickly laughed and said, "You've got nothing to worry about, no one you know reads Chinese. And I'm sure it says what you think it does."

Loquita told me that homeboys get this tattoo when their girlfriends dump them. "If his girlfriend sleeps with another guy," she said, "he loses trust in all women." When I asked Joker's girlfriend, Giggles, an MS homegirl, how she felt about his "trust no bitch" tattoo, she said, "He got it before we met. One of his girlfriends probably burned him. But it's hypocritical. The homeboys say they don't trust us, but they always end up with another girl. They don't trust us, but they don't avoid us either." To retaliate, Giggles said the homegirls came up with an expression of their own: *El amor es un pedo*. Literally this means *love is a fart*, but Giggles said it means that love of a guy is a waste of time. "We girls got t-shirts made up with this written in bold letters," she told me, "Joker got *soooo* mad when he saw it, but I didn't care. It was our way of getting back at the guys."

The reality that male gang members were just as likely as female gang members to be sexually unfaithful or rat out one of their fellow gang members was lost on most of the homeboys. They preferred to operate under the premise that females are untrustworthy, partly because it was a safer, more cautious approach. Most of these MS homeboys never knew Tiny, an MS homegirl who spent four years in prison for a crime she did not commit because she refused to give up any information about her homeboys. Cases like this tend to go overlooked by male gang members. The stereotype or myth of the untrustworthy women is powerful and is reinforced each time a female gang member rats out or spies on her fellow gang members. One example of the dangers of spying was Puppet, an MS homegirl who was killed by the Harpies because she was suspected of spying on them. "Puppet was hanging with the Harpies," Psycho explained. "And then she would go back to hang out with her homies in MS. When she returned to the Harpies, they killed her. She was actually spying for the Harpies, but they didn't believe her, so they killed her. She was playing both sides and got burned."

In the minds of MS gang members, no case better illustrates the untrustworthiness of women than that of Brenda Paz.[29] Brenda, who was born in Honduras, was thirteen when she joined the gang in Los Angeles and took the nickname Smiley. A year after joining the gang, Smiley ran away from home, staying with various MS members, and eventually ended up in Virginia in 2002. Soon after, Smiley was arrested with her boyfriend, Conejo, for stealing a car. Conejo was a suspect in a murder investigation. Fearing a long prison sentence for having witnessed a gang-related homicide, Smiley decided to cooperate with law enforcement. She entered the FBI's witness protection program and was relocated. But feeling isolated and alone in Minnesota, where she had no friends, Smiley started calling her fellow homeboys on the phone, and within a few months she moved back to Virginia. Smiley threw a party and invited all her homeboys to her apartment, telling them that her father was paying the rent. Her homeboys got suspicious and launched an investigation. They found her diary in which she had written of her encounters with FBI detectives. In addition, the diary had one of their business cards tucked inside. The gang members called a meeting to decide her punishment, and she was green-lighted by unanimous vote, meaning an order of execution.

On July 13, 2003, three gang members lured Smiley to go on a "fishing expedition," where she was brutally murdered on the banks of the Shenandoah River. Autopsy reports indicate she was stabbed between thirteen and sixteen times, and her throat was slit. As one law enforcement official said, "Her head was almost decapitated."[30] The autopsy also revealed that she was four months pregnant, though it is not known whether or not the executioners knew this at the time. The gang's rule, immortalized in the title of the History Channel's *Gangland* program on her life, is "You rat, you die." Brenda was well aware of the consequences of her actions. According to videotaped testimony she gave to the FBI, she says, "MS never forgets. If you break the rules, they will hunt you down."[31]

Most of the MS homeboys I interviewed thought that Brenda got what was coming to her because she was a rat. But Loquita had a different perspective on Brenda's case. "It was not the first time that a gang, any gang, had killed a snitch," she said. "I think the reason why Brenda Paz was such a big thing is because law enforcement screwed up. They had a *minor*, an underage girl, in their possession. The FBI had made promises to protect her in exchange for information. They had custody over her and should have protected her. And they didn't." After a pause, Loquita added, "And no one asked about her parents."

Loquita thinks this part of the story won't get told. "The FBI was successfully able to deflect the attention of what happened to Brenda away from the bureau and onto the gang," she said. "Everything was spun to further demonize these guys, when they were just doing what everybody knows that they do." Loquita did not condone what the homeboys did to Brenda Paz, but as a hard-core member of the gang, she knew the gang's rules and was willing to live by them. She understood that the worst thing a gang member can do is to spy on or rat out one's fellow gang members, and that if you get caught, you might get killed. There is another rule violation within street gangs, however, for which few people get punished. Although this unwritten rule is not strictly enforced, it still leads to distrust and conflict within the gang. This rule, which was mentioned above, states that gang members should not sleep around with more than one fellow member at a time. That this rule is applied more forcefully to female members is reflective of androcentric, *machista* bias within street gangs.

The Sexual Double Standard

> It's a guy thing.
>
> — Angel

Because it applies only to female gang members, the sexual double standard within street gangs is quite sexist. This unwritten rule within the gang is a general societal prohibition, which views women who have multiple partners as "loose" or "immoral." This rule is a double standard because there is a different standard for male gang members.

Whereas homegirls who sleep around are considered sluts or hoodrats, homeboys who participate in the same activity are considered players, who are manly or virile. This double standard becomes amplified in the gang, where young women who have sexual relations with more than one man are greatly stigmatized. Although both males and females are jealous and suspicious of their sexual partners, there is a general attitude within street gangs that women are possessions or chattel. When asked to explain this sexist rule, Angel shrugged her shoulders and sighed. "It's a guy thing," she said, exasperated.

Angel said that that it's rare, but MS homegirls can get courted or punished for sleeping around. "And the guys?" I asked. "Do they get court for it, if they sleep with a lot of women?" Angel laughed at the naiveté of my question. "No. *Para un hombre es mejor para uno.* (No, for a guy it's good)," she said. When I asked why the rules are different for guys than gals in the gang, Angel said, "Because in a man it doesn't look bad if he's fucking. They feel more like a player, *mas pisosa, mas aca.* But if a homegirl is going around fucking everyone, she's not worth a damn (*no vale verga*)."

> *Mona cochina chuca* [She's a dirty girl]. Because a girl in the gang can choose who she wants, anyone she wants. She can get one and leave him, get another and leave him, get another and leave him. But she shouldn't be going out with more than one at a time. *Putasona* [Super-slut]. If you sleep around, they call you a slut. They'll call out to you, "Hey slut, come here."

Because having sexual relations with more than one fellow gang member causes conflict within the clique, the rule makes sense. That it applies only to female gang members makes no sense at all, unless viewed from the male bias. Although homegirls like Angel are well aware of this double standard, they have little power to change it. In order to get along, they accept this bias, but it doesn't mean that they're happy with the status quo. Feeling the disparity, some female gang members rebelled, and many of the homegirls did what the homeboys did and slept around. Needless to say, this was a major cause of conflict within many cliques of MS. Another major source of conflict within the gang was sleeping with the enemy, an unwritten rule that both homegirls and homeboys also violated quite frequently.

Dating the Enemy

If you want to fuck, that's what the homeboys of your clique are for, so you can fuck within the clique. But if you fuck an enemy, *mala onda*.[32]

— Loquita

Despite this rule against dating the enemy, it is common within street gangs for their members to fraternize with the opposite sex who happen to belong to an enemy gang. "All is fair in love and war," said Loquita, quoting a popular phrase. The reason why gangs have this rule is fairly obvious. "If girls sleep with enemy members, gang secrets will be exposed," said Joker. As mentioned above, there is the problem of divided loyalty. "If a homegirl is dating an enemy gang member, there is a very good chance that she is going to betray her own homeboys," said Trouble. "Even if she doesn't want to, her boyfriend is going to pressure her to help them out." She might give up information about her gang's hangouts or, worse, set up a fellow gang member for attack. Despite the risks involved, however, both homeboys and homegirls violate this rule frequently. However, homegirls are much more likely to be punished for dating the enemy.

Loquita said that two times her gang members disciplined her for dating someone from another gang. Her first boyfriend was from Primera Flats, an enemy gang. When her homeboys found out, she received a severe beating. Loquita was given a beating a second time for dating a member of 18th Street, the worst enemy of MS. However, these beatings did not prevent Loquita from dating outside her gang. Because of her defiant personality, she was not going to let her homeboys dictate who was an acceptable mate. "Who am I going to date?" she asked rhetorically. "I had my pride and I wasn't going to be told who I could date and who I couldn't."

Another example illustrates the hypocrisy of MS homeboys. At one point in his gang career, Sniper was dating Chola, a well-respected member of 18th Street, a founder and shot-caller of a female auxiliary of the gang in East LA. When Sniper was in court proceedings, I spent a good deal of time with Chola. As a veteran of her gang, Chola was well aware of the contradictions of gang dating. When I asked her about the frequency of dating an enemy gang member, she laughed and said that it happens all the time. She was introduced to Sniper by one of her homeboys, who was locked up with him in LA County Jail. They exchanged letters and when Sniper was released, they started going out together. She lamented that it had brought her nothing but trouble with her own gang members. One time, she said, she had to break up a fight that was about to start in a gas station. "We were filling up the car in my barrio, and some of my homeboys spotted Sniper," she told me. "The fool [referring to Sniper] wanted to start a fight even though he was outnumbered four to one." Chola successfully diffused this confrontation, but it did nothing to endear her to her boyfriend.

Chola was very critical of Sniper and his MS homeboys, who she viewed as "stupidly belligerent" and hypocritical when it came to dating the enemy. Many times she would accompany Sniper to his local hangout, and each time his homeboys would query her about her fellow homegirls.

> It was strange. They're supposed to be the enemy and they're asking you to bring one of your homegirls [from 18th Street] down to meet them. They seem to make the rules up as they go.

For some unfathomable reason, Chola stuck by her man until he was arrested and later transferred to a federal prison in Texas. By this time, she had given up on him. "He sent me letters," she said, "and I wrote back a few times. But he's going to be *torcido* (locked up) for a very long time, so what's the point?" Chola didn't know why her gang was the worst enemy of MS, but she learned that dating an enemy gang member was not her best decision. "Well, it would be good, you know," she said. "It would be cool if we could get along. But, I don't know. I don't think it will work." Another aspect of gang life for homegirls that didn't work in their favor was a double-bind with regard to respect.

The Catch-22 of Respect

> Female gang participation has generated much public concern and media attention, in part because they are becoming more visible, and also because they are presumed to be rebelling against traditional notions of femininity. The popular image of female gang members portrays these "bad girls" as even more problematic than their male counterparts because they challenge traditional gender roles.
>
> —Hunt and Joe-Laidler[33]

Theoretically speaking, a female gang member can get the same status as a male gang member. However, Loquita said that a homegirl in her gang has to work much harder to earn her status than her male counterpart. "Some of his status comes from just being a man," she told me, "whereas I have to *earn* it. I earned my status in the gang by putting my foot down, not letting others push me around, by putting in work, and being faithful." Indicative of this male dominance, Miller's excellent ethnography of female gang members in Missouri and Ohio is entitled *One of the Guys*.[34] To be accepted within the gang, homegirls must act like one of the guys, and they gain status within the gang the same way that guys do, by committing acts of violence.

Within this gang ideology, femininity is seen as a weakness. This is because street gangs, like armies on the battlefield, are mainly violent proving grounds for boys who want to be men. "If you want to join the gang, *hay que tener huevos* [you have to have balls]," said Joker, referring to testicular fortitude, or the willingness to fight for the gang and be killed for the cause. As a paramilitary group, street gangs tend to value its male members over its females. "We're in a hierarchy," said Loquita, "where the men are on top. It's a machista world we live in. Even if a woman is independent, there's always going to be some critics. She will never get the same status as a man, who gets it just 'cuz he's a man. That's just the way it is." Loquita went on to say, "The gang is an equal opportunity enterprise. A homegirl has to decide for herself what role she is going to play in the gang. The attitude toward homegirls is different than it is for homeboys. A homegirl has to earn it from the day she joins until the day she dies. She can't be told what to do. She has to refuse to be disrespected. She has to throw down with a man to get respect. I threw down with guys."

To illustrate this point, Loquita told me how she gained the respect of Criminal, one of her fellow homeboys. One day Criminal asked her to cook something for him and she answered, "I'm not your maid. And I'm not your wife. Do your own damn food!" Loquita said that Criminal tried to hit her, but she dodged the blow. "I told him, 'I'll throw down with you,'" she said. Criminal answered, "I'm not going to fight with a woman." When Loquita insisted, Criminal told her he would "kick her ass." In response to this, Loquita said, "You may kick my ass, but I'm going to get some good punches to your face." They went outside and began to fight. "We went at it," said Loquita. "Then, in the middle, he began to laugh and said, 'I can't believe I'm fighting a woman.'" They stopped fighting and Criminal changed his attitude toward Loquita. "Now he respects me," she said. "He won't let anyone touch me."

This story illustrates the necessity for homegirls to show masculine aggression in order to get respect. "You've got to be willing to throw down with guys," said Loquita, "Or they will never give you props. They will disrespect you and use you." However, what I noticed over many years of observation of gang members was a general tendency of the homeboys to view the most violent homegirls, those with the most respect, as less than desirable mates. This gets to the point of the Catch-22 for female members of street gangs. A Catch-22, taken from the novel by the same name, is a double-bind syndrome, which can be summarized in the phrase *you're damned if you do, you're damned if you don't*.[35] The Catch-22 of homegirls is that respect means acting aggressively masculine, but this comes at some sacrifice of their femininity and sexual attractiveness.

When I asked MS homeboys about their ideal mates, the vast majority of them said that they wanted the equivalent of a "church girl," one who is pious, pure, subservient, and extremely feminine. Needless to say, this is the opposite of a hard-core homegirl, who is rebellious, independent, and aggressively masculine. Although a few of the homeboys ended up living with female gang members, most of the ones who found successful, long-term partners married females who had never associated with or belonged to a street gang. For MS homegirls, it was much more difficult to find mates that had nothing to do with gangs, although this was their expressed preference. As the quote at the beginning of this section states, "because they are presumed to be rebelling against traditional notions of femininity" these homegirls were judged to be "bad girls." In the gang, each of these young women had to navigate the difficult waters of their sex and gender. If they wanted to be respected by their fellow gang members, they had to be violent. If they were willing to be passive and submissive, they would gain in sexual attractiveness, but at the cost of equal status to the guys in the gang. Yet another limitation imposed on female gang members that males never have to confront is the limitation imposed by pregnancy.

Pregnancy and Motherhood

There is much variability as to how a pregnancy will affect a female gang member, depending on her level of dedication and how she sees her role within the gang—i.e., how invested she is in her gangster identity. Some homegirls decide not to let pregnancy get in the way of their gang activities. However, these women risk the loss of status within their gangs because of the expectation that they should curb their participation in order to protect the baby. This is particularly true if the father of the child is an active member of the gang. He is likely to put pressure on his pregnant wife or girlfriend to "chill out," at least until the baby is born. Female gang members also typically discourage their fellow homegirls from committing crimes, getting into fights, and hanging out. Drinking alcohol or taking drugs are also generally frowned upon, for obvious reasons. All of these activities are seen as putting the fetus in danger. In addition, pregnant homegirls are seen as a liability in gang warfare because of the perception of pregnancy as a physical handicap. Most gang members do not want to be put in the position of having to defend a pregnant woman if a fight breaks out. There is also a general sense that expectant homegirls who ignore these warnings are violating a cardinal rule of womanhood—to be a good mother.

When I asked Angel if pregnant MS homegirls were expected to "chill out," she said, "It's not expected, but it's the reality. You *have* to take care of your kid." She emphasized the fact that caring for one's offspring is unquestioned. Not taking care of one's child is tantamount to betrayal and abandonment, issues close to the hearts of these gang members. A homegirl loses respect in her gang if she abandons her baby, choosing instead to act like a gangster. Homeboys, on the other hand, do not lose respect in their gang if they choose to ignore their offspring and continue to act like criminals. In fact, the opposite is true. Homeboys who chose to take on the lion's share of responsibility for childcare lose some of their gangster status. There is a misperception that male gang members are always dead-beat dads, but I observed a handful of MS homeboys who took on this role despite their loss of status.

Both homeboys and homegirls tend to see their babies as trophies. However, it is only the female gang members who are expected to take care of their children. Because the baby's father is often incarcerated, the mother is expected to take up the slack. Angel's boyfriend was in and out of jail, so she had to take care of her baby girl as well as her boyfriend. A homegirl who takes her baby out into the street so that she can continue gangbanging or hanging out, will lose respect within her gang. Said Angel, "It's like playing Russian roulette with your baby's life." For these reasons, most of the pregnant homegirls of MS curtailed their gang activities to some degree. However, there were a few homegirls who completely ignored all of these proscriptions against active participation. They were unwilling to give up their hard-won status within the gang and continued to hang out, party, fight, or commit crimes.

Giggles was one of these exceptions. Because he was the father of the baby, Joker put tremendous pressure on Giggles to chill out, what the gang members call becoming *calmada*. But Giggles was not going to listen to her boyfriend. Loquita and Lonely also tried to convince Giggles to stay at home, away from the dangers of drive-by shootings or gang fighting, but to no avail. Fortunately for all involved, Giggles did not get hurt during her pregnancy and she successfully gave birth to her baby girl, Jeannette. However, Giggles lost quite a bit of status within her clique afterward because she chose not to be a stay-at-home mom. She left the care of her baby to her aunt and continued to pursue her gang career on her own terms. As the father, Joker lost none of his gangster status even though he chose not to be a stay-at-home dad.

The gang literature suggests that female members are affected by pregnancy in one of three ways, each of which can lead to the termination of gang affiliation.[36] First, a deterioration of affiliation can be caused by abandonment. Often when a female gang member becomes pregnant, her boyfriend abandons her. As Fleisher states, "Males lose interest in pregnant females and in the mothers of their children ... especially if these women cannot offer males a place to hang out, sleep and sell illegal drugs."[37] The sense of family that is initially associated with gang affiliation is sometimes removed once female gang members are no longer able to actively participate in gang life. The abandonment by individual gang members or the gang as a whole causes many mothers to move away from the gang life, disillusioned with a group that no longer satisfies their current needs.

The second effect of pregnancy is the influence of the young woman's family. In many situations parents become more actively involved in their daughter's life because she needs support raising the child, and parents are then able to set rules and standards that they were unable to do before. Often parents of these teenage mothers become involved in their daughter's life due to concern they may have over the protection and raising of their grandchild. Female gang members can face the threat of losing their child to their parents or the state if gang affiliation continues. Thus, the family often puts pressure on the daughter to disassociate from her gang.

Sometimes in combination with the previously mentioned factors, pregnant gang members decide for themselves to disassociate from the gang. Self-disassociation occurs because these new mothers acquire new responsibilities and a change in identity once their child is born. Many pregnant homegirls have a positive outlook toward how pregnancy will affect their lives. Having a child usually helps a young woman's reputation if she is viewed as a good mother. The new role as a mother brings with it many responsibilities. She can improve her status within her biological family by proving that she can provide for and protect her child, and she loses little status within her gang family. This is because most gang members view motherhood as a perfectly legitimate excuse to leave the gang.

Motherhood often causes these female gang members to re-evaluate their relationships and encourages disassociations with people who might cause her harm or harm to her child. "Having a kid changes everything," said Angel. "One's effort towards the gang changes." Pregnancy enables these young women to mature out of gang life because of their new responsibilities. Those who chose gang life as a form of rebellion are brought back to the traditional role as mother. Many of these young women searching for familial ties within the gang are able to find that comfort through the birth of their child. Gang membership is no longer needed because the responsibilities of having a baby change their outlook on the future. The entrance into motherhood creates a fulfillment of the needs that caused these young women to join gangs and therefore allows them to exit the gang life much earlier than their male counterparts. This brings us to an often unacknowledged aspect of females' participation in street gangs, namely their crucial role as caretakers.

"Mothers of Us All"

> You support me. You make sure that I'm fed, that I'm taken care of, and if I go down, you'll be there to help me.
>
> —Angel

In this quote, Angel is commenting on the general attitude of the homeboys toward the women in their gang. "In a very twisted way, it's like what they would have wanted their mothers to do for them," she said. "They expect us to always support them. And they expect us to be like their mothers and forgive or forget everything they'd done to us in the past." Here, Angel is referring to homegirls' expected role as *caretakers* of male gang members. These caretaker duties include everything from the domestic—cooking meals, washing dishes or clothes, ironing pants, and vacuuming carpets—to the paralegal—contacting lawyers or parole officers and bailing male gang members out of jail. Female gang members are also expected to be the primary messengers for care packages, money, and/or letters to homeboys in prison. And they are expected to visit their homeboys when they get hospitalized. Part of the reason for this is that homegirls are less likely to have legal problems and can freely visit these places, but the more compelling reason is traditional gender roles. Young women are expected to fulfill these roles and often they willingly accept them.

Those female gang members who have children are not only expected to care for their offspring but are also expected to take care of their partners in prison. As Angel describes above, in the gang ideology, a homegirl is expected to be the ultimate caretaker, the "mother" of her clique. In some rare cases, she becomes responsible for an extended network of kinfolk, including her baby, her boyfriend, her homeboys, and her biological parents. Needless to say, the more she takes on the role of caretaker, the less she will be able to be active in criminal and violent activities.

However, female gang members do not get credit for these caretaking duties. Taking care of one's homeboys does not count in the same way as committing crimes or fighting the enemy. Although caretaking is an essential task within the gang family, the young women who take on this role do not gain status as gangsters. The role of "mothers" to the clique is a combination of wife and mother, meaning that the woman cares for the others as a wife would, providing companionship and friendship, and as mothers, providing support, cooking, and cleaning up the mess. Those women who decide not to take on these roles violate the unrealistic expectations of homeboys who want their homegirls to "be there to help them" unconditionally. Female gang members who rebel against these norms, carving out their own identities within their cliques, are seen as rebelling against traditional notions of femininity.

> You have women who break all those molds. You have women in the gang who don't want to be wives or mothers. You have some that are full-fledged lesbians, or are bi-sexual. You have some that just totally

decide not to have relationships within the gang. You have some that have decided to have relationships even with enemy gang members. And all of those things are major offenses, because they don't fall in line with what's expected of them.

—Loquita

A few of these runaway and rebellious homegirls violate another prohibition within the gang that prevents them from being caretakers. Becoming alcoholics or drug addicts causes some of these young women to become persona non grata. Loquita told me that she thought drugs and alcohol were worse than the violence itself because of the damage they caused to gang members. Sometimes drugs and alcohol become the coping mechanism of choice as an escape or form of self-medication. Many of these young men and women do not know how to regulate their own emotions. Males and females are socialized to deal with their emotions in different ways. There is a tendency in males to suppress certain emotions, to pack everything in. Homeboys are socialized not to show fear but are given free rein to express anger.

Drugs and alcohol are disinhibitors, which allow the expression of frustrations. "When homeboys are drunk or high, everything comes rolling out," said Loquita. "And usually with detrimental effects, involving violence against somebody else, often those who are near and dear to them—like their girlfriends or their wives or their kids or even their own homeboys. They figure that it's safe to let that [anger/frustration] out with those people, even it means that you're going to hurt them in the process. Because if they love you, they will forgive you." In contrast, females tend to be more inner-directed and self-destructive in their expression of frustration. Drugs and alcohol fuel this process.

Homegirls are much less likely than their male counterparts when drunk or high to go out and commit acts of violence against others and much more likely to direct the violence to themselves. The next line of harm for frustrated women is their children, a form of self-harm against innocent victims that won't fight back. Drugs and alcohol become a conduit by which these negative feelings are expressed. Some depressed homegirls don't know how to deal with the pain, the sorrow, and the anger or rage and turn to inebriants for solace. Alcohol and drugs become an excuse to vent these feelings, but rarely with positive outcomes. There is a general feeling that if "the victim loves me, he or she will understand that I was drunk or high, and forgive me for the damage done." It took Angel many years to forgive herself for the damage she did by taking drugs.

Angel's Descent

Getting jumped into the gang was only the beginning of Angel's descent. Her introduction to crack cocaine sent her into a spiral that would eventually lead to her "excommunication" from the gang. It was Angel's boyfriend, Tricky, who initiated her to the explosive power of crack cocaine. Angel described its high as "a kick in the head, but a good one." When I first met Angel, she had just gotten out of Cybil Brand, the Los Angeles County jail for women, where she spent three months for drug possession. Although only fifteen years old at the time, Angel told the police she was an adult, because she didn't want to get sent to Juvy or Juvenile Detention and have the police look for her aunt. After her incarceration, Angel was more careful about carrying drugs in public. With her father out of the picture and Tricky locked up in jail, she began to go out with other guys from the gang. Her need for affection trumped Angel's initial resistance to dating fellow gang members. But these other homeboys turned out to be just as unreliable as Tricky, and Angel sought solace and escape in crack cocaine.

Angel's descent into drug addiction caused her isolation from her fellow gang members and eventually led them to consider her an outcast. Drug addicts or crackheads are considered to be liabilities within street gangs because they can't be counted on to bring in resources or fight the enemy. Within MS, homeboys are given somewhat more leeway in terms of taking drugs because of the suspicion against women as snitches or rats. During my fieldwork, both homeboys and homegirls were warned against becoming addicts, and some were punished if they ignored these warnings. Angel knew that it was against her gang's rules to smoke "too much pipe," as they say, but this did little to deter her from what became her addiction.[38] Eventually, this led to her ostracization.

It was incredibly sad to watch Angel waste away, transmogrified from a plump, cheery girl into a thin, depressed teenager with sad sunken eyes. What led to Angel's addiction to crack will ultimately remain a mystery, but one suspects that her feelings of rejection from her biological family combined with the heartbreaks of her boyfriends' betrayals and the death of her homegirl, Lonely, played their parts, sending her into deep depression. Whatever the reasons for her addiction,

Angel's habit became a liability for the gang. She began to spend more time away from her clique as she spent increasing time searching for and smoking crack. By becoming a crackhead, Angel knew that she had violated a taboo within her gang, but she didn't care. Because crack had addled her mind, she also didn't care that her fellow gang members considered her an outcast. It took many years for Angel to finally break the habit, but by then she was too old and disillusioned to consider going back to the gang. Her descent into drug addiction caused her exit from the gang life, but it was an unintended consequence. Prior to joining, Angel had never wanted to be part of a street gang, and postaddiction she had no interest in going back. Although she was grateful to her homies who had provided her protection, shelter and camaraderie, having paid the high price of gang membership, Angel wanted to forget the past and start a new chapter in her life. What she learned, the hard way, was that the fast life of a gang member is not all that it was cracked up to be.

Notes

1. 1997, p. 35.
2. Literally a "female goat," but in this context it means "punk" or "sissy."
3. This is the disparaging name MS gang members used to refer to their enemy, the 18th Street gang.
4. 1991; 1994.
5. Chesney-Lind, 1986; Chesney-Lind, Shelden, and Joe, 1996; Maher and Daly, 1996; Maher, 1997; Chesney-Lind, 1999.
6. Moore, 1991; Curry, 1998; Joe and Chesney-Lind, 1995; Hagedorn and Devitt, 1999.
7. Lauderback, Hansen, and Waldorf, 1992; Brotherton, 1996; Miller, 1998; Venkatesh, 1998; Joe and Chesney-Lind, 1999; Moore and Hagedorn, 1999; Nurge, 1999.
8. DeCesare, 1998.
9. Thrasher, 1927; Campbell, 1991; Cohen, 1955; Short and Strodtbeck, 1965.
10. Moore, 1991; Fishman, 1995; Chin, 1996.
11. Campbell, 1991; Swart, 1991.
12. Miller, 1973; Quicker, 1974; Brown, 1977; Harris, 1988; Brotherton, 1996; Hagedorn and Devitt, 1999; Joe and Chesney-Lind, 1999; Hunt, MacKenzie and Laidler, 2000; Nurge, 1999.
13. Cf. Miller, 2001.
14. 1984; 1990.

15. 1984, p. 182.
16. 1995.
17. 1995, p. 90.
18. 1992.
19. 1991.
20. Ciordano, Cernkovich, and Pugh, 1978; Moore, 1990b.
21. 1991; 1994.
22. Moore and Hagedorn, 1996; Chesney-Lind, 1999; Miller, 1998, 2001; Nurge, 1998.
23. 1993, p. 118, quoting a female gang member.
24. Sikes, 1997.
25. It never occurred to Trouble that this young woman might have psychological problems, particularly problems of identity and self-worth, stemming from abuse.
26. Chesney-Lind, 1999; Miller, 1998, 2001; Huff, 2002.
27. Law enforcement officials from the LAPD and the LA Sheriff's Department have told me that one of the best sources of information about street gang criminal activities are angry girlfriends who have been betrayed by their boyfriends.
28. Barrio is a slang term for clique or gang. It derives from the term for neighborhood.
29. Cf. Diaz, Tom, 2009, pp. 178–188; Logan, Samuel, 2009, *This Is for the Mara Salvatrucha: Inside the MS-13, America's Most Violent Gang*. New York: Hyperion; Getlin, J. Book it *.Los Angeles Times*, May 29, 2008, E3.
30. Logan, 2009.
31. National Geographic Explorer. 2006. *World's Most Dangerous Gang*.
32. Literally speaking, this means "bad wave," ' but figuratively speaking it means "it's a problem."
33. 2006, p. 245.
34. 2001, *One of the Guys: Girls, Gangs, and Gender*, Oxford University Press.
35. Bloom, Harold. 2009. *Joseph Heller's Catch-22*.Bloom's Literary Criticism.
36. Chesney-Lind and Hagerdorn, 1999; Moore and Hagedorn, 2001; Miller, 2002.
37. Huff, 2002, p. 214.
38. Female gang members' drug use varies greatly between and within particular gangs. Moore and Hagedorn (1996) found a significant difference between Latinas and African-American girls in Milwaukee gangs. Drug dealing can lead to sexual exploitation: one girl reported that she was prostituted out to drug distributors to induce them to lower their prices (1996, p. 210).

CHAPTER 6

....

Live Fast, Die Young

We Salvadorans are the way we are because we came from a country at war with itself. One of my neighbors was a sergeant in the army. During one offensive, he lost an eye when a bomb exploded nearby. They put in a glass eye, but he was never the same. He started drinking and became a drunk. Then he killed himself. It's like that with the homeboys—you live fast and then die young.

— TROUBLE

Every homeboy wants to be *más felón* or *el mero chignón*.[1] Each guy wants to be more than the other. That's where it begins. Each guy has his *cora*.[2]

— PSYCHO

In the minds of hard-core gangsters like Trouble and Psycho, the gang is like a paramilitary group, and its members are barrio warriors prepared to die in battle. Many of these hard-core gang members are fatalistic and find the idea of living fast and dying young as a glorious goal. For these gangsters, living fast means having fun and being cool. It combines the dangers and excitement of fighting the enemy with the delinquency of committing crimes and the hedonistic excesses of having a lot of sex, taking drugs, and constant partying. Because of these excesses, the gang life expresses a feeling of *joie de vivre*, living for the moment and not having a care in the world. As Trouble expressed it, "We don't give a fuck what happens." This bravado expresses an idealized form of gang life in which one is liberated from the conventional rules that limit opportunities for adult pleasures, whether they are the pleasures of sex, drugs, alcohol, cars, guns, or fighting to the death.

Hard-core gang members like Psycho are quick to claim their willingness to give their lives for their gang. "This is not a game we're

FIGURE **6.1 Los Angeles, CA, 1994. Mara Salvatrucha members on Santa Monica Blvd in Los Angeles Copyright © Donna DeCesare, 1994.**

playing," he told me. "Everyone knows you can die." Such statements are part bravado. But having already attended several funerals for fellow homies, Psycho was realistic about the risks he was taking by being a hard-core member of MS. The devil-may-care attitude of these gang members meant that they sometimes put their lives in danger, but it did not mean that they were completely suicidal. Sniper took risks and claimed not to care what happened. But this did not prevent him from complaining to his girlfriend, Chola, that enemy gang members were trying to kill him. Chola scolded him, saying, "You told me you didn't care if you died or not. So why are you suddenly worried now?" Sniper's attitude was typical of gang members who claimed not to care about dying but still took precautions to prevent it. When they are being honest, gang members who are active in gang warfare admit that fear grips them at some point in their gang careers. But hard-core members learn to suppress these feelings or at least not express them, for fear of appearing weak. According to the street gang code, one should "show no fear."

MS gang members took pride in their willingness to fight, which gave their gang its reputation. Most of the MS homeboys I hung out with enjoyed what they called *throwing down*, their term for fistfighting. The gang life gives these more aggressive gang members ample opportunities to hone their skills. For these homeboys, fighting was a sport that provided catharsis, a physical release from psychological stress or pent up emotions. Psycho told me that throwing down demonstrated that these homeboys were not *culeritos* (little punks or cowards) and that they have *cora*. The Spanish word *cora* combines the meanings of heart, courage, and anger. For these homeboys, cora meant one was willing to fight and take a beating, or get stabbed or shot. Hard-core MS gangsters like Psycho saw their scars and bullet wounds as badges of honor, and they were more than willing to show them to me. These scars made these homeboys feel more like a gangster and served as proof of their *cora*.

Hard-core gang members are thought to enjoy fighting more than their peripheral or core members, and my observations in the field confirmed this. In addition, several gang members told me that the main difference between homeboys and homegirls in terms of fighting is the degree to which homeboys find it pleasurable. "Homegirls will fight if they have to, but us homeboys *love* to fight," said Trouble. "*Me encantaba*. I loved it because when you fight, you learn how to fight. When you fight, even if you lose, it doesn't frighten you—you lose your fear." Among the hard-core gang members, Trouble was the most opportunistic fighter. Any excuse would serve him well. "You lift up your shirt, and you're ready to go," he told me. Trouble took pride in his ability and willingness to fight.

> For whatever reason, you're ready to fight. Maybe it's because you've been drinking beer or whatever. *Como sea.* Because they say that Salvadorans *pelean por gusto*,[3] to see who has more courage, toughness and stamina.

Trouble was unconcerned about the pain he suffered or inflicted upon others. "It doesn't matter," he said. "We don't care about that. After a good fight, we'll say, 'What's up, homie? Gimme five. Let's throw down again.'" On at least a dozen occasions I witnessed Trouble's fights with fellow gang members, and on many more occasions I prevented him from fighting with those he perceived as enemy gang members.[4] When asked how many fights he had been in, he answered,

Uncountable. *Way* too many to count. In school, on the streets, in jail, one fights everywhere. One learns to fight from an early age, and from there, *aii* [gesturing with the hand to indicate "many"]. I couldn't tell you how many times I lost and how many times I won. But I can tell you that I was never afraid to throw down with anybody.

When I asked Trouble why he liked to fight so much, he echoed the words of Psycho, "It's the *felonía de cada quien*.[5] Each one wants to be *más felón*. One guy wants to be tougher than another. That's where it begins. Each guy has his *cora*. No one can take it away from you." It was his love of fighting that drew Trouble to boxing. Like his homeboys, he loved watching boxing matches. Over the years I saw several professional boxing matches with MS gang members on stolen Pay-Per-View.[6] To make these matches more interesting the homies always gambled, though the stakes were small. The winner rarely took home more than seventy dollars. These matches provided an opportunity to watch professional fighters, and no doubt served as vicarious thrills.

Trouble saw himself as a boxer, and he laid claim to almost being a contender. No doubt he had the mental tools of a boxer. At 5 foot 10 inches tall, he also had a boxer's build, with broad shoulders, muscular arms, and thick legs. He was athletic, quick on his feet, and could throw a punch. He told me he had been working out in a local gym and was recognized as a good fighter by one of the coaches there. This coach began training Trouble, developing his technique and honing his skills. After months of working out with this trainer, Trouble was invited to box in Las Vegas for a $10,000 purse. Needless to say, he was excited about the possibility of getting paid to fight.

That would have made a big difference in my life. Man, I loved to fight. And I'd been beat up so many times. I got beat up on the street, in the joint, and in the pen. Sometimes it was like ten guys jumping me, five guys, three guys, it didn't matter. Yeah, I got beat up badly. But, I never got paid for it. If I was gonna join boxing, I was gonna get beat up, but at least I was gonna get paid for it.

Trouble worked hard to qualify for this fight in Las Vegas. So when his parents refused to grant him permission to go, his elation was replaced by anger and frustration. Denied this great opportunity, Trouble focused his attention on street gang warfare. Although this fighting had none of the glamour of Vegas, it earned him respect within his gang. Among the hard-core gang members I met in the gang, Trouble seemed to sustain the most injuries, each of which only increased his reputation. Some of the gang members considered Trouble lucky that he wasn't already dead. Over the years of his gang career Trouble had been stabbed thirteen times, shot four times—once in the head—clubbed on his head with a baseball bat, cut with razor wire several times trying to escape police by jumping over fences, and separated his left shoulder in a jailhouse fight with another inmate. He had a slight indention in his shoulder as a result of its not being properly set.[7]

Trouble, like other gang members, often instigated these fights with enemy gang members by flashing hand signals that represent his gang. Flashing several signals together is called stacking. In addition to flashing these signs at enemies, MS gang member flash these signs at each other in order to not get shot when entering their own barrios in a foreign car. In the early stages of research, before they came to recognize my truck, gang members I was transporting would flash their gang signs at their fellow homies standing on the corner or in the alleyway in order to indicate that we were "friendlies."

All MS members are supposed to throw up their gang sign at any threat or to provoke a fight. This is an important way to "represent" the gang. But some homeboys had a hard time distinguishing real enemies from imitations. Sniper would throw his gang's sign at any suspicious car that drove by—and most of them looked suspicious to Sniper. His girlfriend Chola, from 18th Street, once commented to me about the stupidity of Sniper's penchant for throwing up gang signs. "He used to come over to my neighborhood," she said. "And if a car came up, he would start throwing signs at them. Often they were not even gang-bangers. There *are* people who don't gangbang. Just because they dress like it, doesn't mean they are one. They wouldn't do *nothing*, and yet he would still pick a fight with them." Sniper was not the only hard-core member who picked fights with anyone who appeared to be an enemy gang member. When many non–gang members dress the part, it is difficult to properly identify the enemy.

Who's the Enemy?

During the war I felt nothing seeing a dead body. We were at war. In training, they were constantly telling you and forcing into your mind

that if your father was on the opposite side, he was your enemy. So,
you would have to kill him. We had no emotions, no feelings.

— MS gang member[8]

We're not supposed to feel for them. If you do, you're gonna feel bad.
You're gonna feel weak. We don't want *weak*.[9]

Much of the excitement of what the homeboys call gangbanging comes
from the thrill of fighting an enemy. "We go search them out to fight,"
said Psycho. "Sabemos donde se cliquean—We know where they hang
out."[10] As the quotes above suggest, one must shut off one's feelings when
fighting an enemy. To "feel" for the enemy is a sign of weakness. Most
gang fights are with enemies, however this is defined. Trouble defined
an enemy as "someone you can't get along with, someone that you can
never forgive. He's never going to forgive you. You hate him and he hates
you because you're enemies. If he has a chance, he will kill you and if
you get a chance you will kill him." Enemies are the fuel that runs the
engine of a fighting gang like MS. Generally speaking, the larger the
street gang, the more enemies it has, in terms of the numbers of individuals or the numbers of different gangs. In the 1980s, as MS grew in
size, taking over more territory, the gang bumped into other, older street
gangs that became their enemies.

Enemies are usually created by proximity. MS gang members told
me that there are approximately eighty enemies of their gang in southern
California. Initially, the enemies of MS were the Harpys, the Playboys,
Easy Riders, Crazy Riders, the Rebels, Florencia, TMC (The Magician
Club), White Fence, and many other Latino gangs that were well established in Los Angeles prior to the arrival of Salvadoran refugees fleeing
the civil war. MS gang members told me that they also have enemies in
Armenian, Korean, and Filipino gangs. However, the definition of the
"enemy" has shifting boundaries. For MS, as other street gangs, these
boundaries shifted over time, place, and opportunity.

The most glaring example of this shift was MS's relationship with
the 18th Street gang. 18th Street started in Los Angeles in the 1960s
and is reported to be the largest Latino gang in southern California.
"With as many as 20,000 members in Southern California alone, the
gang called 18th Street is 20 times the size of the region's typical gang,
dwarfing even the notorious Bloods and Crips."[11] In the early 1980s, MS
and 18th Street got along with each other. Part of this may have had to

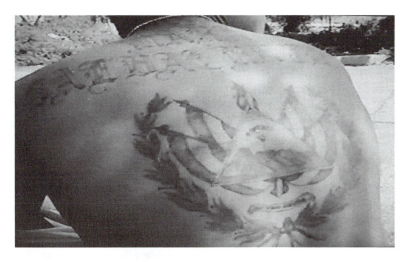

FIGURE **6.2 Los Angeles, CA, 1994.** MS gang members sometimes tattoo the flag of their country as a form of nationalistic pride. Here, the flag of El Salvador is drawn below the words "Mara Salvatrucha." Copyright © T. W. Ward, 2011.

with the fact that 18th Street had many Central Americans, including Salvadorans in its ranks. However, sometime in the mid to late 1980s, fights broke out between members from these two street gangs.

When I questioned both MS and 18th Street gang members about the reason for the breakdown in their relations, they gave me different answers. The two primary reasons given for fighting between MS and 18th Street gang members were arguments over a woman at a party, and disagreements regarding recruitment and leaving the gang. In the first case, as Joker put it succinctly, "It only takes one fool to mess things up." According to the MS version of this story, an MS homeboy by the name of Scrappy was gunned down with an Uzi submachine gun by an 18th Street gang member because of a fight over a girl. This fight started at a party with fists, but escalated when an 18th Street gang member returned with an automatic weapon and killed him. Word of this killing quickly got out and a feud began that continues to this day.

According to the second version, a conflict arose because some Salvadoran members of 18th Street decided to quit their gang in order to join MS, which they felt better represented their nationality. 18th Street gang members did not like the idea of their members changing allegiances, which is seen as betrayal. According to some MS homeboys, members of their gang also changed allegiances to 18th Street. This inevitably led to fighting between the gangs and the rest is history. A third account I was told by MS homeboys is that a homeboy from 18th Street by the name of Torrito was accidentally killed by MS gang members doing a jale on enemies from another gang. Because MS gang members felt Torrito shouldn't have been kickin' it with these enemy homeboys, they felt no punishment was needed. Needless to say, 18th Street gang members wanted retribution for the death of their homeboy. Whichever of these stories is true, the fact remained that fighting broke out between these gang members and a feud began.

For this reason, MS homeboys said, "We can't get along with them." Because these two street gangs are fairly large, other, smaller Latino gangs in Los Angeles were relieved when MS started to square off against 18th Street, and vice versa. The end result of these conflicts was that 18th Street and MS became their worst enemies.[12] Once two gangs become enemies, the reasons for the feud are often forgotten, and with passing generations it is believed that these gangs have always been enemies. The vast majority of MS and 18th Street gang members who joined their gangs after the mid-1990s that I interviewed in Los Angeles and El Salvador thought that their gangs had always been enemies. The typical response of these gang members was, "Just 'cuz. It's always been that way." For example, I interviewed 18th Street gang members in a prison in Cabañas, El Salvador, in 2007, and all of them thought that their gang had always been an enemy of MS. I gave them a short charla or lecture to correct this misperception. This was also true for MS gang members I interviewed. Those who had joined their gang long after this feud began believed that 18th Street had always been their enemy. Once a feud is started, it is extremely difficult to diffuse it. Blood feuds tend to take on a life of their own. Because the idea of 18th Street as its worst enemy is ingrained in the minds of MS gang members it is highly unlikely that these gangs will ever revert back to their former friendship.

There is another illustrative example of the shifting boundaries of the meaning of an "enemy," which at first glance appears to be contradictory. Today, MS and 18th Street gang members are the worst of enemies, and constantly fight each other on the city streets of southern California. But when these supposed enemies get to a California state prison, they suddenly become *compas*, or the best of friends. I knew of a few cases where an MS gang member shared a cell with an 18th Street gang member and they got along well together. This is because of a significant change of context. In prison, both of these street gangs are currently under the umbrella of the Mexican Mafia, a large prison gang. All of the street gang members under this umbrella call themselves sureños, or South Siders. When they get to prison they are part of a much bigger family, and they are not allowed to fight.

MS and 18th Street gang members in California prisons acquire new enemies. Usually the new "enemy" is defined around racial or ethnic lines.[13] For MS and 18th Street gang members in these prisons, their new enemies are African-American or white prison gangs, such as the Crips and the Aryan Brotherhood. Over the past twenty years, riots between these prison gangs have been common. But the worst new enemy for these sureños is la Nuestra Familia, a large Latino prison gang that started in northern California. This example shows how quickly enemies can change for street gang members once they get *torcido*—or locked up in jail or prison. These shifting boundaries in street gangs in what it means to be an enemy has parallels in nation-states, whose axis powers over time become allies.

The notion of police as the enemy of street gangs has been grossly distorted in the media, drawn from a small sample of attacks on law enforcement officials. Although there is variability with regard to the perceptions of individual gang members, most street gangs do not see law enforcement as their enemy. As Trouble explained to me, "I don't have a problem with the cops, but they have a problem with me." Most of the MS gang members I interviewed had the attitude that the police, or what they call *la jura*, were just doing their job. Joker told me that most police officers he met were fair, but he said there were a few who were "assholes." "They would slam me up against the car and use their batons to hit me in the balls," he said. Joker had no problem with law enforcement officials who stuck by the book, but he hated those few belligerent officers who cut corners or broke the law.

One example of this is a practice that most law enforcement officials have denied for years but is commonly known in the barrios. This is the practice of capturing gang members and then dropping them off in enemy neighborhoods, as a deterrent or form of punishment. Evidence of this was provided by Alex Salazar, a former Los Angeles Police Department officer in the Rampart Division.

Police officers would take gang members to rival neighborhoods and drop them off. This was done usually to scare the gang member or to teach them a lesson in respecting the police—that you didn't mess around with law enforcement, for whatever reason. Sometimes the gang member would be beaten up or, worse, who knows, maybe even killed. And so, this was something that was commonly done. I did see this happen and I did actively take part in it myself. You hear about someone who didn't have a weapon on them who was shot. There's basically more of a "oh shit" moment, "let's cover our ass," and, you know, "because we're gonna get in trouble," and because fear paralyzed us and made us do something that we shouldn't have done.

—Alex Salazar, Former LAPD Officer[14]

Needless to say, this practice, or the practice of framing gang members by planting drugs or guns on them in order to make arrests, does not endear gang members to law enforcement officials. The most notorious case of the latter is known as "the Rampart Scandal."[15] In March of 1998, when officials in the Los Angeles Police Department's property room discovered that six pounds of cocaine evidence were missing, detectives focused their investigation on a fellow officer Rafael Perez, a member of the Rampart gang suppression force, called the CRASH unit.[16] Perez cut a deal with prosecutors under which he pled guilty to cocaine theft and agreed to provide prosecutors with information about two "bad" shootings and three other Rampart CRASH officers involved in illegal activity. In exchange, Perez received a five-year prison sentence and immunity from further prosecution.

Perez told investigators of how he and his partner Nino Durden had shot, framed, and testified against Javier Ovando, a nineteen-year-old Honduran member of the 18th Street gang. Ovando was unarmed when these officers entered his apartment, and the shooting left him paralyzed from the waist down. At the time of Perez's admission, Ovando was in jail, serving a twenty-three-year sentence he had received for allegedly assaulting the two officers. Ovando was released from prison after serving two and a half years. Based upon Perez's allegations and investigations by the Task Force, nearly 100 more convictions were overturned. As a result of this scandal, in March of 2000, LAPD chief Bernard Parks announced that he was disbanding the department's CRASH units and creating new anti-gang details that would include more rigorous requirements for membership. In November of 2000, in the largest police misconduct settlement in city history, Javier Ovando was awarded $15 million. An additional 29 civil suits were settled for nearly $11 million. City officials, faced with more than 140 civil suits stemming from the corruption scandal, estimated that total settlement costs would be about $125 million. Four months after his settlement, Ovando was arrested in Nevada and charged with the possession and trafficking of drugs.

This case speaks to the fact that, like street gangs, law enforcement has a small percentage of its membership that cause problems and get public attention. Sniper expressed this sentiment, saying of the police, "They're a gang just like us." I doubt that law enforcement officials would agree with Sniper's unflattering comparison. Regardless, it has been noted in the gang literature that street gangs feed off of oppositional structures, and to the extent that officers engage in discriminatory or unlawful behaviors, they unintentionally reinforce gang cohesion.[17] This is significant because, generally speaking, the more cohesive a street gang is, the more criminally oriented it is.

Similar to the myth of street gang members as "baby killers," there is another misperception that they are "cop killers." Among other media sources, gangster rap music has done much to fuel this myth. However, most gang members do not see law enforcement officials as enemies worthy of targeting for execution, for the simple reason that it "brings the heat."[18] If a law enforcement official is fatally shot by a member of a street gang, the gang can expect to receive increased suppression efforts against it. For example, in 2009, a member of the Varrio Hawaiian Gardens gang made the mistake of killing a sheriff's deputy as he was headed to work. *Operation Knock Out* was launched against this street gang, with a massive number of raids against its members.

The raids were organized by the FBI and resulted in the indictments of 147 members with murder, attempted murder, drug trafficking, weapons trafficking, extortion, kidnapping, and witness intimidation.[19] I know of no cases where MS gang members have killed a law enforcement official in the United States, but if they did, they could expect the same treatment. Because it attracts too much attention to the gang, a member who carried out such a crime could expect to be punished by his own members. Realizing that cops are basically off-limits, gang members focus their attention on enemy gangs. The major victims of gang homicides are other gang members, young males of the same ethnicity as the offenders.[20] Law enforcement is less concerned when gang members kill off each other. Klein reports hearing more than one cop in more than one city expressing the view that "they'd just as soon see the gang members knock off one another."[21] As Trouble said of the police, "They don't care if we kill off another homeboy. They consider that we're doing them a favor. One less gangster to lock up." However, for gang members this is a serious offence, which requires retribution. It is the murder of street gang members that spurs gang warfare and often starts feuds.

Gang Warfare—"You're never more alive than when you're almost dead"

> We are violent when someone provokes us. We can't allow anyone to kill a member of the gang without fighting back. Violence breeds violence.
>
> — MS gang member[22]

> There's nothing like the thrill of the kill. Nothing gets us going like when we're being shot at.
>
> — Psycho

There is nothing more exciting than fights between enemy gangs. Although MS gang members claimed they didn't need an excuse to fight, there are many reasons for fighting. These include jealousy, status, rank, power, turf, wealth, resources, revenge, and, most particularly, insults to pride, or disrespect in the form of personal affronts such as *maddogging* or staring with menace or distain. Fights over women are common. "Envy can cause a lot of fights," said Joker. "One guy has a pretty girl and the other guy doesn't. One guy tries to take her. That's enough to start a fight." Another common reason is status within the gang. All gang members want respect within their own gang as well as others, but this must be earned. In order to earn respect and maintain it within the gang, one must be willing to fight. Some gang members fight to prove to their fellow gang members that they are "down for the gang." Younger gang members, who have not yet earned their stripes, are more likely to seek out fights with enemy gang members than someone who has already achieved the status of a respected veteran. To gain a reputation within the gang, some of these young hard-core gang members are eager to participate in gang warfare.

Defense or control over gang turf is another reason for fighting. Street gangs fight over territory because it is their way of securing and expanding their borders. In addition to protecting their barrio against robbery or theft, MS gang members collect taxes from drug dealers and sell drugs in their neighborhoods so they must be willing to fight to keep enemy gang members out. Gang turf is seen as scarce resource, and if members are not willing to fight to keep it, there are often eager enemies who are all too willing to take it from them. *Maddogging*, or menacing stares, or disrespectful comments are another reason to fight. Because the issue of respect lies at the core of gang membership, most gang members are quick to defend their honor.

Among the many reasons for fighting, nothing coalesces gang members to warfare like the death of one of their own. Street gangs have an eye-for-an-eye, tooth-for-a-tooth mentality regarding the death of one of its members. The murder of one of their homies spurs gang members to seek revenge. Street gangs that are actively involved in feuds with other street gangs keep counts, or mental lists of their fellow warriors who have fallen in the line of battle. "We don't want to seem weak," said Psycho, "If we know who did it, we'll get him. They're not going to come up to you and say, 'Leave us alone.' They're going to shoot first, and ask questions later." A case in point is the example mentioned above of the accidental murder of an 18th Street gang member by MS gang members that served as a legitimate excuse to begin a war between the two gangs.

Most gang warfare does not end in fatalities. The vast majority of fighting is done with fists. However, if one of the gang members is carrying a weapon, the likelihood is that someone is going to get shot. The first time Psycho was shot, he was in middle school. He told me he got into a fight with an older homeboy and was twice beaten to the ground. The older guy told Psycho to "get out of here," but Psycho had his *cora* and wouldn't back down. "I grabbed a tree branch and tried to hit the guy with it," he said. "Then the guy took out a .380 and started shooting. As I was running away I got hit once in the upper back. That's how we live the dangerous life." For MS gangsters like Psycho, fights like this proved their machismo. Contrary to stereotypes, shootings like this one are rare, but for obvious reasons they garner the most public attention and give the gang members bragging rights. As Klein notes, gang members spend a lot more time talking about their exploits than they do creating them.[23]

MS gang members took pride in the fact that they never backed down in the face of enemies. Joker told me of his homeboy Ghost, who had a reputation for being really crazy. Ghost told Joker, "When the enemy gets me, I'm not going to run. If they kill me, then kill me." Joker was impressed with Ghost's *cora* and *locura*—bravery and craziness. "That vato is loco," he said. ""He didn't fear death." Trouble was also a friend of Ghost and admired his courage under fire. He told me that Ghost, Smokey, and Trigger were hanging on the street when the enemy showed up. The other two ran, but Ghost just stood there. They shot him three times in the chest with a 9-millimeter, and he died from his wounds. "That *chavala* that shot him is serving life in prison," said Trouble.

When I asked Trouble what he thought about Ghost's lack of fear, he said, "In the life of a gangster, if you are going to be afraid of death, better to remain at home watching television or helping your mother wash dishes. You can't fear death. You know that it's *certain* that you're going to die." He added, "I didn't fear death. I don't fear death now. I always say, 'Whatever is clever.'" Hard-core gang members like Trouble learn to suppress whatever fears they may have about gang warfare. "It's like you don't think about it much," he said. "With all the experiences you have in the streets you lose fear of everything. So many things that you experience, like getting shot, picking up your homeboy all shot up or stabbed. I have seen *un chingo* de homeboys *en caja*—a lot of homeboys in the casket. I've been to the funerals of about forty homeboys, not counting those who died in El Salvador, like Fantasma and Shy Boy. From my clique, about sixteen homeboys have been killed."

Trouble said the worst years were from 1989 to 1995. "*Eramos cholos*, puros Nike, puros Vans; 50, 60 size pants; white or black shirts. Things have changed quite a bit since then. There aren't nearly as many homies, nor as many shootings. If the police see a gangster on the street now, they stop him immediately. The laws are more strict." It's interesting and ironic that Trouble thought these stricter laws were beneficial. "For me, it's good," he said, "Because things were too tough back then." By this he means that too many people were getting killed. Death is a heavy price to pay for being a gang member, but it was the excitement of these gang battles that got the heart pounding and the blood boiling for hard-core homeboys like Trouble. He summed it up, saying, "You're never more alive than when you're almost dead."

With excitement comes the stress and nightmares that result from gang fighting. Like combatants from warfare, some gang members suffer from posttraumatic stress disorder (PTSD).[24] PTSD occurs following exposure to extreme stress or trauma.[25] One study of twenty male gang members from South Central Los Angeles found that gang members experienced anxiety, anger, guilt, insecurity, dysphoria, fear, and affective sensitivity to varying degrees.[26] But what most characterized these gang members was a strong mistrust of other people. Gang warfare also results in injuries and disabilities. Several times during fieldwork I visited gang members in hospitals and transported others to the Rancho Los Amigo Medical Center, an LA county hospital with a major rehabilitation program. The leading cause of spinal injuries treated at this center in the late 1980s was gunshot wounds, "almost all of them involving gang members from the inner city."[27]

Joker was one of the gang members I transported to Rancho. As I mentioned at the beginning of Chapter Two, in the late 1990s he was gunned down with an Uzi submachine gun. "I got shot at 2 in the morning," said Joker. "That night we were kicking back on the roof of a building. We were hanging out there when some of the other homeboys, who were on the street, began to fight amongst themselves. I went below to stop them from fighting. I separated them and then suggested that we go kick it at another place. We went to the local 7-Eleven. A yellow cab passed by. When I crossed the street at the light, I saw the taxi again. But because the windows were tinted, I couldn't see who was inside. I didn't suspect anything because it was a cab. When it turned around, they rolled down the window and stuck an Uzi submachine gun out the window and started firing."

"Five bullets hit me, and four bullets hit my homeboy who was with me. I only heard them shout out, 'Calle Feighteen!' [18th Street]. Two bullets hit me. That's when I fell. When my homeboy saw that I was hit, he came back to help me. He was in front of me when I got hit. He came back to lift me up so that we could get out of there. When he lifted me up, that's when I got the last three bullets, which threw me against the wall. And four bullets hit him. One in his left side, one in his leg, and two in his stomach. I got hit once in the arm, once in the leg, and three times in my body and my back. One bullet broke two ribs, another broke my spinal column. I still have two bullets inside my body that they couldn't take out. There were too many nerves, and they couldn't operate to take them out. It would have been too risky to try to take them out. If they touch a nerve, I could end up a vegetable or not be able to move at all."

"When I was hit a bunch of my homeboys came running up to help me. They were giving me air, trying to keep me alive. Someone at the 7-Eleven called the paramedics. The last thing that I remember was seeing the tires of a black and white [a police car]. I was thinking that I was gonna die, and I thought about all the shit I'd been through. I thought about El Salvador and my family. And then I lost consciousness. My homies told me I was taken to the General Hospital, in East LA. I spent a month in a coma and another month recuperating. When I woke up in the hospital, at that time my daughter was only three months old, and it's for her that I kept on living. It was for her that I fought for life. Because when they told me that I was going to be in a wheelchair, I tried to commit suicide in the hospital. Then my homies started coming, and my mother cried a lot. They brought my daughter so that I could see her. So I started fighting more and more to stay alive. Then they transferred me to Rancho Los Amigos in Downey, and there I spent six months to learn how to live in a wheelchair. At first I couldn't even move my arms, I could only move my neck a little bit. I could only move my head a little because a bullet was stuck in my neck. After six months I got well. Now I'm in a wheelchair. And that's it."

Joker was not alone at the rehab center. "There were a lot of other homies at Rancho," he told me. "I was with Snoopy—he had been shot by Armenian gangsters in Hollywood." Joker said he now has many fellow homies in wheelchairs. "My homeboy Wino, my homeboy Shaddy, my homeboy Medio-muerto, my homeboy Angel, my homeboy Lil' Snoopy, my homeboy Pirata, my homeboy Caballo, about eight homeboys in all." Joker said the ordeal hit his mother hard. "My mother was crying so much that her eyelashes fell out. The whole month that I passed in a coma, the doctors gave no guarantee that I would live. Each day they didn't know if they would find me alive or dead. Every night, at 2 a.m. my mother would visit me. She was on her knees praying to God to help me. And then she had to go to work at 7 a.m. She went all disheveled and at that time she got very thin. Mothers suffer a lot when one walks the crazy life."

Joker doesn't really know who shot him. "It was probably 18th Street," he told me. "But it could have been any of 20 other gangs that we don't get along with. Even though they shouted "18th Street" it could have been anyone. Sometimes they shout the wrong gang so that they won't get attacked in return." Joker said that getting shot is just a normal part of gang warfare. He had learned to accept the high cost of being a hard-core gangster. During the course of fieldwork, I attended three funerals and four wakes for MS gang members. However, even in a large gang like MS, most of its members do not end up in a wheelchair or a casket. Those who are killed in battles with the enemy are mourned, and they serve as a reminder of the dangers of gangbanging. However, for most MS gang members there is a danger much closer to home.

The Enemy Within—On Intragang Fighting

In Los Angeles, MS gang members gained a reputation for fighting other members of their own gang, what is called intragang fighting. Although gang members didn't like to admit the extent to which they fought each other, their rebellious dispositions and their democratic anarchic form of decision making ensured such fights. Very few MS gang members wanted to be told what to do, and none of them would permit other members to disrespect them. Disagreements and disrespect almost always led to arguments, which would lead to fighting or worse. In order to understand the nature and character of intragang fighting within MS, I recount three examples of different types of fighting that I encountered during my fieldwork with MS gang members. Each of these types represents a different level of aggression and severity. The first was a fistfight that resulted from the failure of one gang member to loan his bicycle to another. The second was a fight between two gang members from different cliques that escalated into an attack with a broken bottle. And the third involved an argument between two large cliques of MS that resulted in several drive-by shootings.

The first case is an example of *intraclique* fighting. Joker was hanging out in his neighborhood with his homeboy Ghost, who was sitting on his bike. When Joker saw his girlfriend in the distance, he asked Ghost if he could borrow it. "*Prestame la bika*," he said to Ghost. But Ghost refused to loan it to him. Joker pressed the issue, "Hey, chill homie, just loan me your bike for a second." Annoyed, Ghost said, "Shut the fuck up, before I knock you on the head."[28] Joker responded to this with his own *felonía* or anger. "Sure. If you want to hit me, let's get it on."[29] These were fighting words, which Ghost perceived as disrespect. "We took off our shirts and threw down," said Joker. "*Bueno y sano*" (Good and clean).[30] This fistfight ended somewhat in a stalemate, each inflicting pain and getting his punches thrown. But Joker was not satisfied with the result, and over the next week he instigated three more fights with Ghost.

"The other homies said that if we didn't stop we'd both get court," said Joker. "They said we could fight again tomorrow if we wanted, but no more today. If they hadn't stopped us, we would have been fighting into the night and who knows what would have happened." The next day, Joker and Ghost prepared to fight a fourth time.

> And the funny thing that happened was that I showed up the next day and all the homies were there. Almost the whole clique was there, around thirty guys sitting down in a circle, ready to see the fight. It was in an abandoned parking lot. *El Amazona* we called it.[31] We had huge placasos painted there, really big. And we were going to fight, but both Ghost and I had swollen eyes and so we decided to wait until our eyes cleared, until the swelling went down.

"A few days passed," said Joker. "We robbed together, partied together. And we bought about $500 worth of crack. There were about seven of us *loquiando* [partying]. We were really high and Ghost says to me, 'You know what, Joker? You got your balls. Are you still angry with me?'[32] I told him, 'Chale homes, nah, forget it.' We shook hands and then *nos hicimos peritos* [we became really good friends]. We became Big Homies." Joker told me that he wasn't going to let Ghost disrespect him. "He had his felony and I had mine," he said.[33] "And I wasn't going to let anyone put down my felony. It's better to fight and get it over with than to let your fellow homie insult you, *culero, callado se queda* [only a punk keeps quiet]. You fight, and even though you might get beat up, you shake hands afterward. You say, 'Okay, homie. That's it. You have your courage.' But if you don't give your hand to shake then you're saying that you are still carrying a grudge. That's when fights escalate."

Joker's fellow gang members were concerned that if their argument continued it could escalate into fighting with bottles, knives, or guns. If this happened, the fear was that it could end with the murder of a fellow gang member. Lethal fighting within a gang will often lead the group to fission. Because there is strength in numbers, gang members do not want their group to break apart as a result of internal battles for respect, status, or women. Sniper knew all too well how these internal fights could escalate. He was almost killed as a result of a continuing dispute with a homeboy from another clique of his gang. Sniper told me about getting cut by one of his homeboys, who was wielding a broken bottle.

"I was hanging out with my homies and we were drinking," he said. "I was pretty fucked up. None of the homies had any drugs on them, so I walked over to Hoover to see if Blackie could help me out. I asked him, 'Hey, *que honda* [what's up]? Hook me up with a dime [bag of marijuana] or a line [cocaine] so that I can calm down.' He said he didn't have anything, so I left to walk home. As I passed by Roberts Park[34] I saw a bunch of the homeboys there, from another clique. I was really gone. I didn't know what I was doing. My homeboys Razor, Micky, and Gacho were there. I had already fought twice with Gacho. We had a grudge. Our blood did not mix.[35] He started talking shit to me, so like fuck it. We started fighting."

"And Gacho had me on the ground and was hitting me. I said to him, 'You know what, *puto* [male whore or "faggot"], you want to kill me or what? Because if you don't, afterward I'm going to kill you, homes.' And the vato was hitting me and then put his hands around my throat and was strangling me. After I tired out and couldn't fight anymore, he got a broken glass bottle and began to beat me with it. He hit me in the face, on the side of the head and on the body.[36] The last cut was on my neck. I was fucked up. I was gone. And my homeboys were standing there watching. These were homeboys I had helped out. And I was thinking, 'What's up with this? Are they my homeboys or what?' But they did nothing."

"When Gacho cut my neck, he got up and ran. Everybody ran. As they were running, I heard one of them say, 'He killed that vato.' But I got up and started walking. I was dizzy from so many hits. I was bleeding. And my shirt was all ripped and I didn't have any shoes. I had lost them. And as I was walking, some people on the street saw me and asked, 'Hey, what happened to you?' They asked if I wanted a ride. I was so fucked up I said 'No.' They said, 'No, no, get in.' I was bleeding a lot all over. The gash in my neck was deep. Then the guys came up and helped me into the car. I was bleeding all over the seat. They asked, 'Where do you want to go?' And I said, 'You know what, leave me at 6th and Jackson St.' They took me there and left me. They didn't want to get into trouble, so they took off. I started walking to the house of one of my homies. As I was walking, I began to feel like I was suffocating in blood. But somehow I managed to get to his house. It was like 3 o'clock in the morning."

"I started knocking on the door, but they didn't want to open it. I said, 'This is a matter of life and death. I'm dying.' My homie finally opened the door and when he saw me, he said, 'Fuck, what happened to you? His wife saw me and said, 'Damn, I can't look at you.' She got scared. And I said, 'You know what, it's nothing serious. It just happened. Something stupid, but shit happens.' I told them I wanted to fix myself up. They brought me a bottle of alcohol and I threw it on myself. I didn't want to go to the hospital because I was so gone. I lay down. My eyes were swollen shut from so many blows to the face. And then my homie called my mom. She came over and took me to the General Hospital, and I was there for three days. They put, like, eleven stitches inside and then seventeen stitches on top. They had to sew up two layers. It missed my artery by about an inch. By an inch he missed killing me." Afterward, Sniper said his homeboys wanted to get him. "They were going to take me over there to get the guy." But Sniper did not want revenge. "I don't want to kill my own homeboy," he told them. "If I'm from MS I have to take care of my barrio. I didn't get into the gang to kill my own homeboy. That's not my business."

It was also not the business of members of one MS clique to be committing armed robbery and selling drugs in the neighborhood of another MS clique. This was a violation of two unwritten rules of the gang. At that time, MS gang members were not supposed to rob in their own neighborhoods because it brought too much police attention. Furthermore, gang members were not supposed to sell drugs in another clique's territory without permission and paying taxes. The violation of these rules led to the third example of intragang fighting. In the mid-1990s, several members of one large clique of MS in Los Angeles began to rob, steal, and sell drugs in the neighboring turf of a slightly smaller clique of MS. When word got out, several meetings between members of these two cliques were called, ostensibly to put a stop to this activity.

However, several members of the offending clique refused to go by the rules. The arguments escalated to the point that drive-by shootings occurred. More meetings were called, and the end result was group fission. Some of the members of the larger clique split off and formed a new gang, giving themselves a new name.

Outnumbered, this new gang eventually disappeared and most of its members were re-incorporated into MS. This example shows the fragility of maintaining peace between gang members. Given a democratic anarchic leadership structure, a few rebellious and opportunistic individuals can influence others to break the rules, which causes havoc within the gang. Generally speaking, the larger the gang, the more difficult it is to maintain peace and prevent fighting between its numerous subgroups. Another example of this principle is the Crips gang of Los Angeles. Today, there is more fighting between different sets of Crips than there are fights with their archenemy, the Bloods.[37] Intragang fighting is a major source of conflict for large street gangs with shifting definitions of their enemies. However, for hard-core gangsters who live by the motto live fast and die young, there is another enemy within. This is the enemy that lives within their heads, and causes some members to commit suicide.

Suicide—Grief and Loss

> When you hear *The Unforgiven* think of me.
>
> —Demon

Some gang members fall into a deep depression and feel an unbearable sense of guilt for all the damage that they have done to themselves and others. Although many gang members, if they are being honest, will tell you that they feel this sense of guilt, only a few sink deep enough to take their lives. Within street gangs there are three forms of suicide. The first two are symbolic. Actively participating in gang violence or becoming addicted to drugs is self-destructive behavior. Gang members express bravado when they say they do not expect to survive past twenty-one, but this feeling reflects their fatalistic perspective. When gang members put themselves in the line of fire of enemy gang members or law enforcement, this can be considered a form of suicide.

Second, gang members usually kill the people who look most like themselves. They are their "mirror reflections." Some have commented that this is a form of self-hatred, directed outward.[38] These are symbolic forms of suicide, but there is also the literal form of suicide, death by one's own hand. Homeboys usually use a gun to the head, because it is the most effective method. All of the hard-core MS gang members I interviewed knew of at least one of their fellow gang members who had committed suicide. Some of these gang members had buried several victims of suicide. Five of Loquita's homeboys committed suicide, but of these, Demon's suicide hit her hardest because he was a dear friend and she was there to witness him take his own life.

"It happened on Friday," said Loquita. "Several of us were kickin' back in a hotel room, because back then the homeboys would rent a room on a daily basis. Especially on weekends, the hotel rooms would get packed with homeboys from the same clique that rented the room, and other people would come from other cliques. There were about six of us there. The TV was on, music was playing, and Pizza Loca had just been delivered. Happy from Hollywood was taking a shower. Demon was standing off to the side, dancing, and looking at himself in the mirror. And the boom box was playing and the TV was playing, and Demon was dancing. And he pulled out a .380. He was dancing with it, and he stuck it in his mouth. So, I took a piece of pizza and threw it at him, and I'm all like, 'What are you doing, don't play like that!'

"And then he opened up the chamber and one bullet popped out and he let it go. He looked at me and said, 'See, it's empty.' But, you know, Demon had been in the military in El Salvador. He had been a child soldier. He knew his guns. And that .380 was his. So, he knew what he had in there and what he didn't. Some of the homies tried to justify it as an accident, but it wasn't an accident. So, I just go, like, 'Man, don't play like that.' I'm watching TV and minding my own business. He keeps dancing. The next thing I know, in the corner of my eye I see a flash, and I see Demon fall. And I'm like, 'What the hell?' I get up off the bed. I'm the only one that's sober. I'm the first one to go over there, and he's lying face up, with his eyes wide open. I got down on the floor and I lifted his head. When I lifted his head I felt something wet and warm. And when I pulled out my hand, I saw the blood. And then I put his head to one side, and I saw the hole. And then I looked at the other side and he had another hole."

"The bullet must have just cleared the back of his brain and come out the other side. One of the homeboys picked up the gun and left.

I ran outside. I opened both of the doors of my car and I ran back inside. I told another homeboy to help me lift him and carry him to the car, so we could take him to the hospital. I was gonna pick up his legs, and the homeboy was going to pick up the rest of his body. But when he saw the blood and felt the blood, he wigged out. He got up, and he went and punched a hole in the wall. And, I'm like, 'Man.' And I thought to myself, 'Okay, obviously he's not working with a full deck of cards here.' I ran back outside and tried to use the pay phone. But the damn thing wasn't working."

"I went and told the hotel clerk, 'Call 911. Someone's shot in room blah blah blah. Can you please call?' And this Asian lady, God save her soul—I say, because I wanted to strangle her—'cuz she's asking me all these stupid questions. And I'm saying, 'Just call 911.' And I stayed there until she called. And then I ran back over to the room. The two homegirls were yelling and screaming. I told them both to shut up and do something useful. Demon was already beginning to feel cold. He was beginning to spit up blood. I was talking to him, telling him to think about his two sons. I went back to the clerk and had her call again, because no one had shown up. I went back to the room. Finally, the paramedics showed up. They took Demon and the cops took me and the other two women and a homeboy to the police station."

"Demon had shot himself around 7:30 at night. He was still alive when the paramedics took him. They told me he died en route to the hospital. We were kept at the police station for a couple of days, until someone coughed up the gun. And the police were able to determine by the paraffin test that it was suicide. None of us had gunpowder [residue], except for Demon. Once they made a match with the gun and Demon's bullet, they let us go. But that wasn't the end of it. A bunch of guys from 18th Street were waiting outside for us, waiting to kill us. Luckily the police were smart enough to know that this was going to be a gang thing, and they were out patrolling and they caught these guys and arrested them. The day after, we went to bury Demon in the San Gabriel Valley."

The gang members reacted to Demon's suicide with sadness and anger. "I remember at the cemetery," said Loquita, "Some of the homeboys went to pick a fight with some people that were visiting someone at their grave because they looked like cholos. A lot of homeboys were drinking. There was a lot of pain. There was lot of crying. It's one thing when someone is killed by a rival gang. It's a whole other thing when they take their own life. Because who do take out your anger on? Who do you get mad at? How do you take revenge?"

On reflection, Loquita said they should have seen it coming. Demon had been laying the foundation to commit suicide. He was no longer living at home. He gave all of his possessions away, including his car. "You know," said Loquita, "Most of the people receiving these things were like, 'Wow, what a generous homeboy.' None of them understood what he was doing." Loquita said Demon was a fan of Metallica. "He told all of us, 'When you hear *The Unforgiven* think of me.' That was his song." Many of the gang members felt guilty for not having prevented Demon's suicide. Others were looking elsewhere for blame. Some of them were angry with his girlfriend. "But you know what," said Loquita. "He's not the only one from the neighborhood that's committed suicide. There have been many others. Payaso from Hollywood, I knew him also. He killed himself. Muerto from Leeward, I knew him. He also committed suicide. It's like all these people, you know what I mean—" her voice trailed off into silence. After a long pause, Loquita told me that Demon's suicide sent her into a spiral.

> It was huge. I can't even begin to tell you. You know, witnessing the death of someone, let alone it's someone you love, it's like—I can't even begin to explain to you. It was horrible. Three months after, I was such a wreck that I literally lived 24/7 in the neighborhood. Less than three months after, I myself got shot. Ten days later, I got busted. The only way that I could get myself to sleep was by drinking very heavily. I mean, before, I used to drink, but it was like partying—drinking for partying. This was drinking because I just could not—I mean, I would close my eyes, I would see him dying. I couldn't get the smell of blood out of my hands no matter how much I washed, and washed, and washed. I would have these flashbacks. I couldn't sleep. The only way I could get myself to sleep was to totally get wasted.

Loquita was particularly eloquent and perspicacious in her views on Demon's and her other fellow gang members' suicides. "I think that what they had in common was that they got to that point in their lives when they realized, 'I can't do this forever. And I've got all this stuff on my conscience that I can't deal with.' Some of them start having thoughts about all the people they had hurt. They thought, 'I've done things to people I don't *know*, and people that I *love*.' And they couldn't deal with it." Most of these deaths go unnoticed except to those closest to the victims. However, when gang violence results in deaths of non–gang members, it gets a lot of public attention. Most of the stories about street gangs covered by the media involve this type of violence. Although most of what gang members do is nonserious crime, including hanging out, public intoxification, and petty vandalism,[39] members of street gangs also victimize many civilians. Large street gangs like Mara Salvatrucha get their notorious reputations because of the number of serious crimes committed by their hard-core members. And there are few gangs today that have garnered more attention than MS.

"The World's Most Dangerous Gang"

> There is a cliché about today's news media that says, "If it bleeds, it leads." By that standard, the highly publicized Latino gang Mara Salvatrucha, or MS-13, has earned its place in the nightly news reports.
>
> — Chris Swecker, FBI[40]

The media and law enforcement have presented a stereotypical picture of MS as an extremely organized, extremely dangerous transnational gang, disrespecting national boundaries, involved in a wide variety of crimes, including rape, armed robbery, kidnapping, extortion, drug dealing, human smuggling, aggravated assault, attempted murder, and homicide.[41] In addition, MS gang members have been reported to be involved in drive-by shootings, extortion, theft, graffiti, and disorderly conduct.[42] In El Salvador, in addition to homicides and drug trafficking, MS has also reportedly been involved in kidnappings and use of explosive devices, such as hand grenades.[43] The FBI has characterized MS as a criminal enterprise and successfully used RICO against the gang.[44] According to law enforcement, MS has expanded into some thirty four U.S. states, with *Newsweek* magazine calling it "the most dangerous gang in America."[45]

> The presence of MS-13 has been reported in 147 cities across the United States. It is no longer confined to big cities like Los Angeles,

New York, Chicago, and Miami. The cities now include Fairfax, Virginia; Charlotte, North Carolina; Tulsa, Oklahoma; Alpharetta, Georgia; and Colorado Springs, Colorado.

— Swecker, FBI[46]

According to the Department of Homeland Security, MS has also spread into Canada, Mexico, El Salvador, Honduras, and Guatemala, with an estimated size of 50,000 to 100,000 members.[47] Given this large transnational street gang's reputation for violence and heinous crimes, it has been called "The World's Most Dangerous Gang."[48] Sensationalistic accounts of atrocities committed by MS gang members have only furthered the gang's reputation. According to one report, "The Mara Salvatruchas are known to cut the 'testicles' of their enemies and feed them to their vicious dogs. Other times they have cut the heads off their opponents to play soccer with them."[49] Furthermore, an unsubstantiated rumor was spread that MS gang members in Honduras were aiding and abetting radical Islamic terrorists from Al Qaeda and smuggling them into the United States for profit.[50] Although this claim has been indisputably refuted, it can still be found on the Internet.[51] Another part of MS's notorious reputation was gained through its members' use of machetes.

> The victim of a machete attack outside a Marrifield multiplex appeared in court yesterday, both hands in casts, three fingers missing and his head marked with pink scars as long as six inches.... The victim has tattoos, including three dots under one eye...and what appears to be a number inked on his neck, [which] could suggest gang involvement.[52]

In another case involving the use of a machete, eighteen-year-old Hayner Flores, a reputed member of MS-13, was charged with the malicious wounding of a sixteen-year-old member of a rival gang, the South Side Locos.[53] The victim's hands were mutilated in the attack. All four fingers of his left hand were sliced off, and his right hand was nearly severed. Detectives suspected this was in retaliation for a confrontation between the two gangs that occurred ten days earlier at a carnival at Potomac Mills in Prince William County. A member of SSL punched a member of MS-13 in the face, after the rival gang member "bumped his girlfriend" and then flashed the MS-13 hand sign.

The use of machetes by MS gang members makes sense considering their backgrounds growing up in El Salvador. Machetes are the main tool of Salvadoran campesinos or farmers for clearing brush. Trouble said when he was six years old he witnessed a fight between two drunken campesinos armed with machetes, which ended with one of the men decapitated. "The headless body took two steps before it fell to the ground," he said. "I couldn't sleep for three nights." Having become desensitized to this violence, many years later Trouble learned to adopt a machete as a favored weapon. He demonstrated to me how he once frightened his girlfriend, waving his machete around like a madman and banging it on the wall. He said that there is nothing that scares people more than a sword wielded by an angry man. In his mind, it is this power to terrorize that makes the machete such an effective weapon. MS gang member promote their notoriety for using machetes because it creates a sensation and furthers their gang's notorious reputation.

Media depictions of the worst of the gang violence have painted all MS gang members as heartless, cold-blooded killers. Because it serves their interests, gang members and law enforcement are not about to correct this misperception. Media reports of MS violence in the United States and El Salvador have unintentionally served to build the gang's reputation and boost the egos of its active members. These stories have also provided the gang with a powerful tool for recruitment. For example, Joker told me that the National Geographic film *World's Most Dangerous Gang* had been a boon to his gang. He held up the yellow box that contained the DVD and said, "This is our best recruiting tool!"

No one would argue that hard-core members of MS are not violent or that these gang members have not caused innumerable pain and suffering to innocent civilians. However, if we step back and look at the big picture, a different view of MS emerges. All large street gangs, MS included, have different types of members. Some members are peripheral, some are core, and a tiny portion is hard-core. It is this tiny portion, about 5 percent of its members, that commits most of the crimes and gives the gang its reputation. Another consideration is the amount of violence committed by gang members. Although research has found that street gang members are disproportionately represented in violent acts, gang violence represents a small proportion of violent crimes in the United States.[54] According to the Bureau of Justice Statistics for the period 1993 to 2003, "Violent crimes for which victims identified the offender to be a gang member peaked in 1996 at 10% of all violent crime and decreased until 1998 to about 6%, not significantly changing since."[55] MS gang violence represents a small proportion of these violent crimes committed in the United States.

Yet another consideration is the extent to which MS represents a criminal organization like the Mafia. I would argue that MS falls far short of the criteria for organized crime because of the lack of coordination between its innumerable cliques in different cities, states, and countries. MS has not been able to rise to the level of a Mafia because of its democratic anarchic leadership structure and the belligerence of its membership. Gang members in El Salvador are unwilling to take orders from MS gang members in Los Angeles because, as the gang members say, "We don't have leaders." This is not the place for a lengthy discussion regarding the many prosecutions of shot callers of MS in the United States. Suffice it to say that although there are cases where individual members have exerted influence over others in their clique, even giving them orders to commit crimes, MS prides itself on its egalitarian nature, and all active members are given a vote in meetings.

Contrary to some reports of law enforcement, MS is much too large and disorganized to qualify as an organized crime family.[56] The evidence suggests that MS has become a large, traditional, international gang that is loosely organized, involved in a variety of criminal endeavors—mainly extortion, robbery, and drug dealing —and heavily active in fighting its enemies.

> It is important to understand that gangs like MS-13 and 18th Street are different from traditional criminal "syndicates," such as La Cosa Nostra or Russian organized crime, whose "families" are highly regimented, hierarchal, and almost businesslike. Street gangs are less evolved on the criminal ladder. They are criminal networks whose structure is more informal and less disciplined.
>
> — Chris Swecker, FBI[57]

This is also not the place for a lengthy discussion of all of the various ways in which MS gang members make money through illegal endeavors. To do it any justice would require another book. Surviving on the streets is a complex process, and there is an incredible amount of diversity between gang members in their crimes for profit. I will limit my comments to a few points about the economics of gang life. First, highly profitable crimes, such as drug dealing, prostitution, extortion, or robbery, involve risks and competition. Generally speaking, when the stakes are high, the level of competition is equally high. In Los Angeles, some MS gang members make money by extorting "taxes" from drug dealers. Some gang members sell drugs full-time and some part-time, and many not at all. Those that want to sell drugs must compete with fellow members for a corner of the market. In addition, money made selling drugs is often spent on personal consumption of drugs or alcohol. As Joker said, "I became my own best customer."

Some MS gang members make money through armed robbery or stealing cars. Some gang members are involved in little illicit activity. Some peripheral members are involved in none at all. In addition, some active members have part-time or full-time jobs. What should be evident to anyone who knows anything about street gangs is that very few gang members ever get rich in their illegal endeavors. It is the poverty of economic opportunities that drives some of them into the gang. But, financially speaking, the vast majority of them find out eventually that the gang is not a realistic long-term option. Most gang members, even hard-core members, eventually burn out or mature out of their gang. The vast majority who survive the gang life, escaping the grave or life in prison, find low-paying jobs and start a new family. MS gang members call this retirement from their gang "becoming calmado."

Notes

1. Más felón means more criminal; Mero chingón literally this means the biggest *fucker*; metaphorically it means being the *top dog* [Rodriguez, 1993, p. 52].
2. *Cora* is a Spanish word that combines the meanings of heart, courage, and anger.
3. "Como sea" means "that's how it is"; "pelean por gusto" means "they fight for pleasure."
4. Trouble was always looking for a fight. When I was alone with him, providing him rides to various places, he would often try to pick a fight with any male who had a shaved head and the dress of a gangster. I warned him that if he got into a fight, I would leave him there and he'd have to find his own way home. He didn't believe me at first, but it only took one encounter at Los Angeles Community College for him to realize that I was serious. "Where'd you go?" he asked me later. "I told you if you threw down, I would split," I responded. This was one of many boundaries I set with these gang members, for their protection and my own.

5. Roughly translated, this means "one's willingness to fight." Literally, it means "each one's felony." "Más felón" means "meaner" or "more criminal."
6. Cable television.
7. Although Trouble is a composite character, this list of injuries was sustained by only one hard-core gang member. It is not a combination of injuries sustained by several. Although most of the hard-core MS gang members had been stabbed or shot, this is not typical of most gang members. Trouble stands out for the number and variety of his injuries.
8. Fuchs et al., 2007.
9. Connell and Lopez, 1996, p. A33 (emphasis added).
10. This literally means "where they clique it."
11. Connell and Lopez, 1996. An inside look at 18th St.'s menace. *Los Angeles Times*, October 20, pp. A1, 32, 33, 35.
12. Cf. Diaz, Tom, 2009, pp. 118–23.
13. Race is a cultural construct, and does not exist as a biological, empirical truth. However, this matters little to members of street gangs.
14. Fuchs et al., 2007.
15. Cf. http://www.pbs.org/wgbh/pages/frontline/shows/lapd/scandal. It should be noted that MS has several cliques in the Rampart area of Los Angeles, near downtown.
16. CRASH stands for Community Resources Against Street Hoodlums. The original name for this unit was TRASH, or Total Resources Against Street Hoodlums.
17. Klein, 2004.
18. Cf. Alex Alonso, 2011. "Between 1988 and 2003 there were a total of 72 law enforcement officers in Los Angeles County that were killed in the line of duty [by members of street gangs]. Although gang members have been responsible for several murders of police officers, several of these murders occurred in the context of domestic violence calls, traffic stops, and armed robberies, where the suspect's gang identity played little to no role in their decision to murder a police officer. Although there exists an extremely fragile relationship between some gang members and the police, the overwhelming majority of gang members would never condone or approve the murder of police officers." http://www.streetgangs.com/features/060704_police_gangs.
19. Scott Glover and Richard Winton, Massive raids target Hawaiian Gardens gang. *Los Angeles Times*, May 22, 2009, pp. A1, A14.
20. Klein, 1995, p. 72. As Klein notes, victims "look pretty much like the suspects."
21. 1995, p. 73. A citizen expressed a similar view in a letter to the *Los Angeles Times*: "What we must do is get angry enough...and get down to the

business of exterminating these hopeless vermin." *Los Angeles Times*, November 22, 1996, p. B8.

22. Fuchs et al., 2007.
23. Klein, 1995.
24. Whitney, Catherine. 2009. Broken warrior. *Los Angeles Times*, May 25, p. A33.
25. Archibald, H., and Tuddenham, R. 1965; Van der Kolk, Bessel A. 1987; Groves, Betsy McAlister. 2002; Bustamante, A. L., et al. 1990; Helzer, J. E., et al. 1987; Cervantes, et al. 1988; Hoffer, 1991. See also Diaz, Tom, 2009, pp. 16–22.
26. Bustamante et al., 1990.
27. Mydans, 1990b, cited in Spergel, 1995, p. 33.
28. "Mejor callate si no queres que te pege un descontón."
29. "Como asi, como que vas a pegarme un descontón, nos vamos a la verga."
30. This means a fair fight.
31. "The Amazon jungle."
32. The word he used is "rencor." *Rencor* is Spanish for *rancor*, which is bitter resentment, deeply held and long-lasting ill will, or disdain for another.
33. Vos con tu felonía, y él con su felonía.
34. Roberts Park is a fictitious name.
35. Teníamos un pedo, así como—la sangre no llegaba, homes.
36. I saw Sniper a week after this incident. He was still in bandages. Later he showed me his scars. The one on his neck is two-and-a-half inches long.
37. Crips and Bloods: Made in America, http://www.cripsandbloodsmovie.com/; Alonso, Alejandro, *Black Street Gangs in Los Angeles: A History*, http://www.streetgangs.com/history/hist01.html.
38. Rodriguez, 1993, p. 9.
39. Klein, 2004.
40. Foreward, in Diaz, 2009, p.vii. Swecker was assistant director of the FBI's Criminal Investigative Division.
41. Mara Salvatrucha Street Gang: An International Criminal Enterprise with Roots in El Salvador's Civil War, March 2005. Report prepared by: Alvi J. Castro, Supervisory Immigration Enforcement Agent, Immigration and Customs Enforcement / Department of Homeland Security.
42. Jackman, 2005; Flores, 2005; Lopez et al., 2005; Martel, 2006; Werner, 2005.
43. Cruz and Carranza, 2006; Escobar, 2002; Portillo, 2005; Salamanca, 2005.
44. This is a U.S. federal law that provides for extended criminal penalties for acts performed as part of an ongoing criminal organization. Cf. Diaz, Tom, 2009, pp. 223–30.
45. Campo-Flores, 2006.

46. Foreward, in Diaz, Tom, 2009, *No Boundaries*, p. xi.
47. Castro, 2005; Cruz and Carranza, 2006.
48. In 2007, National Geographic produced a documentary on MS, calling it *The World's Most Dangerous Gang.*
49. Cienfuegos, Ernesto. 2005. Violent Latino terrorist gang (MS-13) threatens American Minuteman protestors! *La Voz de Aztlan*, March 1. http//www.alipac.us.
50. Cf. Seper, Jerry, 2004. Al Qaeda seeks tie to local gangs. *The Washington Times*, September 28. MS-13 smuggles Muslim terrorists into U.S., http://familysecuritymatters.org.
51. The MS-13 gang and Al Qaeda connection, http://kea.hubpages.com/hub/Gangs-and-Terrorists.
52. Whoriskey, Peter. 2005. Fairfax machete victim testifies he played dead. *The Washington Post*, March 2.
53. Glod, Maria, and Shapira, Ian. 2004. Fairfax teen is charged in machete wounding: Gang retaliation wuspected. *The Washington Post*, May 14.
54. Thornberry, Terence P. 2006. Membership in youth hangs and involvement in derious and violent offending. In Egley, Jr., et al. (eds.), *The Modern Gang Reader*, ed. Los Angels: Roxbury Publishing Company, pp. 224–32.
55. Bureau of Justice Statistics, Crime Data Brief, Violence by Gang Members, 1993–2003, cited in Justice Policy Institute, *Ganging Up on Communities? Putting Gang Crime in Context*, Policy Brief, 2005.
56. Mara Salvatrucha Street Gang: An International Criminal Enterprise with Roots in El Salvador's Civil War, March 2005. Report prepared by Alvi J. Castro, Supervisory Immigration Enforcement Agent, Immigration and Customs Enforcement / Department of Homeland Security.
57. Foreward, in Diaz, 2009, p.viii. Swecker is a former street-level FBI agent working gang detail and later became assistant director of the FBI's Criminal Investigative Division.

CHAPTER 7

Becoming Calmado

God forgives us all.

—Trouble

A ctive participation in a street gang is a transitory phenomenon. For the vast majority of members, the gang is like a seriously delinquent Boy Scouts club in which they participate for a time and then move on to other endeavors. Many gang members are active for a very short amount of time, as little as a year.[1] For those who are active in their gangs for a longer period of time, getting out of the gang is a gradual, fluid process rather than a distinct incident.[2] As they get older and wiser, gang members gradually find other activities to occupy their time. There are many different ways to exit a street gang. Most gang members mature out or "age out" of their gangs. Other ways of exiting the gang include going to prison, getting jobs, joining another organization such as the military or law enforcement, or leaving as the gang subdivides.[3] Marriage and parenthood are other factors that cause members to leave the gang. Some gang members are beaten out of their gang in a ritual similar to gang initiation.[4] Others become incapacitated and use their handicap as an excuse to cease and desist. Obviously, death is a permanent exit from the gang, except to the extent that one lives on in the memories of fellow gang members. MS gang members are no different from these other gang members. Most of the members of the gang mature out as they start families and get legitimate jobs. They call this process of retirement "becoming calmado," which means calming down or chilling out.

The transition from active gang member to calmado is a process that can be enacted in a short time—spurred by a violent crisis—or can take an extremely long time, depending on the individual's circumstances

FIGURE 7.1 San Salvador, El Salvador, 2010. Having children is one reason that gang members decide to become "calmado." Copyright © T. W. Ward, 2011.

and his or her commitment to the gang. Generally speaking, a gang member needs some means of economic support in order to replace the income generated from illegal activities. In order to successfully retire from the gang, the person must be able to provide for the material needs of the family or have sufficient economic support from family members.[5] Work is a crucial aspect of retiring from a street gang because it keeps the individual occupied, gives him or her a sense of self-worth and responsibility, and provides one with an excuse not to hang out with fellow members. This is important because, as the saying goes, idle hands are the devil's playthings.

In addition, a calmado must also undergo a transformation of consciousness, or a change in perspective. The gang member must be sufficiently disillusioned with the gang life in order to be sufficiently motivated to retire. One has to get tired of the gang life and see that there are other positive alternatives available. Although the gang member may still have strong emotional ties to the gang or to particular gang fellows, he or she must be able to distinguish between a strong feeling of affection and camaraderie and the need to participate in gang activities. In the broadest sense, joining a gang can be seen as a search for survival and meaning. The gang family provides its members with a sense of belonging and purpose, however dysfunctional. Therefore, the gang member must find some other family to replace these important functions.

For MS members there are often pressures to stay active in the gang. But according to the gang's unwritten rules, once one has paid one's dues—suffered and sacrificed for the gang by "putting in work"—he or she has permission to become calmado. What qualifies as a sufficient amount of work or active time in the gang varies over time and place and between different cliques and different individuals. Nonetheless, no one expects a gang member, even a hard-core MS gang member, to be active forever. Although rarely stated, there is an expectation in the street gang subculture that members will eventually get too old and too tired to continue gangbanging. Old and tired are relative terms, but no one expects a sixty-year-old to be hanging out on the street corner or shooting up the neighborhood. These veterans of the gang are allowed to rest on their laurels. However, one of the obstacles to finding a new meaningful life for hard-core members is the psychological torment of guilt feelings for having done "bad things" as a gangster.

Sentence

The air weighs with guilty oppression
Can barely lift my face
I focus on a point on the floor
Waiting for it to open and swallow me into its space
I am my own judge and jury
My eyes accuse me, fixed and morose
What worse punishment can I have
Than my own unforgiving soul?

— Susan Cruz[6]

Different gang members handle this problem differently, some through denial or rationalization, and some through remorse and repentance. A few use drugs or alcohol in an attempt to forget the past. Many of the hard-core MS gang members I got to know well over the years of field-work found spiritual salvation or psychological comfort in the church.

Even those who do not choose this path find comfort in the idea that they will be forgiven for their sins. When I asked Trouble if he felt like God would forgive him for his misdeeds as an MS gangster, he answered, "Who is the father that does not forgive his children? God forgives us all." This sense of having been forgiven is a great aid to those who decide to leave the gang family. For all too many of these gangsters, the gang was the only family that provided them with a heart connection.

De Corazón—The Heart Connection

> They're there for you. Whatever it is, they'll help you out.
>
> — Psycho

> What gives you life? *Your heart.* If you have no heart, then you don't have blood. You can't survive. It is the source of life.
>
> — Joker

One of the most misunderstood aspects of the gang life is that it does not last forever. Gang members and law enforcement support the myth of "once-a-gangster-always-a-gangster." When asked, gang members typically say "Blood-in, blood-out," meaning that death is the only exit from the gang. Psycho told me, "I'll always be an MS gangster." By this he means that he will always be loyal to the gang and feel a sense of camaraderie with his fellow homies. But what he *doesn't* mean is that he will always be active committing crimes and violence. MS gang members do not like the term "ex-gang member." To them, this is a sign of disloyalty and weakness. For this reason they say they are calmado or retired from the gang, but most of them still claim to be a member forever. This is because of the heart connection they have with fellow gang members, which finds expression in the phrase "de corazón."

The Spanish word *corazón* has the triple meanings of heart, courage, and love or affection. This includes the feeling of empathy or compassion, which is the wish to relieve the suffering of others. When I asked MS homeboys what was the core of the gang, it's meaning to them, they pounded their chests forcefully, at heart-level, with a clenched fist, declaring *"De Corazón, Tomás. De Corazón!"* By this they meant that the gang provided them with an opportunity to show their courage, strength, and toughness, but more importantly, it gave them a connection to the human heart. For humans, there is no better example of the heart connection than the family. The ideal family is that group of people who will take you in, no matter the circumstances, and give you shelter, protection, and love. As Psycho says in the quote above, referring to his gang family, "They're there for you. Whatever it is, they'll help you out."

When gang members speak of their gang as *la familia*, they are referring to the role that street gangs play as surrogate families, a form of fictive kinship. This central role of the street gang speaks volumes to their needs for protection, affection, and a sense of belonging. The gang family provides comfort and fulfills the emotional needs of stressed and often-traumatized members. Although the emotional bonds created by this fictive kinship are fragile and usually impermanent, the sacrifices they make for each other are real. In spite of the endemic violence in street gangs, many of its members experience, for the first time, true caring and compassion in their gang family. We hear much more about the culture of violence in street gangs than we do about the culture of compassion. But it is this hidden culture of compassion—the sharing and caring—that drives many youth to join street gangs. To call a fellow gang member a *homie* is a term of endearment. A homie is someone who shares your dwelling, someone who's got your back, and cares about your suffering. On the surface, it seems absurd to look at street gangs as compassionate organizations—but not for the members who have experienced this heart connection within their gang.

Although the heart connection can be an obstacle to their transition to their afterlives, most active members of street gangs undergo a process of disillusionment. Hard-core veterans of street gangs understand, better than most, that the gang mimics the dysfunction of their highly dysfunctional families. Gang members are loath to talk about their feelings of disillusionment because it is a sign of weakness and opens them up to harsh judgment and punishment. Most gang members also think that complaining about their gang or their fellow members is a sign of disrespect and for this reason keep these feelings to themselves. However, given enough maturity and time to reflect, most of the active members of the gang come to realize that gangbanging wasn't all that they thought it was cracked up to be. This gradual process of disillusionment is a major factor in these gang members' decisions to leave the gang.

More Die of Heartbreak—The Process
of Disillusionment

> I don't miss attending funerals, because it hurts too much. I don't
> miss getting to know somebody and then they're dead or facing life in
> prison. And I'll *never* get to see them again. After a while, you don't
> want to get too close to people.
>
> — Joker

If they spend enough time in the gang, most active members go through
a process of disillusionment. Eventually these gang members come to
realize the dysfunctional nature of their gang family. In moments of
honesty, most will tell you that their gang turned out to be something
other than what they expected when they joined. What these street gang
members discover, over time, is that their surrogate family is more a
family of convenience than a family that will always stand behind them,
unconditionally lending them a helping hand. Gang elders of MS often
complained to me about the deviant behaviors of their fellow homies,
who acted stupid or did them wrong. These complaints ranged from
the trivial—their lack of hygiene—to the essential—such as sharing resources or visiting a fellow homie in the hospital or jail. Angel
complained to me that some of her homies were not only *chuchos*—
dirty—but they also did not live by the street gang code that prohibited
members from stealing or robbing from one's own neighborhood.

> Some of our homeboys look homeless. They're all dirty and they don't
> shave or nothing. All they care about is booze and drugs. That's what
> they do. Then they don't have money and they're jacking [robbing]
> their own people. There was a lady in our neighborhood who sold
> food on the streets and they jacked her. She helped them out when
> they were hungry. She fed them. And yet they still jacked *her*. They
> did. They're scandalous.

Angel attributed much of this scandalous behavior to intoxification by
drugs or alcohol. "They only care about getting drunk," she said. "And
when they're drunk, they don't care if anyone gets hurt or not, including themselves. They would jack their own family for money. Jacking
your own people is just stupid." In the early days, MS had a proscription

against preying on one's neighbors. This rule was meant to prevent police attention, which interferes with the gang's criminal activities, such as extortion, robbery, and dealing drugs. But some of the younger gang members decided to violate this rule, which was later dropped in some of the cliques. Angel was one of many who criticized fellow gang members. Trouble told me that some of homeboys and homegirls violated the rule about not getting addicted to drugs. MS had a prohibition against *pipiando*—what they called smoking crack cocaine in a pipe. "Some gangs will pass out drugs," said Trouble. "But if my homeboys were pipiando they'd be courted out. We were strict on that, because if you're *cliqueando* [gangbanging], you're there to take care of your things. If you want to get high, do it at home in your spare time. People started criticizing us for that."

Another area of complaint was sharing resources. Within MS, there was an unwritten rule that one should share what they had with fellow members of the clique. What one was expected to share varied between different cliques and different members. Generally speaking, there was no expectation that individual income generated by illegal activities would be shared. Collections would be taken at local meetings, and this money would be spent on purchasing weapons that could be borrowed by active members of the gang for commission of a crime or to fight the enemy. Members would pay what they could, based on their personal income and generosity. Some of this collection might be spent on rent of an apartment, which they called "destroyer." This was a place where gang members could hang out, sleep, shower, and store weapons.

Resources that gang members were expected to share included food, shelter, alcohol, and drugs. However, there was a great deal of variability regarding the extent to which individual members would share these resources. Often when I was transporting gang members to meetings, we would stop at a fast food restaurant to pick up a meal. I was surprised by the rapidity with which these gang members wolfed down this food. What I discovered was that they knew they would have to share with other gang members whatever was left of the food they were eating. Being a slow, meticulous eater, I was usually the only one who ended up sharing my hamburger and fries. Because I was not a member of the gang, I was not expected to provide shelter to these gang members, though it never stopped them from asking. However, there was an expectation that active members would provide a place to sleep for their fellow clique members. Sniper was an iterant solicitor for a place to sleep, but more often than not he was rebuffed by fellow gang members because he tended to overstay his welcome.

Despite the gang failures to live up to its exalted ideals of sharing and caring, many gang members have a hard time completely severing ties with their gang. Many gang members miss aspects of the gang life after they leave it behind. "I miss kickin' it with my homies," Joker said, referring to the camaraderie he felt. Echoing this sentiment, Psycho said, "They're still a part of me, and I'm still a part of them." Most non-gang members do not understand this aspect of gangbanging. "The whole thing with *corazón* is that no matter where you go, you carry it with you," said Trouble. "It's a part of your life and it makes you *feel* alive. When you're not with your homies, you feel alone. But when you're with them, okay—*no hay pedo* (no problem). Even though they get on your nerves, and you get on their nerves, when you're with them you feel *alive*. Because you feel like you're a part of something." Sniper also stressed the importance of belonging, the sense of comfort he enjoyed with his gang family. "I can't describe it," he said. "It's not the same with others. Like I'll be with a group of people that are not gangbangers—and it seems like I am such a stranger, such a foreigner to them."

The street gang as surrogate family provides its members with this sense of belonging to a group of people who share their interests and background. In contrast, the surrogate gang family is highly dysfunctional, and most gang members go through a process of disillusionment. Although gang careers rarely end in death or life in prison, they do not provide its members with a healthy, satisfying quality of life. Despite this sad fact, hard-core gang members have a hard time disconnecting or dissociating from their gang family because of the heart connection they feel with fellow homies. In addition, the gang has been an important part of their formative years as adolescents. Having spent so much time gangbanging, they became accustomed to this way of life. Familiarity breeds comfort. Humans are resistant to change, even if it means a positive change in their lives. Change brings uncertainty, and some gang members have doubts about their abilities to make the necessary changes to ensure a successful transition to becoming calmado. It is this sense of uncertainty that causes some gang members to continue relying on their gang, which is the devil they know.

"The Devil We Know"

Better the devil you know than the one you don't.

—Joker, quoting a popular refrain

Having gone through the process of disillusionment, gang members discover that the gang does not serve their better interests. However, if they do not have opportunities for gainful employment or a support network, they are unlikely to see gang retirement as a viable option. Similar to abused children who long to go back to their parents who abused them, gang members fall back on what they know, which is the gang life. This is expressed in the saying in Spanish, "*Mejor Diablo conocido que no*." "I think one of the important things about MS, or any gang, is that it becomes *family*," said Joker. "It's the evil you know, and it's better than the one you don't know." In spite of being disrespected, abused, or neglected by their fellows, gang members tend to cling to what they know. "MS is like a family," said Joker. "Yes, it's abusive and yes, you're abandoned and sometimes you're neglected. All these bad things happen to you, but it's the only thing you know." In the absence of positive alternatives, the gang provides its members with certainty.

> Everywhere you go, you know it's there. And it's consistent and it's *always* there. And you're *connected* to it...because it belongs to you and you belong to it, like the parent and the child. So, that's what makes it so powerful, and I think that's the most important thing people need to understand about the gang. That lacking a normal, loving, nurturing, family environment, and not feeling accepted and embraced by society, the gang is the evil we know and it's better than the one we don't know.
>
> —Joker

When I asked Trouble about this aspect of gang life, he had a slightly different take. "It's like an addiction," said Trouble. "You fight to get out. You say, 'I'm not gonna go back. I'm not gonna go back.' But, next thing you know, you miss it. You wanna be back. You wanna see your homeboys. Yeah, it's like an addiction. It's hard to get out, to forget about everything." Among all the hard-core gangsters, Lil' Silent had the most reason to stick with his gang despite its many failings. "I never really had a family," he said. "I never knew my mom or dad. The gang was really the only family I had."

When one considers the lack of positive alternatives, it makes sense that these gang members would feel a close attachment to their gang. They grew up in a country during its civil war and were traumatized by the sight of dead bodies. They were socialized to violence from an early age by harsh discipline at home. Feeling abandoned by their families, they had trouble reconnecting with their parents after a difficult undocumented journey to a new country. When they arrived in Los Angeles, they experienced culture shock and the difficulty of learning English. At school, they were teased and picked on by bullies at school or in the neighborhood. Joining a street gang that had been started by stoners or "devil worshippers" provided them with protection, feelings of self-worth and belonging. For most of these hard-core gangsters, severing the heart connection with the gang family would take many years.

Despite the difficulties, most of these hard-core MS members survived the gang warfare and made the transition to calmado successfully. A few of them had less luck and found themselves incapacitated, in prison, or deported. And a small, significant minority did not survive the gang battles. Some died from shootouts with the enemy, and a few committed suicide. For the vast majority of the hard-core members who successfully retired from the gang, their lives after the gang were not easy. Exiting the gang does not insure against enemy confrontations, for enemies are often not willing to forgive and forget. Those MS gang members with felonies found it extremely difficult to find jobs and start new families. The transition to retirement was smoother for those who had support from family and the church. This support helped them deal with drug addiction and alcohol abuse. Growing older, getting jobs, having children, and joining the church gave them an excuse to stop gang-banging. But they still had to deal with their inner demons. Some kind of support was needed for these gang members to stay on the straight and narrow. Some kind of positive support was needed to give them feelings of self-worth. Moving beyond the devil they knew was necessary if they were going to have any kind of success in their afterlives.

Afterlives

Once you've paid your dues, *no hay pedo.*[7]

— Trouble

Research indicates that for those gangsters who are able to break their strong emotional attachment to the gang, it is fairly easy to get out.[8]

This is somewhat true for MS, depending on the context. The general rule in MS is reflected in Trouble's quote above. "If you haven't paid your dues, you just don't go 'No more. That's it,'" he told me. "You have to put in work for the clika [clique]. But if you've kicked it with your homies and backed them up, then they will give you a pass. Then, if they ask you, 'Why don't you come around no more?' you just say, 'Ah, nah. I'm working. I'm doing this and that.' Then they will say, '*Orale*, that's cool. Kick back. *Firme*.'[9] That's it. They will let you retire. In fact, some of the older homeboys told me, 'Kick back now. Go to your house, get an education, or see if you can get a job. This shit's no good no more.'" Trouble went on to say that if you are old enough, it's okay to retire. But if you just started and you want to get out, it's not so easy. "You have to have at least four or five years or more doing good stuff for the barrio," he said. "Then, yeah, they'll let you go." By "doing good stuff," Trouble means fighting the enemy and bringing in resources for the gang.

Of the five MS composite gangsters documented here, all but Sniper successfully retired from the gang. Sniper had begun the process of chilling out by starting a family and getting a job in a restaurant as a cook. But when one his homeboys stopped by his house one night, he was unable to resist temptation. Despite his wife's warning, he accompanied his homie to a party, after which they robbed a couple at knifepoint. "We were drunk and stupid," said Sniper. "We needed money and it seemed like a good idea at the time." Sniper regretted his decision afterward. He felt guilty that he had abandoned his wife and daughter. But he could not turn back the clock. Because it was his second strike, Sniper was sentenced to twenty-eight years in a California state prison. This wasn't the first time Sniper had spent time in prison, so he knew the rules. In order to adapt to his surroundings, Sniper chose to keep his gangster identity. For him, protection meant strength in numbers. It is impossible to predict what will happen to Sniper in the future. He will be a late middle-aged man when he gets out, if he survives his stay in prison. Sniper stays in contact with a couple of his fellow gang members, but he gets fewer and fewer letters as he does his time. One thing is certain—when he gets out, Sniper will not be expected to return to the gang. As an old MS veteran of gang warfare, he will have paid his dues.

As mentioned in the last chapter, Joker was shot five times with an Uzi submachine gun in a drive-by shooting and is now a paraplegic who will spend the rest of his days in a wheelchair. In the parlance of the gang members, he has paid his dues. The good news is that he has gone back to school to learn computer and website skills, and there is little risk that he will return to the life of a gangster. However, the transition to calmado was not easy for Joker, who continued to gang-bang for four years after he was incapacitated. Although he now needs an oversized spoon to eat his meals, he told me how his fellow gang members helped him hold a gun so he could fire at the enemy. But eventually the long years of gangbanging finally took its toll on Joker, and he decided, as do most veterans of gang warfare, that there was no future in the gang life. Separated from his wife, who finally grew tired of trying to change her man, Joker still sees his son regularly, and he credits the support he got from his mother with his successful transition to retirement.

> *Fue demasiado duro*. It was really tough for me to retire from the gang. First, you have to be away from it long enough to see a difference. When you're around your homeboys, they don't know what you're thinking or feeling. In order to be calmado you have to hide the fact that you're a crazy gangster, until it kicks in. If you're in the street, the other crazy gangsters are going to want to cause problems for you. First, you have to get off the streets.

For Joker, it wasn't a question of pride or fear. "I wasn't afraid," said Joker. "It wasn't a question of humbling myself, but of calming down. Once you've paid your dues, there is nothing to be ashamed of, nothing to fear." Joker said that for a long time he was tempted to go back to his gangster ways. "If one of your homeboys comes around, you've got to be strong enough or have a good excuse to say no." For Joker, it was a question of changing his point of view. He said he thought a lot about his homie who died as a result of the drive-by shooting that put him in a wheelchair. "Maybe it was because of me he died," said Joker. "It was my fault because they [the enemy] were looking for me, and my homie paid for this. After awhile this made me think that if I continue doing the same shit, the people around me are going to die, and it'll be my fault."

> I think the definite way to become calmado is to change one's mind. One has to finally stop doing bad and only do good. You make a commitment to yourself, or God, or your family to change for the better.

After getting picked up by the police for drug possession, Trouble was deported to El Salvador. According to Trouble they planted that one rock on him, but despite the fact that this sometimes happens to gang members, who's going to believe Trouble?

> One of the things that would be done to secure the conviction of a gang member would be what we termed as "testi-lying." We would fabricate an arrest, plant drugs or a gun, and that would be it. The gang member would go to the police station, saying, "Oh, they planted drugs on me. They did this. They did that." And of course no one would believe the gang member because the police officer was obviously the one in control.
>
> — Alex Salazar, former LAPD officer[10]

Although he didn't want to be back in El Salvador, Trouble adjusted to his new life in his home country. It was not an easy adjustment; it took time, effort, and rehabilitation. Among his many obstacles, Trouble had to deal with enemy gang members. Cranky from 18th Street was a childhood friend of his, but not when they saw each other on a bus in San Salvador. Both were deported in 1995. As Trouble tells it, "Cranky got on the bus with about seven guys, and I heard him say, 'Hey, you see that vato' and 'If I don't get down' and this and that. He was right in the front of the bus, talking loud. And then he came to the back. I knew he wasn't going to say, 'Hey Trouble, what's up, homie?' I knew he wasn't going to do that."

"So, I was thinking if I have to get down, I hope it's one-on-one. But, no, it wasn't like that. He got up and walked up to me and he goes, 'Uh, Trouble.' And I said, 'Que honda?' He says, 'Nada. Whas up?' I got up, 'Wach you want?' Da-da-da, and we started getting down with it, boom-boom-boom. Everybody was yelling. Cranky knew I would fight for it. His homeboys had knives. So one of them stabbed me right here in my neck [he shows me the scar]. I turned around and hit him and another guy stabbed me in my back. He got me in the ribs, too. And I didn't know what to do, because there were eight of them. There were a lot of cars around, and the bus was packed because it was lunchtime. And the people were yelling and we kept fighting. At first, I didn't feel the stabbing because I was so mad. I was hitting Cranky in the face. And the people saw I was bleeding and they were yelling, but I didn't listen."

"I was bleeding so much I didn't have no more energy to keep going. Cranky turned me around and stabbed me two times in my stomach. He ran to the back to try to get out of the bus. And another guy tried to stab me in the stomach, but I put my hand up and it got cut. And there was another one, you can see it right here [he shows me two little scars on his hand]. They were all trying to stab me. And I didn't even have no knife. My cousin was with me, but he was just a little guy and he wasn't going to get involved. It was eight of them against me. I got hurt pretty bad, but I was trapped. I couldn't get off the bus. Then bus stopped and they ran off. There was a lot of blood. I was gonna die because I was losing too much blood from my neck. It was just shooting up, like that [with his hands he indicates a fountain of blood]."

"Everybody left. Somehow, in the fight I lost my shoe, I don't know how. I got it back and I put it back on. And I grabbed my stomach. I remember seeing something green and something white coming out of my stomach. And I was just holding it because I was seeing my guts trying to come out. I got out of the bus when it stopped. The people on the bus were just looking at me. I got out, and I got to the sidewalk. And I was just sitting there, bleeding out. My cousin got out of the bus and he goes, 'Are you okay?' And I said, 'Yeah.' But I was feeling sleepy, real sleepy. This lady comes over, and she goes, 'Oh my God. Baby, what have they done to you!' And I go, 'Nothing. I don't know. Can you please let me sleep? I'm so cold, I want to go to sleep. Please.' 'No!' Pow! Slap! I remember she slapped me, 'No, you're not going to go to sleep. Don't go to sleep,' she said."

"And she says to a guy standing nearby, 'Get a taxi!' And three guys came over, a vato from White Fence, a vato from MS, and a vato from Diez y Ocho [18th Street]. At that time, they used to get along in El Salvador, but not any more. They came over and they asked me, 'Hey, what happened to you?' I go, 'These fools…' 'Yeah, who?' I didn't say who. And one of the guys put some things on me to stop the bleeding. And I told the lady, 'Let me go to sleep, please. I'm too cold.' I was freezing to death. And she goes, 'Nah, it's alright. It's alright, baby, you're going to be fine.' And a taxi came and they picked me up and put me in the taxi. My cousin and the three guys took me to the hospital."

"I passed out, so I don't know what happened, but they told me about it later. They had to operate on me. They put the shocks on my chest to get my heart beating again. It had stopped. And they put handcuffs on me and locked me to the bed so I wouldn't get up. They said that I got up and got all my things and was trying to walk out of the hospital. I don't how I could get up, but I did. I don't remember a thing. I was there in the hospital for two months. I couldn't eat nothing. I was just there with tubs all over my body. When I left, my wife had to take me out in a wheelchair. I was in a wheelchair for seven months. I had therapy to learn to walk again."

Since then, Trouble has managed to avoid his enemies, and after years of struggle he managed to get a job answering telephone orders, a job he got because he speaks perfect English. Trouble has become a good husband and father—he now has two daughters, a ten-year-old and a three-year-old. In addition to his job, Trouble began volunteering to visit one of the prisons in El Salvador where his fellow homeboys were locked up, taking them toiletry essentials, such as soap, toothpaste, and toothbrushes. This ended when the authorities moved his homeboys to a prison in San Miguel called Ciudad Barrios. It would have taken Trouble several hours on a bus to make the trip to this eastern department, and because of work and family obligations time would not permit.

Trouble's transition to calmado was not an easy one. There were many factors that influenced his decision to change his life. First, and foremost he decided he wanted to live for his daughter and his mother. "When time passes and you get to be an adult, you look at things different," he said.

> I saw my daughter growing up, and I didn't want her to see me as a gangster. And I didn't want her to follow in my footsteps and become a gangster. I figured it was time to try something else. I got tired of being persecuted and arrested by the cops. I got tired of fighting enemy gangsters. I also saw how much my mother suffered for my gang life, and I didn't want her to think that her son was an assassin, a thief, or a drug addict who respects nothing and no one. Now, I want to pay her back for all that she has suffered, so that she can forgive me for being such a bad son. I am calmado, trying to give love to my family that I neglected because I was cliquing it for the barrio.

Once he had decided to change for his family, Trouble knew he had to stop taking drugs and drinking alcohol. "You have to break the habit," he told me. "You have to stop thinking about the fun and excitement of hanging out with homies and getting high. All these things make you return to your past. You think about wanting to get revenge on your enemies, the ones you fought for so many years and killed your friends. When you are kicking it, all you think about is vengeance." Like Joker, Trouble felt guilty for the death of a friend in Los Angeles. I knew about this incident because the day before I had been hanging out with him in the very spot where this young woman was shot. I remember the little shrine of flowers and candles and a photo that they erected for her. An enemy gang member had walked up to a group of them, hanging out in the front yard of Trouble's apartment building. Without warning, he pulled out a gun and started firing. Trouble was hit twice, once in the arm and once in the leg. His friend, however, was hit in the chest and died. Only seventeen years old and pregnant, she was not a member of the gang. Her friendship with Trouble had cost her life.

"I think about her a lot," he told me. "It hurts. She died because of me. I started thinking about the future and that it could have been my daughter or my mother who got shot. And I decided I didn't want that future." When I asked Trouble how long it takes to become calmado, he said, "I'm still in the process. Sometimes I still think like a gangster. Although I'm not kicking it with the homies anymore, sometimes I miss it. It's really tough—*cuesta mucho* [it costs a lot]—but you have to keep going and not look back. You have to change your way of thinking, and that's not easy." I asked Trouble how he stays calmado, and he said it's a matter of handing your life over to God. "You have to have patience not to act like a gangster. I do it by thinking that God is going to take charge of everything in my life. If I continue to react like a gang member, I'm always going to have problems."

In order to break his drug habit, Trouble sought out the Evangelical church and entered a rehabilitation program. "Going to church helped me start a new life," said Trouble. "It forced me to focus on other stuff. The people at church gave me the support I needed. Their rehab program allowed me to break my addiction to drugs and alcohol." Although becoming an Evangelical Christian is not the only way to become calmado, it is the most legitimate and respected within the gang subculture in El Salvador.[11] Because he dedicated his life to God, Trouble said that his decision to become calmado was respected by his fellow gang members.

He did not ask permission from the gang to make this transition. But when they found out, he got approval from the "big fellows"—the older veteranos who have influence in the gang—because he was following the straight and narrow. "I started going to church," said Trouble, "And when my clique members found out they said, 'Keep on going, don't slip up. Keep doing good.'" His fellow members advice not to "slip up" meant that if he was caught "slipping"—getting drunk, taking drugs, or robbing—there would be consequences. The possible consequences include a severe beating, being ordered to re-engage in gang activities, or being assassinated.

The Evangelical church's rehabilitation program helped Trouble start a new life. "I knew I needed the Victory outreach program," he said, "They gave me *animo, ayuda,* and *automotivación*"—courage (spirit, or purpose), help, and self-motivation. To this list I would add a sense of belonging to a spiritual family. "In the program, I was focused on other stuff besides drugs, alcohol, and *cliqueando* (hanging out) with the homies," said Trouble. "I couldn't get high, and being in the program separated me from the gang life." There were four other MS gang members in the program when Trouble attended, but he said that thousands have been helped to make the transition to calmado. "Most of the homeboys that successfully became calmado did it for Christ," he said. "After having been great criminals, they became great Christians."

Trouble stayed in the live-in center for two years. He said that some gang members make the transition quicker. While in the program he was required to work, which gave him a sense of responsibility. Without the program, Trouble does not think he would have been able to successfully make the change to calmado. In addition to the support he received from the church, Trouble was fortunate to find a decent job after completing the rehab program. Trouble credits his supportive wife for successfully completing the program and becoming calmado. "Before I entered the program, my wife supported me. Whenever I wanted to go visit the homies, I told her, 'I'm just going to say hello.' But she told me not to go. She reminded me about my girls. She wanted me to stay off of the streets because she knew that being on the streets means getting beaten up by the cops or encountering enemy gang members and getting shot. When you're at home, it's about love. Your family wants the best for you and you see the difference. My wife always helped me, and that's the way I measured things."

Trouble said that when you're "young and stupid," you don't care about family, because the gang is your family. "When you get older and more mature, and more involved in family," he said, "you experience a new life and realize that the gang is not one's real family." It took years for Trouble to come to this realization. "Eventually, I was glad to have a real family. My girls would ask me, 'Dad, is there something wrong with you?' They gave me kisses or a hug and they made me feel good. They gave me the motivation to change." Regarding his job, Trouble said that he was surprised he could find work. "It gave me a new way to think, a new purpose, and I realized I have skills," he said. He received on-the-job training in computer skills. "They gave me a chance," said Trouble. "I was surprised and amazed that I could do computer graphics. I became curious. I realized that there is something else to learn, and that I can defend myself in the workplace."

> When you know nothing but the gang life, you think that nothing will happen. But when you're given a chance, you think, "Why not give it a try?" It was a new experience for me. I was really surprised I got the job for a company buying things from the States, processing orders for toys, furniture, and stuff like that. It gave me a push to keep going—to go for it.

Above all, Trouble said that one must have a willingness to change. "You get tired of the old shit and decide to try something different," he said. "You start over, and little by little you realize that you can do it." What brought Trouble to this point? "I saw myself in a critical condition," he said. "I was into drugs and alcohol, and I knew that was going to die if I kept using them. One night I had a dream and I saw myself with my little baby girl, and I thought, 'What's going to happen when she grows up and sees her father as a drug-addicted, alcoholic gang member?' That changed my mind. I didn't want to give her a bad example. When I woke up, I decided to go to the rehab place." This dream was a tipping point that motivated him to try something else, to see if he could make the transition to a calmado. The church, his family, and work provided Trouble with the support to make it.

> So, what I do is ask for patience from God. I tell the homies that I'm done with that. "Sabes que, I'm retired." It's a question of staying calm—that's

why we call it *calmado*. You have to *bajar la queda* [early curfew]. You
have to stay calm and accept what comes, leaving it to God.

Like Trouble, Psycho had a supportive mother and was lucky enough
to get a job. A fellow homeboy helped him get this job working as a
deliveryman for UPS. At around the same time, Psycho was involved
in a serious relationship with a Mexican-American woman who moved
in with him, and eventually they got married and had two children
together. A few years later, Psycho got an even better paying job install-
ing glass in expensive houses, apartments, and office buildings in
Los Angeles. Another homeboy who was working for this company
helped Psycho get this job. This, as you can imagine, requires highly
technical skills, for which Psycho put in the long hours learning as an
apprentice.

Over many occasions I observed Psycho interacting with his wife
and children, and I can say, unequivocally, that he surprised me. My dire
prediction that he would end up in prison or dead fortunately did not
come true. Over time he became a good husband and a loving father. An
extremely important part of what made this possible was the fact that
he was older and more mature, and he had a good job that enabled him
to support his wife and children. Psycho liked his job and it gave him
a sense of meaning and self-worth. Among all the hard-core members,
Psycho was the most critical of the gang and his decision to actively participate in crime and violence. Like his homies, he had attended many
funerals for fellow members of his gang and seen the damage done to
others. He told me, "Getting in the gang was by far the stupidest thing I
ever did. *Pendejadas* (silliness or stupidity), I did it because I was young
and thought being a gangster was cool. But there is nothing cool about
seeing your homies get shot and killed. I had one of my homies die
bleeding in my arms. It affects you. After awhile, you say, 'This shit ain't
worth it.' Being a gangster brought me nothing but trouble."

Psycho never expressed these feeling to other homies, but not
because he thought they wouldn't understand. He kept these thoughts
to himself because he didn't want to seem disrespectful to his gang or
his fellow gangsters. I think another reason Psycho doesn't talk about
these negativities is because of his feelings of guilt for having contributed to the spread in violence. He was a co-founder of his clique and
had initiated many youngsters into the gang. Psycho doesn't know what

happened to all these little gangsters, but he has a good idea. As he said, being a gangster brings one nothing but trouble. Psycho now spends his time working and taking care of his wife and daughters. He still sees some of his former homies and occasionally invites them over to his house for parties. But all of these homies are calmado, because he doesn't want to invite trouble. Psycho still smoke marijuana occasionally, but he prefers to smoke on camping trips to northern California. He told me that getting stoned, gazing up at the stars at night, gives him a feeling of comfort. "I don't think too much about the past," he said, "Because now I have a good life."

Unlike Psycho, Lil' Silent was unable to find a permanent job. He was forced to work intermittently in construction. Although Lil' Silent never took drugs or drank alcohol, he slipped into depression. With his fellow gang members growing old and moving on to other things, he had less opportunity to hang out with them. For whatever reason, Lil' Silent was unable to make his relationship with his girlfriend work out, and eventually she left him. Unable to find enough work to support himself, he eventually became homeless again, sleeping in city parks. He was too shy or embarrassed to ask his homies for help. Lil' Silent's gang career was circular in nature. He had started out on the streets and now he was there again, trying to survive.

The last time I saw Lil' Silent he looked disheveled. His clothes were dirty and his hair was uncombed. He had become alienated from the gang life, which had promised him protection but now failed to meet his needs for safety, security, and stability. Lil' Silent told me he was getting too old for this "gangster shit," and it was time to look for something different. With no job or family or friends to support him, Lil' Silent drifted along the streets, and eventually I lost contact with him. Rumors about Lil' Silent spread within the gang. A fellow gang member who had once been good friends with Lil' Silent told me that heard that Lil' Silent had been shot and killed. Another gang member told me that Lil' Silent had ratted out a homeboy and was therefore persona non grata. No one knows what really happened to Lil' Silent, but it is doubtful that his transition to calmado was successful. Without family or friends to support him, it is unlikely that he found redemption on the streets.

I'd like to end this book on a positive note. The fates that befell Sniper, Joker, and Lil' Silent—prison, life in a wheelchair, and homelessness—are not typical for MS gang members. As I noted above, most MS gang

Figure 7.2 La Paz, El Salvador, 2011. Retired gang members pay last respects to their Evangelical brother, Napoleon Cruz. Copyright © T. W. Ward, 2011.

members, even the hard-core, find meaningful lives beyond the gang. As they get older and more mature, they realize that the gang isn't worth the sacrifices it requires. Having buried fellow homies or seen them get locked up for long periods of time, they know that the gang life is not going to end well. Most of these gang members find jobs and start families. Many of them have children and become good fathers and mothers. Although it is difficult for them to severe ties with "the devil they knew," most of them are able to make a successful transition to retirement. Some of these gang members were aided in their transition to calmado, finding meaning in spirituality.

In August of 2011, I attended an all-night wake in La Paz, El Salvador, for Napoleon Cruz, an MS calmado who had become an Evangelical preacher. I drove Trouble and a carload of former gang members to this wake, where a congregation of over a hundred people was present. Many of these attendants were former gang members, some of whom, like Napoleon or Macizo, as he was known in the gang, had joined MS in Los Angeles. I was deeply impressed by the spirit of camaraderie and the positive energy that spirituality provided to these former gang members. Standing, with arms upraised, singing their dedication to God, they had found a suitable substitute for their former dedication to the gang. Their conversions speak volumes to the potential power of spirituality for healing. Having dedicated their lives to God, they have found redemption in their afterlives beyond the gang.

Notes

1. Decker and Lauritsen, 1996.
2. Maruna, 2001.
3. Pyrooz, David C., Decker, Scott H., and Webb, Vincent J. 2010. The ties that bind: Desistance from gangs. In *Crime and Delinquency*, September 8; Decker, Scott, and Lauritsen, Janet. 1996. Breaking the bonds of membership: Leaving the gang. In Huff (ed.), *Street Gangs in America, II*; Sanchez-Jankowki, 1991, p. 61.
4. Vigil, 1988.
5. Shute, Jon. 2011. Family support as a gang reduction measure. In *Children and Society*.
6. A former member of a street gang in Los Angeles. This is an excerpt from a longer poem.
7. 'No hay pedo' literally means 'there is no fart,' but figuratively speaking it means 'it's not a problem.'
8. Cf. Decker, Scott, and Lauritsen, Janet. 2002. Breaking the bonds of membership: Leaving the gang. Inn Huff, R. (ed.), *Gangs in America III*.
9. "Orale" means "alright"; "firme" means "firm' or "with reason."
10. Fuchs et al. 2007.
11. Brenneman II, Robert. 2009. *From Homie to Hermano: Conversion and Gang Exit in Central America*, dissertation, University of Notre Dame.

CHAPTER 8

....

Epilogue

The ongoing difficulties with youth gangs make one lesson very clear: there are no quick fixes or easy solutions for the problems that youth gangs create or the problems that create youth gangs.

—WYRICK AND HOWELL[1]

As indicated in the quote above, the street gang phenomenon is quite complex, and therefore society's response to them must reflect that complexity. In the previous chapter, the afterlives of the hard-core MS gang members I described suggest that there is much that can be done to help gang members get out of their gangs earlier. There are practical solutions to curbing gang crime and violence, but they require smart policies. Past efforts to curb street gang activities have generally been centered on law enforcement suppression. But as experienced gang cops will tell you, suppression alone will not put an end to the damage done by street gangs.[2] We cannot incarcerate our way out of the problem. In fact, incarceration only adds to the problem, because as gang members say, "Prisons are finishing schools for criminals." Until we devote more efforts toward prevention and intervention—i.e., keeping adolescents out of gangs and helping active members find positive alternatives to 'gangbanging'—youth will continue to join gangs and cause suffering to themselves and others.

As suggested by theses stories of hard-core MS gangsters, many gang members are in need of effective programs to rehabilitate them from drug addiction and alcoholism.[3] Obviously, opportunities for gainful employment are also necessary. Most hard-core gang members would greatly benefit from psychological counseling to deal with PTSD and feelings of shame and guilt. Church programs and nonprofit social organizations have filled this gap somewhat, but the need is much greater than current services provided.[4] Classes in parenting, conflict resolution, and life skills would do much to help these youth deal with important issues they confront on a daily basis. Although education and job training are important aspects of both prevention and intervention, they still only represent a small part of a holistic approach to a solution to gang crime and violence.

One example of a holistic approach to stop gang violence is that provided by David Kennedy, Director of the Center for Crime Prevention and Control and professor in the Department of Anthropology at John Jay College of Criminal Justice in New York. Recognizing the fact that a small fraction of gang members, approximately 5 percent, cause most of the problems, Kennedy created a successful gang violence prevention model by focusing on these individuals. In his book, *Don't Shoot*, Kennedy shows how this model has been effectively implemented in over seventy cities within the United States.[5] A key element in his model is the creation of a "firebreak" in gang violence. The Boston Gun Project, a problem-solving policing exercise that Kennedy directed, used a "pulling levers" approach to curb serious youth violence. Its chief intervention, Operation Ceasefire, was implemented in mid-1996 and appears to have been responsible for a more than 60 percent reduction in homicide victimization among those age twenty-four and under citywide.

Kennedy's plan involves many traditionally adversarial constituencies working together, confronting racial mistrust, and aligning the hopes of underserved communities with the goals of law enforcement. This model requires the cooperation of police departments, leaders in the affected communities, the judicial system, and the criminals themselves—active gang members and drug dealers. Kennedy applied a radical approach of hanging out and carefully listening to members of each of these groups. What he found was that each of these groups misunderstood and distrusted the others. The first step in his model was to inform the main offenders—the 5 percent—that the violence must stop. They are told that even the cops want them to stay alive and out of prison and that most of their family members support swift law enforcement suppression if the violence continues. They are told to spread the word in their gangs and that they are being watched and will be arrested for even the most minor infraction (this is the "pulling lever" approach). At the same time, they are given a number to call for whatever services they need. This is a crucial component of the model—providing alternatives to gangbanging or slanging. The church and community organizations are central to making this part of the intervention successful. It was not an easy task to convince these adversarial groups to work together toward a common cause, but Kennedy achieved it by gradually gaining the trust and willingness of each of the various participants in the intervention.

As Kennedy's model demonstrates, a ceasefire is necessary in order to create the space for peace. Having provided a firebreak in gang violence, the next step is to provide pro-social opportunities for these active gangsters. Gang members need hope for their futures. As Joker said, "We need to know that there is something else out there for us." Without options, we cannot expect active members to leave their gangs, or impressionable youth not to follow in their destructive footsteps. If we provide viable options to gang members and to those who are most at risk for joining street gangs then we can expect a different result. Although we cannot solve all of the root causes for gang membership, we can do more than we've done so far. We especially need to provide alternatives to the hard-core members of the gang. For it is these individuals, whom I describe in this book, that cause most of the problems in street gangs and serve as the models for impressionable youth. We can try to help those hard-core members who have become disillusioned with the gang life and are now willing to begin the long, difficult process of becoming *calmado*.

Notes

1. 2004, p. 21.
2. Lieutenant Robert Lopez, LAPD, and Thomas Ferguson, Operation Safe Streets, Sheriff's Department, personal communication. Combined, these two officers have over 40 years working with gang suppression units. Lopez headed the largest CRASH unit of the LAPD in the Northeast Division.
3. A survey conducted by IUDOP at UCA of gang members in Salvadoran prisons indicated that "drug addiction" was the number one problem they confronted. Cf. Cruz and Portillo, 1998; Cruz and Carranza, 2006.
4. In Los Angeles, Jobs for Peace/Homeboy Industries, Father Greg Boyle's organization, is an example that could be replicated throughout the country. Cf. Boyle, G. 2010. *Tattoos on the Heart.*
5. Kennedy, David. 2011. *Don't Shoot: One Man, A Street Fellowship, and the End of Violence in Inner-City America.* New York: Bloomsbury.

APPENDIX: NINE LESSONS ABOUT STREET GANGS

I provide the following list of nine important lessons, some of them new, some reiterations of themes found in the gang literature.[1] Everyone should familiarize themselves with these lessons.

1. Not all gang members are *alike*. They have individual personalities. Some members are "peripheral," some are "core," and a small minority, about 5 percent, is "hard-core." It is the hard-core members who cause most of the damage to society and themselves.

2. All gang members *change* over time.

3. The vast majority of gang members *mature out* of their gang eventually.

4. Gang life is *boring* most of the time. Ironically, boredom is one reason for joining a gang.

5. Street gangs are *patriarchal*, sexist organizations, with double standards for males and females.

6. The street gang is a highly *dysfunctional family*, but a "family" nonetheless. For many members, it is a "matter of the heart."

7. The hardest-core gang members see themselves as "shadow warriors." Some of them are willing to die for their gang. They are fatalistic. Street gangs are part of the cycle of violence, a *process* that extends from infancy to adulthood.

8. Later in life, many gang members feel *guilty* for past actions, but they are highly unlikely to share that sense of guilt with anyone

else. The simple reason is because it is a sign of weakness or vulnerability.

9. *Plus ça change*—the more things change, the more they stay the same: given the current causes and conditions, the future existence of street gangs in America is guaranteed. But it doesn't have to be this way.

Note

1. Cf. Egley Jr. et al., 2006. *The Modern Gang Reader.* Los Angeles: The Roxbury Publishing Company.

BIBLIOGRAPHY

Acevedo, Yesenia, 1999. Iglesia condena grupos de exterminio. In *La Prensa Gráfica*. San Salvador: February 8.

Agency for International Development (Bureau for Latin America and the Caribbean), 1984. *Displaced Persons in El Salvador: An Assessment*. Washington, DC.

Aguayo, S. 1986. Salvadoreans in Mexico. *Refugees* 34: 30–31.

Aguilar, J. 2004. El manodurismo y las políticas de seguridad. En: Asociación Bienestar Yek Ineme, *El Plan Mano Dura y la Ley Anti Maras*. Materiales para la Discusión No. 20, San Salvador.

Alas, H. 1982. *El Salvador: Por qué la insurrección?* El Secretariado Permanente de la Comision para la Defensa de los Derechos Humanos en Centroamerica, San Jose, Costa Rica.

Alegría, Claribel. 1982. *Flowers from the Volcano*. Pittsburgh, PA: University of Pittsburgh Press.

Alegría, Claribel, and Flakoll, Darwin J. 1989. *Ashes of Izalco*. Willimantic, CT: Curbstone Press.

Alonso, Alex. 2011. http://www.streetgangs.com/features/060704_police_gangs.

Alter, Jonathan. 1992. The body count at home. *Newsweek*, December 28, p. 55.

Anderson, Dennis. 1984. Nightmares and culture shock torment children who sought refuge in US. *United Press International*, March 17.

Anderson, Elijah. 1999. *Code of the Street: Decency, Violence, and the Moral Life of the Inner City*. New York: W.W. Norton and Company.

Anderson, Thomas. 1971. *Mantanza: El Salvador's Communist Revolt of 1932*. Lincoln, Nebraska: University of Nebraska Press.

Andréu, Tomás and Ayala, Edgardo. 2010. Moreno: "El negocio en las cárceles está a punto de terminarse." *Contrapunto*, August 8, online news. [Business in jails is about to stop.]

Apfel, Roberta J., and Simon, Bennett. 1996. *Minefields in Their Hearts: The Mental Health of Chilren in War and Communal Violence*. New Haven, CT: Yale University Press.

Arana Ana. 2005. How the street gangs took Central America. *Foreign Affairs* 84, 3 May/June, p. 100.

Archibald, H., and Tuddenham, R. 1965. Persistent stress reactions after combat. *Archives of General Psychiatry* 12: 475–481.

Argueta, Manlio. 1982. *El Valle de las Hamacas* [trans. *Hammock Valley* or the *Valley of Hammocks*], Segunda Edición, EDUCA, Editorial Universitaria Centroamericana.

Argueta, Manlio.1987. *Cuzcatlán: Where the Southern Sea Beats* [trans. by Clark Hansen]. New York: Aventura [Vintage Books].

Armstrong, Robert, and Shenk, Janet. 1982. *El Salvador: The Face of Revolution*. Boston: South End Press.

Arnson, Cynthia. 1982. *El Salvador: A Revolution Confronts the United States*, Washington, DC: Institute for Policy Studies.

Arroyo, William, and Eth, Spencer. 1985. Children traumatized by Central American warfare. In Spencer Eth and Robert S. Pynoos (eds.), *Post-Traumatic Stress Disorder in Children*. Washington, DC: American Psychiatric Press, p. 103.

Arthur, Robert. 2008. *You Will Die: The Burden of Modern Taboos*. Washington, DC: Suburra Publishing.

Bailey, John, et al. 1978. *El Salvdor de 1840 a 1935*. San Salvador: UCA Editores.

Barry, T., and Preusch, D. 1984. *The Central American Fact Book*. New York: Grove Press.

Bauman, Zygmunt. 2007. *Consuming Life*. Malden, MA: Polity Press.

Becerra, Hector. 2003. Taste of combat at County–USC. *Los Angeles Times*, March 8.

Benedek, Elissa P. 1985. Children and psychic trauma: A brief review of contemporary thinking. In Spencer Eth and Robert S. Pynoos (eds.), *Post-Traumatic Stress Disorder in Children*. Washington, DC: American Psychiatric Press, p. 11.

Berryman, Phillip. 1983. *Inside Central America*. New York: Pantheon.

Bjerregaard, B. 2002. Self-definitions of gang membership and involvement in delinquent activities. *Youth Society* 34: 31–54.

Bjerregaard, Beth, and Smith, Carolyn. 1993. Gender differences in gang participation, delinquency, and substance use. *Journal of Quantitative Criminology* 9 (4): 329–55.

Bloch, H., and Niederhoffer, A. 1958. *The Gang: A Study in Adolescent Behavior*. New York: Philosophical Library.

Bloom, Howard. 1995. *The Lucifer Principle: A Scientific Expedition into the Forces of History*. New York: Atlantic Monthly Press.

Bodnar, John. 1985. *The Transplanted: A History of Immigrants in Urban America*. Bloomington: Indiana University Press.

Bogardus, E. 1943. Gangs of Mexican-American youth. *Sociology and Social Research* 28: 55–66.

Bonner, Raymond. 1984. *Weakness and Deceit: US Policy and El Salvador.* New York: Times Books.

Booth, John, et al. 2010. *Understanding Central America: Global Forces, Rebellion and Change.* Boulder, CO: Westview Press.

Bourgois, Philippe. 1989. In search of Horatio Alger: Culture and ideology in the crack economy. *Contemporary Drug Problems* 16(4): 619–50.

Bourgois, Philippe. 1995. *In Search of Respect: Selling Crack in El Barrio.* Cambridge, MA: Cambridge University Press.

Bowditch, C. 1993. Getting rid of trouble makers: High school disciplinary procedures of dropouts. *Social Problems* 40: 493–509.

Bowker, J., ed. 1997. *The Oxford Dictionary of World Religions.* Oxford, U.K.: Oxford University Press.

Bowker, Lee. 1978. *Women, Crime, and the Criminal Justice System.* Lexington, MA: Lexington.

Bowker, Lee. 1998. *Masculinities and Violence.* Thousand Oaks, CA: Sage Publications.

Bowker, Lee, and Klein, Malcolm. 1983. The etiology of female juvenile delinquency and gang membership: A test of psychological and social structural explanations. *Adolescence* 13: 739–51.

Boyle, Greg J. 1995. Victimizers call us to compassion, too. *Los Angeles Times,* September 29, p. B5.

Boyle, Greg J. 2010. *Tattoos on the Heart: The Power of Boundless Compassion.* New York: Free Press.

Brenneman II, Robert. 2009. From homie to hermano: Conversion and gang exit in Central America, dissertation, University of Notre Dame.

Brookman, F., Copes, H., and Hochstetler, A. 2011. Street codes as romula stories: How Inmates Recount Violence. *Journal of Contemporary Ethnography* 40(4): 397–424.

Brotherton, David C. 1996. Smartness, toughness, and autonomy: Drug use in the context of gang female delinquency. *Journal of Drug Issue,* 26(1): 261–77.

Brott, Armin. 1999. Not just another pair of hands. In Wade F. Horn, David Blankenhorn, and Mitchell B. Pearlstein (eds.), *The Fatherhood Movement: A Call to Action.* New York: Lexington Books, pp. 36–41.

Brown, Waln. 1977. Black female gangs in Philadelphia. *International Journal of Offender Therapy and Comparative Criminology* 21: 221–28.

Browning, David. 1971. *El Salvador: Landscape and Society.* London: Oxford University Press.

Browning, David. 1975. *El Salvador: La Tierra y El Hombre.* San Salvador: Ministero de Cultura y Comunicaciones.

Budnick, Kimberly J., and Shields-Fletcher, Ellen. 1998. What about girls? *OJJDP Fact Sheet,* no. 84. Washington, DC: U.S. Department of Justice, Office of Justice Programs.

Bureau of Justice Statistics. 2005. Crime Data Brief, Violence by Gang Members, 1993–2003, cited in Justice Policy Institute, *Ganging Up on Communities? Putting Gang Crime in Context*, Policy Brief.

Bureau for Latin America and the Caribbean and Agency for International Development. 1984. *Displaced Persons in El Salvador: An Assessment*. Washington, DC, March.

Burke, Jim. 1991. Teenagers, clothes, and gang violence. *Educational Leadership* 49(1): 11–13.

Burns, R., and Crawford, C. 1999. School shootings, the media, and public fear: Ingredients for a moral panic. *Crime, Law, and Social Change* 32: 147–168.

Burris-Kitchen, Deborah, 1995. *Sisters in the Hood*. Ann Arbor, MI: UMI Microform.

Bustamante, A. L., Thomas, C. S. and James, C. B. 1990. Psychological characteristics of gang members. Presented at The National Conference on Substance Abuse and Gang Violence, November, 1989.

Callahan, Charles M., and Rivara, Frederick P. 1992. Urban high school youth and hand guns: A school-based survey. *JAMA: The Journal of the American Medical Association* 267(22): 3038–42.

Campbell, Ann. 1990. Female participation in gangs. In C.R. Huff (ed.), *Gangs in America*. Newbury Park, CA: Sage.

Campbell, Ann. 1991. *The Girls in the Gang*, 2d ed. Malden, MA: Blackwell Publishers.

Campo-Flores, Arian. 2005. The most dangerous gang in America, *Newsweek*, 28 March.

Canada, G. 1995. *Fist, Stick, Knife, Gun*. Boston: Beacon.

Carbonero, Nathalie Villarroel. 2004. *Sentencia de Muerte: Ex-pandilleros bajo amenaza [Death Sentence: Ex-gang members under threat]*, vertice@elsalvador. com, May 12.

Carranza, Marlon. 2003. Juventud y políticas en El Salvador, *Estudios Centroamericanos* (ECA). 659, 863–79.

Carranza, Marlon. 2004. *Detención o Muerte: Hacia Donde Van los 'Pandilleros' de El Salvador*. San Salvador: Instituto Universitario de Opinión Pública (IUDOP), UCA Editores.

Casa Alianza Honduras. 2006. *Análisis Mensual Sobre Problemáticas de la Niñez Hondureña*. Tegucigalpa, Honduras, 10 de Octubre.

Castro, Alvi J. 2005. *Mara Salvatrucha Street Gang: An International Criminal Enterprise with Roots in El Salvador's Civil War*, Immigration and Customs Enforcement /Department of Homeland Security, March.

Castro, Rodolfo Baron. 1942 [1978]. *La Poblacion de El Salvador*. San Salvador: UCA Editores.

Cath, Stanley H. 1982. Introduction. In Stanley H. Cath, Alan R. Gurwitt, and John Munder Ross (eds.), *Father and Child: Developmental and Clinical Perspectives*. Boston: Little, Brown and Company.

Central America Crisis Monitoring Team (The). 1985. In *Contempt of Congress: The Reagan Record of Deceit and Illegality on Central America.* Washington, DC: Institute for Policy Studies.

Cerón, Nicolás. 2006. Sombra Negra amenaza a extorsionistas y pandilleros ['Black Shadow' threatens extortionists and gang members], *Redacción Diario Co Latino,* September 1.

Cervantes, R. C., Salgado de Snyder, V. N. and Padilla, A. M. 1988. Posttraumatic stress disorder among immigrants from Central America and Mexico. Spanish Speaking Mental Health Research Center. Occasional paper #24.

CDHES [non-governmental Human Rights Commission of El Salvador]. 1986. *Torture in El Salvador.* San Salvador: CDHES Publications.

Chesney-Lind, Meda. 1986. Women and crime: The female offender. *Signs* 12: 78–96.

Chesney-Lind, Meda. 1993. Girls, gangs and violence: Anatomy of a backlash. *Humanity and Society* 17(3): 321–44.

Chesney-Lind, Meda. 1997. *The Female Offender: Girls, Women and Crime.* Thousand Oaks, CA: Sage Publications.

Chesney-Lind, Meda. 1999. Girls, gangs, and violence: Reinventing the liberated female crook. In Meda Chesney-Lind and John M. Hagedorn (eds.), *Female Gangs in America: Essays on Girls, Gangs, and Gender.* Chicago: Lake View Press.

Chesney-Lind, Meda, and Hagerdorn, J., eds. 1999. *Female Gangs in America: Girls, Gangs and Gender.* Chicago: Lake View Press.

Chesney-Lind, Meda, and Shelden, Randall G. 1998. *Girls, Delinquency, and Juvenile Justice.* Pacific Grove, CA: Brooks/Cole Publishing Company.

Chesney-Lind, Meda, Shelden, Randall G., and Joe, Karen A. 1996. Girls, delinquency, and gang membership. In C. R. Huff (ed.), *Gangs in America,* 2d ed. Thousand Oaks, CA: Sage Publications, pp. 185–204.

Chin, Ko-lin.1995. *Chinatown Gangs: Extortion, Enterprise and Ethnicity.* New York: Oxford University Press.

Chin, Ko-lin. 1996. Gang violence in Chinatown. In C. R. Huff (ed.), *Gangs in America,* 2d ed. Thousand Oaks, CA: Sage Publications, pp. 157–84.

Chinchilla, Norma, and Hamilton, Nora. 1999. Changing networks and alliances in a transnational context: Salvadoran and Guatemalan Immigrants in Southern California. *Social Justice* 26(3): 4.

Chinchilla, Norma, Hamilton, Nora, and Loucky, James. 1993. Central Americans in Los Angeles: An immigrant community in transition. In Joan Moore and Raquel Pinder-Hughes (eds.), *In the Barrios: Latinos and the Underclass Debate.* New York: Russell Sage Foundation, pp. 61–73.

Ching, Eric K. 2007. *Las Masas, la Matanza y el Martinato en El Salvador: Ensayos sobre 1932,* Universidad Centroamericana.

Cienfuegos, Ernesto. 2005. Violent latino terrorist gang (MS-13) threatens American Minuteman protestors! *La Voz de Aztlan,* March 1. http//www.alipac.us.

Clements, Charles. 1984. *Witness to War: An American Doctor in El Salvador.* New York: Bantam Books.

Cloward, R. A., and Ohlin, L. E. 1960. *Delinquency and Opportunity: A Theory of Delinquent Gangs.* Glencoe, IL: Free Press.

Cohen, Albert K. 1955. *Delinquent Boys: The Culture of the Gang.* New York: Free Press.

Colarusso, Calvin A., and Robert A. Nemiroff. 1982. The father in midlife: Crisis and the growth of paternal identity. In Stanley H. Cath, Alan R. Gurwitt, and John Munder Ross (eds.), *Father and Child: Developmental and Clinical Perspectives.* Boston: Little, Brown and Company, p. 325.

Collins, J. 1986. The relationship of problem drinking to individual offending sequences. In A. Blumstein, J. Cohen, J. A. Roth, and C. A. Visher (eds.), *Criminal Careers and 'Career Criminals.'* Washington, DC: National Academy Press.

Connell, Rich, and Lopez, Robert J. 1996. An inside look at 18th Street's menace. *Los Angeles Times,* October 20, p. A1.

Connell, R. W. 1987. *Gender and Power.* Stanford, CA: Stanford University Press.

Cook, James. 1971. *The Explorations of Captain James Cook in the Pacific: As Told by Selections of His Journals.* New York: Dover Publications.

Cotton, Paul. 1992. Violence decreases with gang truce. *JAMA: The Journal of the American Medical Association* 268(4): 443–44.

Cox, V. 1986. Prison gangs: Inmates battle for control. *Corrections Today* 18: 13, 17–25.

Cromwell, Paul, Olsen, Phil, and Avery, D'Aunn. 1991. *Breaking and Entering: An Ethnographic Analysis of Burglary,* Newbury Park, CA: Sage.

Cruz, José Miguel. 1999. Maras o pandillas juveniles: Mitos sobre su formación e integración. In Martínez Peñate, O. (ed.), *El Salvador: Realidad Nacional de Fin e Siglo y Principio de Milenio.* San Salvador, El Salvador: Editorial Nuevo Enfoque.

Cruz, José Miguel. 2001. Pandillas y capital social. *Estudios Centroamericanos* (ECA) 637–638, 1099–118.

Cruz, José Miguel. 2006. *Maras y Pandillas en Centroamérica: Las Respuestas de la Sociedad Civil Organizada,* vol. 4. San Salvador: UCA Editores.

Cruz, J. M., et al. 2000. De la guerra al delito: Evolución de la violencia en El Salvador. In *Asalto al Desarrollo: Violencia en América Latina.* Washington, DC: Banco Interamericano de Desarrollo (BID).

Cruz, Jose Miguel, and Carranza, Marlon. 2006. *Pandillas y Politicas Públicas: El Caso de El Salvador, Juventudes, Violencia y Exclusión: Desafi os para las Politicas Publicas.* Guatemala: INDES, January.

Cruz, José M., and Portillo, N. 1998. *Solidaridad y Violencia en las Pandillas del Gran San Salvador: Más Allá de la Vida Loca.* San Salvador, El Salvador: UCA Editores, (Universidad Centroamericana José Simeón Cañas), v. 9.

Cruz, José M., and Ramos, C. 1998. Transición, jóvenes y violencia. In *América Central en los Noventa: Problemas de Juventud.* El Salvador, San Salvador: FLACSO.

Cruz, J. M., and Santacruz, M. 2005. *La victimizacion y la percepción de seguridad en El Salvador en 2004.* San Salvador. Talleres Gráficos UCA.

Curry, G. David. 1994. *Gang Research in Two Cities.* Washington, DC: U.S. Department of Health and Human Services, Family Youth Services Bureau.

Curry, G. David. 1998. Female gang involvement. *Journal of Research in Crime and Delinquency* 35(1): 100–18.

Curry, G. David.1999. Responding to female gang involvement. In Meda Chesney-Lind and John M. Hagedorn, eds., *Female Gangs in America: Essays on Girls, Gangs, and Gender.* Chicago: Lake View Press.

Curry, G. D., and Decker, S. H. 1998. *Confronting Gangs: Crime and Community.* Los Angeles: Roxbury.

Curry, G. David, and Spergel, Irving A. 1992. Gang involvement and deliquency among Hispanic and African-American adolescent males. *Journal of Research in Crime and Deliquency* 29(3): 273–92.

Dalton, Juan José. 1995. Vigilante groups help step up the violence, *Inter Press Service* (IPS), 27 April.

Dalton, Roque. 1984a. *Poemas Clandestinos* [Clandestine Poems], translation by Richard Schaaf. Willimantic, CT: Curbstone Press.

Dalton, Roque.1984b. *El Salvador: Monografía.* Puebla, Mexico: Universidad Autónoma de Puebla.

Dalton, Roque.1988 [2010]. *Las Historias Prohibidas del Pulgarcito,* 13th ed. San Salvador: UCA Editores.

Danner, Mark. 1993. The truth of El Mozote. *The New Yorker,* December 6, p. 50.

Darling, Juanita. 1999. El Salvador's war legacy: Teen violence. *Los Angeles Times,* August 9, pp. A1, 10.

Davis, Mike. 2001. *Magical Urbanism: Latinos Reinvent the U.S. City.* London: Verso.

Dawley, David. 1992. *A Nation of Lords: The Autobiography of the Vice Lords.* Prospect Heights, IL: Waveland Press.

DeCesare, Donna. 1998. The children of war: Street gangs in El Salvador. *NACLA* 32(1): 21–29.

Decker, Scott H. 1994. Slinging dope: The role of gangs and gang members in drug sales. *Justice Quarterly* 11: 583–604.

Decker, Scott H. 1995. *Gangs, Gang Members, and Drug Sales.* St. Louis: University of Missouri, Department of Criminology and Criminal Justice.

Decker, Scott H. 1996. Collective and normative features of gang violence. *Justice Quarterly* 13(2): 243–64.

Decker, Scott H., Bynum, Tim, and Weisel, Deborah. 2004. A tale of two cities: Gangs as organized crime groups. In Esbensen et al. (eds.), *American Youth Gangs at the Millennium.* Long Grove, IL: Waveland Press, Inc., pp. 247–74.

Decker, Scott, and Lauritsen, Janet. 2002. Leaving the gang. In *Gangs in America,* 3d ed. Thousand Oaks, CA: Sage Publications.

Decker, Scott H., and Van Winkle, Barrik. 2006. The history of gang research. In *The Modern Gang Reader,* 3d ed. LA: Roxbury Publishing Company, pp. 14–19.

Demetrios, N. K., Range, H., Deirdre, A., and Corinne, P. 1999. The relationship between socioeconomic factors and gang violence in the city of Los Angeles. *Journal of Trauma: Injury, Infection, and Critical Care* 46(2): 344–49.

Deschenes, Elizabeth P., and Esbensen, Finn-Aage. 1999. Violence and gangs: Gender differences in perceptions and behavior. *Journal of Quantitative Criminology* 15: 63–69.

Department of Justice. 2010. MS-13 member sentenced 27 years for July 2009 Alexandria murder, Press Release, United States Attorney's Office, Eastern District of Virginia, July 9.

Diamond, Adele. 2002. Normal development of prefrontal cortex from birth to young adulthood: Cognitive functions, anatomy, and biochemistry. In Stuss, Donald T., and Knight, Robert T. (eds.), *Principles of Frontal Lobe Function*. New York: Oxford University Press, pp. 466–503.

Diaz, Tom. 2009. *No Boundaries: Transnational Latino Gangs and American Law Enforcement*. Ann Arbor: The University of Michigan Press.

Domash, Shelly. 2005. America's most dangerous gang. *Police Magazine*, March 16.

Donovan, J. A.1967. *The United States Marine Corps*. New York: Frederick A. Prager, Inc., Publishers.

Donziger, Steven R. (ed.) 1996. *The Real War on Crime: The Report of the National Criminal Justice Commission*. New York: HarperCollins Publishers.

Edgerton, Robert B. 1978a. The study of deviance—marginal man or everyman? In *The Making of Psychological Anthropology*. G. D. Spindler (ed.). Berkeley: University of California Press, pp. 442–76.

Edgerton, Robert B. 1978b. *Deviant Behavior and Cultural Theory*. Reading, MA: Addison-Wesley.

Edgerton, Robert B. 1992. *Sick Societies: Challenging the Myth of Primitive Harmony*. New York: The Free Press.

Egley Jr., Arlen, et al. 2006. *The Modern Gang Reader*. Los Angeles: The Roxbury Publishing Company.

Eliade, Mircea. 1958 [1994]. *Rites and Symbols of Initiation: The Mysteries of Birth and Rebirth*. Dallas, TX: Spring Publications.

Eller, Jack David. 2006. *Violence and Culture: A Cross-Cultural and Interdisciplinary Approach*. Belmont, CA: Thomson/Wadsworth.

Enos, Don, et al. 1984. *Displaced Persons in El Salvador: An Assessment*. Washington, DC: Bureau for Latin American and the Caribbean, Agency for International Development, March 15.

Equipo de Reflexión, Investigación y Comunicación [ERIC] et al. 2004. *Maras y Pandillas en Centroamerica: Pandillas y Capital Social*, vol. 2. San Salvador: UCA Editores.

Equipo de Reflexión, Investigación y Comunicación [ERIC] et al. 2004b. *Maras y Pandillas en Centroamerica: Políticas Juveniles y Rehabilitación*, vol. 3. San Salvador: UCA Editores.

Erdozaín, Plácido. 1980. *Archbishop Romero: Martyr of El Salvador*. Maryknoll, NY: Orbis Books.

Esbensen, Finn-Aage, and Deschenes, Elizabeth. 1998. A multisite examination of youth gang membership: Does gender matter? *Criminology* 36: 799–827.

Escobar, Antolín. 2002. Muertos por explosion de granada fueron sepultados. *El Diario de Hoy*, 25 de junio, elpais@elsalvador.com.

Esbensen, Finn-Aage, Deschenes, Elizabeth, and Winfree, L. Thomas, Jr. 1999. Differences between gang girls and gang boys: Results from a multisite survey. *Youth and Society* 31: 27–53.

Esbensen, Finn-Aage, and Huizinga, David. 1993. Gangs, drugs, and delinquency in a survey of urban youth. *Criminology* 31(4): 565–87.

Esbensen, F-A., Tibbetts, S. G., and Gaines, L. (eds.) 2004. *American Youth Gangs at the Millennium*. Long Grove, IL: Waveland Press, Inc.

Eth, Spencer, and Pynoos, Robert S. (eds.). 1985. *Post-traumatic Stress Disorder in Children*. Washington, DC: American Psychiatric Press.

Evans-Pritchard, E. E. 1964. Foreword In *Sacrifice: Its Nature and Function*. London: University of Chicago Press.

Fagan, Jeffrey. 1989. The social organization of drug use and drug dealing among urban gangs. *Criminology* 27(4): 633–69.

Fagan, Jeffrey. 1990. Social processes of delinquency and drug use among urban gangs. In *Gangs in America*, edited by C. Ronald Huff. Newbury Park, CA: Sage, pp. 49–74.

Fagan, Jeffrey. 1993. Set and setting revisited: Influences of alcohol and illicit drugs on the social context of violent events. In S.E. Martin (ed.), *Alcohol and Interpersonal Violence: Fostering Multidisciplinary Perspectives*. Bethesda, MD: National Institute on Alcohol Abuse and Alcoholism, pp. 161–91.

Fagan, Jeffrey. 1996. Gangs, drugs, and neighborhood change. In Huff, C. R. (ed.), *Gangs in America*, 2d ed. Thousand Oaks, CA: Sage Publications, pp. 39–74.

Faillos, Captain Ricardo Alejandro. 1981. The death squads do not operate independent of the security forces. In Marvin E. Gettleman et al. (eds.), *El Salvador: Central America in the New Cold War*. New York: Grove Press, pp. 146–49.

Farah, D. 1993. Salvador army blocks purge by Cristiani. *Los Angeles Times*, January 1, p. A6.

Farias, P. J. 1991. Emotional distress and its socio-political correlates in Salvadoran refugees: analysis of a clinical sample. *Culture, Medicine and Psychiatry* 15: 167–92.

Ferrara, Matthew L. 1992. *Group Counseling with Juvenile Delinquents: The Limit and Lead Approach*. Newberry Park, CA: Sage Publications.

Fishman, Laura T. 1995. The Vice Queens: An ethnographic study of black female gang behavior. In Malcolm Klein, Cheryl L. Maxson, and Jody Miller, (eds.), *The Modern Gang Reader*. Los Angeles: Roxbury Publishing Company.

Fleisher, Mark S. 2002. Doing field research on diverse gangs: Interpreting youth gangs as social networks. In C. R. Huff (ed.), *Gangs in America III*, 3d ed. Sage Publications, pp. 199–217.

Fleisher, Mark. 1995. *Beggars and Thieves: Lives of Urban Street Criminal.* Madison: University of Wisconsin Press.

Fleisher, Mark. 1998. *Dead End Kids: Gang Girls and the Boys They Know.* Madison: Wisconsin University Press.

Flores, Frank. 2005. Interview with officer of Los Angeles Police Department, special gang investigations unit, expert on MS-13, April 27, LAPD, Hollywood Division.

Flowers, Ronald B. 1987. *Women and Criminality.* New York: Greenwood.

Flowers, Ronald B. 1995. *Female Crime, Criminals, and Cellmates: An Exploration of Female Criminality and Delinquency.* Jefferson, NC: McFarland and Co.

Fong, Robert S. 1990. The organizational structure of prison gangs: a Texas case study. *Federal Probation* 54(1): 36–43.

Fong, Robert S., and Buentello, Salvador. 1991. The detection of prison gang development: an empirical assessment. *Federal Probation* 55(1): 66–69.

Fong, R., Vogel, R., and Buentello, S. 1995. Blood-in, blood-out: The rationale behind defecting from prison gangs. *Gang Journal* 2: 45–51.

Forche, Carolyn. 1981. *The Country Between Us.* New York: Harper & Row, Publishers.

Frazer, James G. 1920. The Scapegoat. *The Golden Bough: A Study in Magic and Religion,* vol. 9. London: Macmillan and Co.

Friedman, Matthew J. 2007. Post-traumatic stress disorder: An overview. US Department of Veteran Affairs, National Center for Post-traumatic Stress Disorder, January 31. http://www.ptsd.va.gov/professional/pages/ptsd-overview.asp.

Fuchs, Alexandre, Belmont, Samantha, and Fourteau, Jeremy. 2007. *Hijos de la Guerra (Children of War).* Documentary film. New York: Flyfilms and Directional Studios Production. http://www.childrenofthewar.com/hijos.html.

Fuqua-Whitley, D. S., Kellerman, A. L., Mercy, J., and Rivara, F. P. 1998. Preventing youth violence: What works? *Annual Review of Public Health* 19: 271–92.

Gahlinger, P. M. 2001. *Illegal Drugs: A Complete Guide to Their History, Chemistry, Use and Abuse.* New York: Sagebrush Press.

Garcia-Robles, Jorge. 1985. *Que Transa con Las Bandas?* México, D.F.: Editorial Posada, S.A.

Garland, Sarah. 2009. *Gangs in the Garden City: How Immigration, Segregation, and Youth Violence are Changing America's Suburbs.* New York: Nation Books.

Getlin, J. 2008. 'Book it.' *Los Angeles Times,* May 29, p. E3.

Gettleman, Marvin E., Patrick Lacefield, Louis Menashe, David Mermelstein, and Ronald Radosh (eds.). 1981. *El Salvador: Central America in the New Cold War.* New York: Grove Press, Inc.

Gewertz, Deborah. 1982. The father who bore Me: The role of Tsambunwuro during Chambri initiation ceremonies. In G. Herdt and R.M. Keesing (eds.), *Rituals of Manhood: Male Initiation in Papua New Guinea*pp. Berkeley: UC Press, pp. 286–320.

Gilligan, James. 1996. *Violence: Reflections on a National Epidemic.* New York: Vintage Books.

Gilly, Adolfo. 1981. *Guerra y política en El Salvador*. México, D.F.: Editorial Nueva Imagen, S.A.

Giordano, P., Cernkovish, S., and Pugh, M. 1978. Girls, guys and gangs: The changing social context of female delinquency. *Journal of Criminal Law and Criminology* 69(1): 126–32.

Giralt, María L. Santacruz, and Choncha-Eastman, Alberto. 2001. *Barrio Adentro: La Solidaridad Violenta de Las Pandillas*. San Salvador: Instituto Universitario de Opinión Publica [IUDOP], Universidad Centroamericana.

Girard, Rene. 1986. *The Scapegoat*. Baltimore, MD: Johns Hopkins University Press.

Girard, Rene. 1987. Generative scapegoating. In Hamerton-Kelly (ed.), *Violent Origins: Ritual Killing and Cultural Formation*. Stanford, CA: Stanford University Press, pp. 73–105.

Glod, Maria, and Shapira, Ian. 2004. Fairfax teen is charged in machete wounding: Gang retaliation suspected *The Washington Post*, May 14.

Glover Scott, and Winton, Richard. 2009. Massive raids target Hawaiian Gardens gang, *Los Angeles Times*, May 22, pp. A1, A14.

Gold, Scott, and Ellingwood, Ken. 2003. Trapped in a trailer, 18 migrants die. *Los Angeles Times*, May 15, pp. A1, 16.

Goldstein, P. J. 1989. Drugs and violent crime. In N. A. Weiner and M. E. Wolfgang (eds.), *Pathways to Criminal Violence*. Beverly Hills, CA: Sage, pp. 16–48.

Gomez, Jorge Arias. 1972, *Farabundo Marti: Esbozo Biographic*. Costa Rica: Editorial Universitaria Centroamericana (EDUCA).

Gonzalez, David. 2000. El Mozote: El Salvador's slain finally rest in peace, *New York Times*, December 11.

Gora, J. 1982. *The New Female Criminal: Empirical Reality or Social Myth*. New York: Praeger.

Gould, Jeffrey, and Santiago, Aldo Lauria. 2008. "Mataron justos por pecadores": Las massacres contrarevolucionarias [Rightly killed as sinners: The counter-revolutionary massacres]. *Trasmallo*, vol. 3, San Salvador, www.museo.com.sv.

Greenwald, John. 1992. Nasty boys, nasty time. *Time*, December 21, p. 15.

Groves, Betsy McAlister. 2002. *Children Who See Too Much: Lessons from the Child Witness to Violence Project*. Boston: Beacon Press.

Guerra, Nancy, and Villalta, Alberto Barillas. 2005. *Evaluación Social: Proyecto 'ÉXITO'—Educación con Excelencia e Innovación para Todos*. San Salvador: Impulsado por El Ministerio de Educación de la República de El Salvador.

Guillermoprieto, Alma. 1997. The harsh angel. *The New Yorker*, October 6, pp. 104–11.

Hackel, Joy, et al. 1985. *In Contempt of Congress: The Reagan Record of Deceit and Illegality on Central America*. Washington, DC: The Institute for Policy Studies.

Hadar, Arnon. 1981. *The United States and El Salvador: Political and Military Involvement*. Berkeley, CA: U.S.–El Salvador Research and Information Center.

Hagedorn, John M. (with Macon, Perry). 1988. *People and Folks: Gangs, Crime and the Underclass in a Rustbelt City*. Chicago: Lake View Press.

Hagedorn, John M. 1991. Gangs, neighborhoods, and public policy. *Social Problems* 38(4): 529–42.

Hagedorn, John M. 1994. Neighborhoods, markets, and gang drug organization. *Journal of Research in Crime and Delinquency* 32: 197–219.

Hagedorn, John M. 2008. *The World of Gangs: Armed Young Men and Gangsta Culture.* Minneapolis: University of Minnesota Press.

Hagedorn, John M., and Devitt, Mary L. 1999. Fighting female: The social construction of female gangs. In Meda Chesney-Lind and John M. Hagedorn (eds.), *Female Gangs in America: Essays on Girls, Gangs, and Gender.* Chicago: Lake View Press.

Handlin, Oscar. 1951. *The Uprooted: The Epic Story of the Great Migrations that made the American People.* Boston: Little, Brown.

Hanson, Kitty. 1964. *Rebels in the Streets: The Story of New York's Girl Gangs.* Englewood Cliffs, NJ: Prentice-Hall.

Harris, Mary G. 1988. *Cholas: Latina Girls and Gangs.* New York: AMS Press.

Harvard Law School. 2007. *No Place to Hide: Gang, State, and Clandestine Violence in El Salvador.* International Human Rights Clinic, Human Rights Program, February.

Harvard Law School. 2008. *No More Children Left Behind Bars: A Briefing on Youth Gang Violence and Juvenile Crime Prevention,* The Charles Hamilton Houston Institute for Race and Justice, March 6.

Haskins, James. 1974. *Street Gangs: Yesterday and Today.* New York: Hastings House.

Heald, S. 1986. The ritual use of violence: Circumcision among the Gisu of Uganda. In Riches, D. (ed.), *The Anthropology of Violence.* Oxford, U.K.: Basil Blackwell, pp. 70–85.

Heath, D. 1975. A critical review of ethnographic studies of alcohol use. *Journal of Operational Psychiatry* 9: 655–61.

Heath, D. 1978. The sociocultural model of alcohol use: Problems and prospects. In Gibbins, R. J., Israel, Y., et al., eds., *Research Advances in Alcohol and Drug Problems,* vol. 1. New York: John Wiley and Sons, pp. 1–92.

Heller, Joseph. 2011. *Catch 22.* 50th Anniversary ed. New York: Simon and Schuster.

Helzer, J. E., Robins, L. N., and McEvoy, L. 1987. Posttraumatic stress disorder in the general population: Findings of the epidemiologic cachement area survey. *The New England Journal of Medicine* 317(26): 1630–34.

Henríquez, Carlos. 1998. Asesinan a dos pandilleros, *La Prensa Gráfica,* San Salvador, August 29.

Herman, J. L. 1992. *Trauma and Recovery.* New York: Basic Books.

Hoffer, Tia Alane Nishimoto. 1991. A measure of posttraumatic stress disorder among Latino gang members. Ann Arbor, MI: UMI Dissertation Services.

Horowitz, M. J. 1976. *Stress Response Syndromes.* New York: Jason Aronson.

Horowitz, R. 1990. Sociological perspectives on gangs. In C. R. Huff (ed.), *Gangs in America.* Newbury Park, CA: Sage.

Howell, J. C. 1998. *Youth Gangs: An Overview* (Juvenile Justice Bulletin, Youth Gang Series, NCJ No.167249). Washington, DC: U.S. Department of Justice, Office of Juvenile Justice and Delinquency Prevention.

Howell, J. C., Moore, J. P. and Egley, A., Jr. 2002. The changing boundaries of youth gangs. In C. R. Huff (ed.), *Gangs in America III*, 3d ed. Thousand Oaks, CA: Sage Publications, pp. 3–18.

Hubert, Henri, and Marcel Mauss. 1898 [1964]. *Sacrifice: Its Nature and Function*, translated from the French by W. D. Halls. London: University of Chicago Press.

Huezo, M. 2001. Cultura y violencia en El Salvador. En: PNUD (ed.). *Violencia en una sociedad en transición*. San Salvador: Programa de las Naciones Unidas para el Desarrollo, pp. 115–37.

Huff, C. R. 1996. The criminal behavior of gang members and nongang at-risk youth. In C. R. Huff (ed.), *Gangs in America*, 2d ed. Thousand Oaks, CA: Sage Publications, pp. 75–102.

Huff, C. R. 2002. Initiation of drug use, drug sales, and violent offending. In F. Esbensen, D. Peterson, A. Freng, and T. J. Taylor (eds.), *Gangs in America III*. Thousand Oaks, CA: Sage Publications, Inc.

Huff, C. Ronald, and Goldstein, Arnold P. (eds.) 1993. *The Gang Intervention Handbook*. Champaign, IL: Research Press.

Hull, Jon D. 1992. No way out. *Time*, August 17, pp. 38–40.

Hunt, Geoffreym and Laidler, Karen Joe. 2006. Alcohol and violence in the lives of gang members. In Esbensen, Finn-Aage, et al. (eds.) *American Youth Gangs at the Millennium*.: Long Grove, IL: Waveland Press, Inc., pp. 229–38.

Hunt, Geoffrey, MacKenzie, Kathleenm and Joe-Laidler, Karen. 2000. 'I'm calling my mom': The meaning of family and kinship among homegirls. *Justice Quarterly* 17(1): 1–31.

Jackman, T. 2005. MS-13 suspected in [machete] attack. *Washington Post*, June 3, p. B2.

Jenkins, J. H. 1991. The state construction of affect: political ethos and mental health among Salvadoran refugees. *Culture, Medicine and Psychiatry* 15: 139–65.

Joe, Karen A.M., and Chesney-Lind, Meda. 1995. Just every mother's angel: An analysis of gender and ethnic variations in youth gang membership. *Gender and Society* 9(4): 408–30.

Johnson, B. D., Hamid, A., and Sanabria, H. 1990. Emerging models of crack distribution. In T. Mieczkowski (ed.), *Drugs and Crime: A Reader*. Boston: Allyn-Bacon.

Johnson, B. D., Williams, T., Dei, K., and Sanabria, H. 1990. Drug abuse and the inner city: Impacts of hard drug use and sales on low income communities. In J. Q. Wilson and M. Tonry (eds.), *Drugs and Crime*. Chicago: University of Chicago Press.

Johnson, Stephenm and Muhlhausen, David B. 2005. North American transnational youth gangs: Breaking the chain of violence. *Heritage Foundation Backgrounder* 1834(21): 11.

Jones, Gareth A.M., and Rodgers, Dennis (eds.). 2009. *Youth Violence in Latin America: Gangs and Juvenile Justice in Perspective.* New York: Palgrave Macmillian.

Juette, Melvinm and Berger, Ronald J. 2008. *Wheelchair Warrior: Gangs, Disability, and Basketball.* Philadelphia: Temple University Press.

Justice Policy Institute. 2005. *Ganging Up on Communities? Putting Gang Crime in Context*, Policy Brief.

Kardiner, A. 1941. *The Traumatic Neuroses of War.* New York: P. Hoeber Publishers.

Katz, Charles M. 1997. *Police and Gangs: A Study of a Police Gang Unit.* Ann Arbor, MI: UMI Microform.

Katz, Jack, 1988. *Seductions of Crime: Moral and Sensual Attractions of Doing Evil.* New York: Basic Books.

Katz, Jesse. 1993a. County's yearly gang death toll reaches 800. *Los Angeles Times,* January 19, p. A1.

Katz Jesse. 1993b. Leaving his turf. *Los Angeles Times,* February 14, pp. B1, 6.

Katz, Jesse.1993c. The Mexican mafia tells gangs to halt drivebys. *Los Angeles Times,* September 26, p. A1.

Keiser, Lincoln. 1969. *The Vice Lords, Warriors of the Street.* New York: Holt, Rinehart and Winston.

Kennedy, David. 2011. *Don't Shoot: One Man, A Street Fellowship, and the End of Violence in Inner-City America.* New York: Bloomsbury.

Kim, Victoria. 2010. Violent slaying retold in cour. *Los Angeles Times,* September 10, p. AA1.

Klein, Malcolm. 1968. From association to guilt: the group guidance project in juvenile gang intervention. Los Angeles: University of Southern California, Youth Studies Center. Prepared by Malcolm W. Klein on behalf of the Youth Studies Center and The Los Angeles County Probation Department.

Klein, Malcolm. 1971. *Street Gangs and Street Workers.* Englewood Cliffs, NJ: Prentice-Hall.

Klein, Malcolm. 1995. *The American Street Gang: The Nature, Prevalence, and Control.* New York: Oxford University Press.

Klein, Malcolm. 2002. Street gangs: A cross-national perspective. In C. Ronald Huff (ed.), *Gangs in America III.* Thousand Oaks, CA: Sage Publications.

Klein, Malcolm. 2004. *Gang Cops: The Words and Ways of Paco Domingo.* Walnut Creek, CA: Altamira Press.

Klein, Malcolm. 2007. *Chasing After Street Gangs: A Forty-Year Journey.* Upper Saddle River, NJ: Pearson/Prentice Hall.

Klein, M. W., and Maxson, Cheryl. 1987. Street gang violence. In Wolfgang, M. E., and Weiner, N. (eds.), *Violent Crime, Violence Criminals.* Beverly Hills, CA: Sage Publications.

Klein, M. W., and Maxson, Cheryl. 2006. *Street Gang Patterns and Policies.* New York: Oxford University Press.

Klein, Malcolm, Maxson, Cheryl, and Cunningham, Lea. 1988. Gang involvement in cocaine 'rock' trafficking. Los Angeles: University of Southern California, Center for Research on Crime and Social Control, SSRI.

Klein, Malcolm, Maxson, Cheryl, and Cunningham, Lea, 1991. 'Crack,' street gangs, and violence. *Criminology* 29(4): 623–50.

knowgangs.com, 2008. 'MS-13.'

Konrad, K., and Skaperdas, S. 1998. Extortion. *Economica* 65: 461–77.

Kramer, Dale, and Karr, Madeline. 1953. *Teen-age Gangs: The Inside Story of One of America's Gravest Perils.* New York: Henry, Holt, and Company.

Krikorian, Gregory. 1997. Study ranks joblessness as top factor in gang toll. *Los Angeles Times*, October 28.

Koegel, Paul. 1992. Through a different lens: An anthropological perspective on homelessness and mental illness *Culture, Medicine and Psychiatry* 16: 1–27.

Konner, Melvin. 1987. The gender option. *The Sciences*, November/December, pp. 2–4.

Konner, Melvin. 1990. *Why the Reckless Survive... and Other Secrets of Human Nature.* New York: Penguin Books.

LaFeber, Walter. 1993. *Inevitable Revolutions: The United States in Central America*, 2d ed. New York: W.W. Norton.

Lane, Michael P. 1989. Inmate gangs. *Corrections Today* 51(4): 98–101.

Lasley, James R. 1992. Age, social context, and street gang membership: Are 'youth' gangs becoming 'adult' gangs? *Youth and Society* 23(4): 434–51.

Lauderback, David, Hansen, Joy, and Waldorf, Dan. 1992. Sisters are doin' it for themselves: A black female gang in San Francisco. *Gang Journal* 1(1): 57–72.

Lawyers Committee for International Human Rights and Americas Watch. 1984. El Salvador's Other Victims: The War on the Displaced, New York, April.

Lee, Jonathan H. X. 2009. Ahora la luz: Transnational gangs, the state, and religion. In Lois Ann Lorentzen et al. (eds.), *Religion at the Corner of Bliss and Nirvana: Politics, Identity, and Faith in New Migrant Communities.* Durham, NC: Duke University Press.

LeoGrande, William M. 1990. After the battle of San Salvador, *World Policy Journal*, Spring.

LeoGrande, William M. 1998. *Our Own Backyard: The United States in Central America, 1977–1992.* Chapel Hill: University of North Carolina Press.

Levitt, Steven D., and Dubner, Stephen J. 2005. *Freakonomics: A Rogue Economist Explores the Hidden Side of Everything.* New York: William Morrow.

Lewis, N. 1992. Delinquent girls achieving a violent equality in DC. *Washington Post*, December 23, pp. A1, 14.

Lewis, S. J., and Russel, A..J. 2011. Being embedded: A way forward for ethnographic research. *Ethnography* 12(3): 398–416.

Logan, Samuel. 2009. *This Is for the Mara Salvatrucha: Inside the MS-13, America's Most Violent Gang.* New York: Hyperion.

Logan, S., and Kairies, K. 2006. Recruitment, redemption in the MS-13. *ISN Security Watch*, Feb. 14, International Relations and Security Network, posted on www.isn.ethz.ch.

Lopez, Robert J., Connell, Rich, and Kraul, Chris. 2005. MS-13: An international franchise: Gang uses deportation to its advantage to flourish in U.S. *Los Angeles Times*, October 30, p. A1.

Lopez, Robert J., and Katz, Jesse. 1993. Mexican mafia tells gangs to halt drive-bys. *Los Angeles Times*, September 26.

Lorenz, Konrad. 1974. *On Aggression.* New York: Harcourt Brace Jovanovich.

Los Angeles Times. 1993. Boy in serious condition after being shot in gang crossfire. January 31, p. B5.

Levitt, S., and Venkatesh, S. 2001. Growing up in the projects: the economic lives of a cohort of men who came of age in Chicago Public housing. *The American Economic Review* 91(2): 79–84.

MacAndrew, C., and Edgerton, R. 1969. *Drunken Comportment: A Social Explanation.* Chicago: Aldine.

MacCoun, R., and Reuter, P. 1992. Are the wages of sin $30 an hour? Economic aspects of street-level drug dealing. *Crime and Delinquency* 38: 477–91.

Maher, Lisa. 1997. *Sexed Work: Gender, Race and Resistance in a Brooklyn Drug Market.* New York: Oxford University Press.

Maher, Lisa, and Daly, Kathleen. 1996. Women in the street-level drug economy: Continuity or change? *Criminology* 34(4): 465–92.

Mann, Coramae R. 1984. *Female Crime and Delinquency.* Tuscaloosa, AL: University of Alabama Press.

Martínez, Ana Guadalupe. 2008. *Las Cárceles Clandestinas* [Clandestine Prisons]. San Salvador: UCA Editores.

Martínez, Mario. 1999. Continúan muertes de presuntos pandilleros. *El Diario de Hoy* San Salvador, February 12.

Marinucci, C., Winokur, S., and Lewis, G. 1994. Ruthless girlz. *San Francisco Examiner*, December 12, p. A1.

Massey, D. S., and Eggers, M. L. 1990. The ecology of inequality: Minorities and the concentration of poverty. *American Journal of Sociology* 95: 1153–88.

Matza, D., and Sykes, G. 1957. Techniques of naturalization. *American Sociological Review* 22: 664–70.

Maxson, Cheryl. 2006. Gang members on the move. In Egley, A., Jr., Maxson, C. L, Miller, J., and Klein, M. W. (eds.), *The Modern Gang Reader*, 3d ed. Los Angeles: Roxbury Publishing Company, pp. 117–29.

Maxson, Cheryl. 2009. Similar but unique: The "peculiar" case of the Mara Salvatrucha (MS-13). *April 16, Youth Violence Prevention Conference, UMSL.*

Maxson, Cheryl, and Klein, Malcolm. 1997. *Responding to Troubled Youth.* NewYork: Oxford University Press.

Maxon, Cheryl, and Whitlock, M. L. 2002. Joining the gang: Gender differences in risk factors for gang membership. In C. Ronald Huff (ed.), *Gangs in America III.* Thousand Oaks, CA: Sage Publications.

Mayer, J. 1989. In the war on drugs, toughest foe may be that alienated youth. *Wall Street Journal*, September 8, p.1.

McClintock, Michael. 1985. *The American Connection: State Terror and Popular Resistance in El Salvador*. London: Zed Press.

McDonnell, P. J. 1993. Central Americans pose an immigration dilemma. *Los Angeles Times*, February 2, Sect.A, p. 1.

McGuire, Connie. 2007. Central American youth gangs in the Washington, D.C. area. Working paper, Washington Office on Latin America (WOLA), January.

Melgar, J. 2006. Extorsión. Cartas, *Redacción Vértice*, January 22, vertice@ elsalvador.com.

Menand, Louis. 1997. How to frighten small children. *The New Yorker*, October 6, p. 112.

Miller, Jody. 1998. Gender and victimization risk among young women in gangs. *Journal of Research in Crime and Delinquency* 35: 429–53.

Miller, Jody. 2001. *One of the Guys: Girls, Gangs, and Gender*. New York: Oxford University Press.

Miller, Jody. 2002. The girls in the gang: What we've learned from two decades of research. In C. R. Huff (ed.), *Gangs in America III*, 3d ed. Sage Publications, pp. 175–97.

Miller, Jody. 2006. Getting into gangs. In Egley, Jr., et al. (eds.), *The Modern Gang Reader*, 3d ed. Los Angeles, CA: Roxbury Publishing Company, pp. 43–59.

Miller, Jody, and Decker, Scott. 2001. Young women and gang violence: Gender, street offending, and violent victimization in gangs. *Justice Quarterly* 18: 115–40.

Miller, Walter B. 1958. Lower class culture as a generating milieu of gang delinquency. *Journal of Social Issues* 14: 5–19.

Miller, Walter B. 1973. Race, sex and gangs: The molls. *Society* 11: 32–35.

Miller, Walter B. 1975. *Violence by Youth Gangs and Youth Groups as a Crime Problem in Major American Cities*. Washington, DC: Government Printing Office.

Miller, Walter B. 1980. The molls. In S. K. Datesman and F. R. Scarpitti (eds.), *Women, Crime, and Justice*. New York: Oxford University Press.

Miller, Walter B. 1981. American youth gangs: Past and present. In A. S. Blumberg (ed.), *Current Perspectives on Criminal Behavior*, 2d ed. New York: Knopf.

Moakley, Joseph. 1990. Introduction. In *The Jesuit Assassinations: The Writings of Ellacuría, Martín-Baró and Segundo Montes, with a Chronology of the Investigation*. Kansas City, MO: Sheed and Ward.

Monti, D. J. 1994. *Wannabe: Gangs in Suburbs and Schools*. Cambridge, MA: Blackwell Publishers.

Monti, Peter. 2001. *Adolescents, Alcohol, and Substance Abuse: Reaching Teens through Brief Interventions*. New York: Guilford Press.

Moore, Joan. 1978. *Homeboys: Gangs, Drugs and Prison in the Barrios of Los Angeles*. Philadelphia: Temple University Press.

Moore, Joan. 1990. Gangs, drugs, and violence. In M. De La Roasa, E. Y. Lambert, and B. Gropper (eds.), *Drugs and Violence: Causes, Correlates, and Consequences*. Rockville, MD: National Institute on Drug Abuse.

Moore, Joan. 1991. *Going Down the Barrio: Homeboys and Homegirls in Change*. Philadelphia: Temple University Press.

Moore, Joan, and Hagedorn, John. 1996. What happens to girls in the gang? In C. Ronald Huff (ed.), *Gangs in America*, 2d ed. Thousand Oaks, CA: Sage Publications.

Moore, Joan, and Hagedorn, John. 2001. *Female Gangs: A Focus on Research*. Juvenile Justice Bulletin. Washington, DC: U.S. Department of Justice, Office of Justice Programs, Office of Juvenile Justice and Delinquency Prevention.

Morales, A. 1982. The Mexican American gang member: Evaluation and treatment. In Becerra, R. M., Karno, M., and Escobar, J. I. (eds.), *Mental Health and Hispanic Americans*. New York: Grune and Stratton.

Morán, Mariano. 1984. *Funcion Politica del Ejercito Salvadoreño en el Presente Siglo*. San Salvador, El Salvador: UCA/Editores.

Morawetz, Nancy. 2000. *Understanding the Impact of the 1996 Deportation Laws and the Limited Scope of Proposed Reforms*. Boston: Harvard Law Review, Vol. 113.

Muncie, John. 2007. Refugee gang youth: Zero tolerance and the security state in contemporary US-Salvadoran relations. In Sudhir A. Venkatesh and Ronald Kassimir (eds.), *Youth, Globalization, and the Law*. Stanford, CA: Stanford University Press.

Nakagawa, Tsuyoshi. 1975. *El Salvador: This Beautiful World*, vol. 54, Tokyo: Kodansha International Ltd.

Nairn, Allan 1984. Endgame: A special report on U.S. military strategy in Central America, NACLA Report on the Americas 18, no. 3, May-June.

Narváez Gutiérrez, Juan Carlos. 2007. *Ruta Transnacional: Á San Salvador por Los Ángeles: Espacios de Interacción Juvenil en un Contexto Migratorio*. Mexico: Universidad Autónoma de Zacatecas: Instituto Mexicano de la Juventud, Miguel Ángel Porrúa.

National Gang Intelligence Center. 2009. *National Gang Threat Assessment*. Product No. 2009-M0335–001. http://permanent.access.gpo.gov/lps125365/32146p.pdf.

National Geographic, Explorer, 2006. *MS-13: World's Most Dangerous Gang* [TV documentary].

The New Yorker. 1992. Notes and Comments: El Salvador. January 27.

Niehoff, Debra. 1999. *The Biology of Violence: How Understanding the Brain, Behavior, and Environment Can Break the Vicious Circle of Aggression*. New York: The Free Press.

Orionce.net. 2009. La Resurrección de la Sombra Negra [The Resurrection of the Black Shadow], October 26.

Padilla, Felix. 1992. *The Gang as an American Enterprise*. New Brunswick, NJ: Rutgers University Press.

Paige, Jeffery. 1997. *Coffee and Power: Revolution and the Rise of Democracy in Central America*. Cambridge, MA: Harvard University Press.

Papachristos, Andrew V. 2005. Gang world: Globalization at work. *Foreign Policy* 147(March-April): 48.

Parker, R. N. 1995. *Alcohol and Homicide: A Deadly Combination of Two American Traditions.* Albany: State University of New York Press.

Payne, Douglas. 1999. *El Salvador: Re-emergence of 'Social Cleansing' Death Squads.* Washington, DC: INS Resource Information Center, March. [QA/ SLV/99.001]

Perera, Sylvia B. 1986. *The Scapegoat Complex: Toward a Mythology of Shadow and Guilt.* Toronto: Inner City Books.

Pernanen, K. 1991. *Alcohol in Human Violence.* New York: Guilford.

Pett, Joel. 2009. Battle lines. *Los Angeles Times*, May 24, p. A39.

Phillips, Susan A. 1999. *Wallbangin'—Graffiti and Gangs in L.A.* Chicago: University of Chicago Press.

Poe-Yamagata, Eileen, and Butts, Jeffrey A. 1996. Female offenders in the juvenile justice system: Statistics summary. *OJJDP report.* Washington, DC: Office of Juvenile Justice and Delinquency Prevention.

Porter, B. 1982. California prison gangs: The price of control. *Corrections Magazine* 8: 16–19.

Portes, Alejandro, and DeWind, Josh (eds.). 2007. *Rethinking Migration: New Theoretical and Empirical Perspectives.* New York: Berghahn Books.

Portes, Alejandro, and Rumbaut, Rubén G. 2006. *Immigrant America: A Portrait,* 3d ed. Berkeley: University of California Press.

Portillo, Edwardo Luis. 1999. Women, men, and gangs: The social construction of gender in the barrio. In Meda Chesney-Lind and John Hagedorn (eds.), *Female Gangs in America: Essays on Girls, Gangs, and Gender.* Chicago: Lake View Press.

Posner, Michael H. 1983. Presidential certification of El Salvador: The case of four U.S. churchwomen, *Church and Society.* New York: United Presbyterian Church, March/April, pp. 37–42.

Price, Mark. 2010. Two MS-13 members plead guilty. *Charlotte Observer,* July 9, p. A1.

Pyke, K. D. 1996. Class-based masculinities: The interdependence of gender, class, and interpersonal power. *Gender and Society* 10: 527–49.

Pyrooz, David C., Decker, Scott H., and Webb, Vincent J. 2010. The ties that bind: Desistance from gangs. *Crime and Delinquency*, September 8.

Quicker, John C. 1983. *Homegirls: Characterizing Chicano Gangs.* San Pedro, CA: International University Press.

Quicker, J., Galeai, Y. N., and Batani-Khalfani, A. 1992. Bootstrap or noose? Drugs, gangs, and violence in South Central Los Angeles. In J. Fagan (ed.), *The Ecology of Crime and Drug Use in Inner Cities.* New York: Social Science Research Council.

Ramos, Wendy. 1999. Matan pandillero a machetazos. *La Prensa Gráfica*, San Salvador, February 7.

Rand, A. 1987. Transitional life events and desistance from delinquency and crime. In M. Wolfgang, T. Thornberry, and R. Figlio (eds.), *From Boy* to Man, from Delinquency to Crime. Chicago: University of Chicago Press, pp. 134–62.

Reedy, D. C. and Koper, C. S. 2003. Impact of handgun types on gun assault outcomes: a comparison of gun assaults involving semiautomatic pistols and revolvers. *Injury Prevention* 9(2): 151–56.

Rice, Constance L. 2004. L.A.'s budding Mogadishus—nearly feral areas need help. *Los Angeles Times*, December 23, op-ed.

Roan, Shari. 2009. Nothing sweet about this type of bitter. *Los Angeles Times*, May 25, p. E3.

Rodriguez, Francisco. 1993. *Vida para Los que Vienen Despues en El Salvador.* San José, Costa Rica: Litografía La Jornada.

Rodriguez, Luis J. 1993. *Always Running: La Vida Loca: Gang Days in East L.A.* New York: Simon & Schuster.

Rodríguez, Mario Menendez. 1984. *El Salvador: Una Autentica Guerra Civil,* Editorial Universitaria Centroamericana (EDUCA).

Rohrlich, Ted, and Tulsky, Fredric N. 1996. Gang killings exceed 40% of L.A. slayings. *Los Angeles Times*, December 5, p. A1.

Rozzell, Liane, and Hollyday, Joyce. 1984. To rise again: A history of repression and hope in El Salvador, in *Crucible of Hope.* Washington, DC: Sojourners.

Russell, Phillip L. 1984. *El Salvador in Crisis.* Austin, TX: Colorado River Press.

Saitoti, Tepilit Ole. 1986. My circumcision. In *The Worlds of a Maasai Warrior.* New York: Random House, pp. 66–76.

Salston, M, and Figley, C. R. 2003. Secondary traumatic stress effects of working with survivors of criminal victimization. *Journal of Traumatic Stress* 16(2): 167–74.

Sampson, R., and Wilson, W. J. 1995. Toward a theory of race, crime and urban inequality. In *Boundaries: Readings in Deviance, Crime and Criminal Justice.* Los Angeles: Pearson Custom Publishing.

Sanchez, Alvaro L. 1990. *La Politica en El Salvador en las Ultimas Seis Decadas 1930–1989,* paperback book, no publisher listed.

Sánchez, George J. 1993. *Becoming Mexican American: Ethnicity, Culture, and Identity in Chicano Los Angeles, 1900–1945.* New York: Oxford University Press.

Sanchez, Reymundo. 2000. *My Bloody Life: The Making of a Latin King.* Chicago: Review Press.

Sanchez-Jankowski, Martín. 1991. *Islands in the Street: Gangs and American Urban Society.* Berkeley: University of California Press.

Sanders, William B. 1994. *Gangbangs and Drive-Bys: Grounded Culture and Juvenile Gang Violence.* New York: Aldine de Gruyter.

Sandoval, Capitan Francisco Emilio Mena. 1984. *Del Ejercito Nacional al Ejercito Guerrillero.* San Salvador, El Salvador: Ediciones Arcoiris.

Santacruz, M. L. 2005. La solidaridad violenta de las pandillas callejeras: el caso de El Salvador. En: Nelson Portillo, Mauricio Gaborit y José Miguel Cruz (eds.), *Psicología social de la posguerra. Teoría y aplicaciones desde el salvador.* San Salvador: UCA Editores, pp. 352–93.

Santacruz, M., and Concha-Eastman, A. 2001. *Barrio Adentro. La Solidaridad violenta de las pandillas*. San Salvador: Talleres Gráficos UCA.

Santacruz, M. L., and Cruz, J. M. 2001. Las maras en El Salvador. En: ERIC IDESO, IDIES e IUDOP (comp.) *Maras y pandillas en Centroamérica, volumen I.* Managua: UCA Publicaciones, pp. 15–107.

Santiago, D. 1992. Random victims of vengeance show teen crime. *Philadelphia Inquirer*, February 23, p. A1.

Sanyika, Dadisi. 1996. Gang rites and rituals of initiation. In L. C. Mahdi, N. G. Christopher, and M. Meade, (eds.), *Crossroads: The Quest for Contemporary Rites of Passage.* Chicago: Open Court, pp. 115–24.

Savenije, Wim. 2009. *Maras y Barras: Pandillas y Violencia Juvenil en los Barrios Marginales de Centroamérica.* San Salvador, El Salvador: Facultad Latinoamericana de Ciencias Sociales (FLACSO).

Schwarz, Benjamin C. 1991. *American Counterinsurgency Doctrine and El Salvador: The Frustrations of Reform and the Illusions of Nation Building.* Santa Monica, CA: RAND, National Defense Research Institute.

Scheper-Hughes, Nancy. 1992. *Death without Weeping: The Violence of Everyday Life in Brazil.* Berkeley: University of California Press.

Shacklady-Smith, L. 1978. Sexist assumptions and female delinquenc. In C. Smart and B. Smart (eds.), *Women and Social Control.* London: Routledge Kegan Paul.

Shakur, Sanyika (AKA Monster Kody Scott). 1993. *Monster: The Autobiography of an L.A. Gang Member.* New York: Penguin Books.

Seper, Jerry. 2004. Al Qaeda seeks tie to local gangs. *Washington Times*, September 28.

Sheley, J., Wright, J., and Smith, M. D. 1993. Kids, guns and killing fields. *Society*, November-December, pp. 84–87.

Short, James F. 1968. *Gang Delinquency and Delinquent Subcultures.* New York: Harper & Row.

Short, James F. 1990. New wine in old bottles? Change and continuity in American gangs. In C. R. Huff (ed.), *Gangs in America.* Newbury Park, CA: Sage.

Short, James, F. 1996. Personal, gang, and community careers. In C. Ronald Huff (ed.), *Gangs in America*, 2d ed. Thousand Oaks, CA: Sage Publications.

Short, James F., and Hughes, Lorine A. (eds.) 2006. *Studying Youth Gangs.* Lanham, MD: AltaMira Press.

Short, James F., and Strodtbeck, Fred L. 1965 (1974). *Group Process and Gang Delinquency.* Chicago: University of Chicago Press.

Shweder, Richard A. 2000. What about 'female genital mutilation'? And why understanding culture matters in the first place. *Daedalus* (fall): 209–32.

Siegel, Daniel. 1999. *The Developing Mind: Toward a Neurobiology of Interpersonal Experience.* New York: Guilford Press.

Siegel, Daniel J. 2007. *The Mindful Brain: Reflection and Attunement in the Cultivation of Well-Being.* New York: W.W. Norton and Company.

Sikes, Gini. 1997. *8 Ball Chicks.* New York: Anchor Books.

Silverman, S. 2003. Prosecutors crack down on drug use: The hard line. *The Pantagraph*, March 10, p. A1.

Simmons, Rachel. 2002. *Odd Girl Out: The Hidden Culture of Aggression in Girls*. New York: Harcourt.

Simon, Rita. 1975. *Women and Crime*. Lexington, MA: Lexington Press.

Skolnick, J., Correl, T., Navarro, E., and Rabb, R. 1989. *The Social Structure of Street Drug Dealing*. Sacramento, CA: Office of the Attorney General, State of California.

Snyder, H. N., and Sickmund, M. 1999. *Juvenile Offenders and Victims: 1999. National Report*. Washington, DC: U.S. Department of Justice, office of Juvenile Justice and Delinquency Prevention.

Smutt, M., and Miranda, E. 1998. El fenómeno de las pandillas en El Salvador. FLACSO, Serie Adolescencia, San Salvador, El Salvador.

Spergel, Irving A. 1989. *Youth Gangs: Problem and Response. A Review of the Literature*. Chicago: University of Chicago.

Spergel, Irving A. 1995. *The Youth Gang Problem: A Community Approach*. New York: Oxford University Press.

Spergel, Irving A. 2007. *Reducing Youth Gang Violence: The Little Village Gang Project in Chicago*. Lanham, MD: AltaMira Press.

Solaún, Mauricio. 2005. *U.S. Intervention and Regime Change in Nicaragua*. Lincoln, NE: University of Nebraska Press.

Solkoff, N., Gray, P., and Keill, S. 1986. Which Vietnam veterans develop posttraumatic stress disorders? *The Journal of Clinical Psychology* 42(5): 687–98.

Spergel, I. 1995. *The Youth Gang Problem: A Community Approach*. New York: Oxford University Press.

Steffensmeier, D. 1983. Organization properties and sex-segregation in the underworld: Building a sociological theory of sex differences in crime. *Social Forces* 61: 1010–32.

Steffensmeier, D., and Steffensmeier, R. H. 1980. Trends in female delinquency: An examination of arrest, juvenile court, self-report, and field data. *Criminology* 18: 62–85.

Steffensmeier, D., and Terry, R. 1986. Institutional sexism in the underworld: A view from the inside. *Sociological Inquiry* 56: 304–23.

Sullivan, Mercer. 1989. *'Getting Paid': Youth Crime and Work in the Inner City*. Ithaca, NY: Cornell University Press.

Swart, William J. 1991. Female gang delinquency: A search for acceptably deviant behavior. *Mid-American Review of Sociology* 15(1): 43–52.

Swecker, Chris. 2009. Foreward. In Diaz, Tom (ed.), *No Boundaries: Transnational Latino Gangs and American Law Enforcement*. Ann Arbor: The University of Michigan Press.

Taylor, Carl S. 1990. *Dangerous Society*. East Lansing: Michigan State University Press.

Taylor, Carl S. 1993. *Girls, Gangs, Women, and Drugs*. East Lansing: Michigan State University Press.

Taylor, Margaret H., and Aleinikoff, T. Alexander. 1998. *Deportation of Criminal Aliens: A Geopolitical Perspective*. Working paper. Washington, DC: Inter-American Dialogue, Carnegie Endowment for International Peace.

*The Jesuit Assassinations: The Writings of Ellacuría, Martín-Baró and Segundo Montes, with a Chronology of the Investigation.*1990. (November 11, 1989–October 22), Instituto de Estudios Centroamericanos and El Rescate, Sheed and Ward.

Thornberry, Terence P. 2006a. Membership in youth gangs and involvement in serious and violent offending. In Egley, Jr., et al. (eds.), *The Modern Gang Reader*, 3d ed. Los Angeles: Roxbury Publishing Company, pp. 224–32.

Thornberry, Terence P. 2006b. The antecedents of gang membership. In Egley, Jr., et al. (eds.), *The Modern Gang Reader*, 3d ed. Los Angeles: Roxbury Publishing Company, pp. 30–42.

Thornberry, T., Krohn, M., Lizotte, A., and Chard-Wierschem, D. 1993. The role of juvenile gangs in facilitating delinquent behavior. *Journal of Research in Crime and Delinquency* 30(1): 55–87.

Thrasher, Frederick M. 1927. *The Gang: A Study of 1,313 Gangs in Chicago.* Chicago: University of Chicago Press.

Tonry, Michael H. 1995. *Malign Neglect: Race, Crime and Punishment in America.* New York: Oxford University Press.

Totten, Mark D. 2000. *Guys, Gangs, and Girlfriend Abuse.* Peterborough, Ont.: Broadview Press.

Trasmallo. 2006. *Memoria de los Izalcos*, No. 2. San Salvador: Museo de la Palabra y la Imagen.

Trostle, Lawrence. 1992. *The Stoners: Drugs, Demons, and Delinquency.* New York: Garland.

Uggen, C., and Thompson, M. 2003. The socioeconomic determinants of ill-gotten gains: within-person changes in drug use and illegal earnings. *The American Journal of Sociology* 109(1): 146–74.

UN Security Council. 1993. *From Madness to Hope: The 12-Year War in El Salvador: Report of the Commission on the Truth for El Salvador*, Annex, S/25500, March 15.

United States Attorney's Office. 2010. MS-13 Member Sentenced 27 Years for July 2009 Alexandria Murder, Department of Justice Press Release, Eastern District of Virginia, July 9.

United States Congress. 2006. MS-13 and counting: Gang activity in Montgomery and Prince George's Counties: Hearing before the Committee on Government Reform. House of Representatives, One Hundred Ninth Congress, second session, September 6. Washington, DC: U.S. G.P.O.

Valdez, Al. 2009. 'MS-13.' Internet article from the National Alliance of Gang Investigators Associations, *NAGIA*, nagia.com.

Valdez, Avelardo, and Sifaneck, Stephen J. 2006. 'Getting high and getting by': Dimensions of drug selling behaviors among American Mexican gang members in South Texas.In Egley, Jr., et al. (eds.), *The Modern Gang Reader*, 3d ed. Los Angeles: Roxbury Publishing Company, pp. 296–310.

Van der Kolk, Bessel A. 1987. The psychological consequences of overwhelming life experiences. In Bessel A. Van der Kolk (ed.), *Psychological Trauma.* Washington, DC: American Psychiatric Press, Inc., pp. 1–30.

van Genep, A. [1908]1960. *The Rites of Passage*, translated by M. Vizedom and M. Caffee. Chicago: University of Chicago Press.

Véjar, R. G. 1980. *El Ascenso del Militarismo en El Salvador*. San Salvador, El Salvador: UCA/Editores.

Venkatesh, Sudhir Alladi. 1997. The social organization of street gang activity in an urban ghetto. *American Journal of Sociology* 103: 82–111.

Venkatesh, Sudhir Alladi. 1998. Gender and outlaw capitalism: A historical account of the Black Sisters United 'girl gang.' *Signs* (Spring): 683–709.

Venkatesh, Sudhir Alladi. 2004. The financial activity of a modern American street gang. In Esbensen, Finn-Aage, Tibbetts, S. G., and Gaines, L. (eds.), *American Youth Gangs at the Millennium*. Long Grove, IL: Waveland Press, Inc., pp. 239–46.

Venkatesh, Sudhir Alladi. 2008. *Gang Leader for a Day: A Rogue Sociologist Takes to the Streets*. New York: Penguin Press.

Vidal, José. 1981. *Monseñor Oscar Arnulfo Romero: A mi me pueden matar, pero no a la voz de la justicia*. ["You can kill me but not the voice of justice"]. Los Angeles: la Organization de Profesionales y Técnicos Salvadoreños.

Vigil, James Diego. 1983. Chicano gangs: One response to Mexican urban adaptation in the Los Angeles area. *Urban Anthropology* 12(1): 45–68.

Vigil, James Diego. 1988. *Barrio Gangs: Street Life and Identity in Southern California*. Austin: University of Texas Press.

Vigil, James Diego. 2004. *A Rainbow of Gangs*. Austin: University of Texas Press.

Vigil, James Diego. 2010. Gangs, poverty, and the future. In George Gmelch (ed.), *Urban Life: Readings in the Anthropology of the City*. 5th ed. Long Grove, IL: Waveland Press.

Villa, Raúl H., and Sánchez, George. 2004. Introduction: Los Angeles studies and the future of urban culture. *American Quarterly* 56(3): 499–505.

Wallace, Scott. 2001. You must go home again: Deported Los Angeles gang members are crime problem in El Salvador. *Harper's Magazine*, August 1, p. 47.

Ward, Mike. 2006. Gang's violent grip: Group with Central American roots leaves a bloody trail across U.S. *Austin American-Statesman* (TX), January 22.

Ward, T. W. 1988. *The Price of Fear: Salvadoran Refugees in the City of the Angels*. Ann Arbor, MI: University Microfilms, dissertation, UCLA.

Waldorf, D., and Lauderback, D. 1993. *Gang Drug Sales in San Francisco: Organized or Freelance?* Alameda, CA: Institute for Scientific Analysis.

Western, B. 2002. The impact of incarceration on wage mobility and inequality. *American Sociological Review* 67(4): 526–46.

White, Christopher. 2009. *The History of El Salvador*. Westport, CT: Greenwood Press.

Whitney, Catherine. 2009. Broken warrior. *Los Angeles Times*, May 25: A33.

Whoriskey, Peter. 2005. Fairfax machete victim testifies he played dead. *Washington Post*, March 2.

Wilkinson, Tracy. 1993. Massacre forces Salvador to come to terms with past. *Los Angeles Times*, A1, pp. 11–12.

Wilson, William J. 1987. *The Truly Disadvantaged: The Inner City, the Underclass, and Public Policy*. Chicago: University of Chicago Press.

Wilson, William J. 1996. *When Work Disappears: The World of the New Urban Poor*. New York: Knopf.

Winfree, L. T., Jr., Fuller, K, Vigil, T., and Mays, G. L. 1992. The definition and measurement of 'gang status': Policy implications and juvenile justice. *Juvenile and Family Court Journal* 43: 29–37.

Witkin, Gordon. 1991. Kids who kill; disputes once settled with fists are now settled with guns. Every 100 hours, more youths die on the streets than were killed in the Persian Gulf. *U.S. News and World Report* April 8, pp. 26–32.

WOLA Special Report [Washington Office on Latin America]. 2006. Youth gangs in central America: Issues in human rights, dffective policing, and prevention, November.

Wolch, Jennifer R., and Dear, Michael. 1993. *Malign Neglect: Homelessness in an American City*. San Francisco: Jossey-Bass Publishers.

Wrangham, Richard, and Peterson, Dale. 1996. *Demonic Males: Apes and the Origins of Human Violence*. New York: Mariner Books.

Wright, R., Decker, S., Redfern, A., and Smith, D. 1992. A snowballs' chance in hell: Doing fieldwork with active residential burglars. *Journal of Research in Crime and Delinquency* 29: 148–61.

Wyrick, Phelan, and Howell, James. 2004. Strategic risk-based response to youth gangs. *Juvenile Justice* 9 (September): 20–29.

Yablonsky, Lewis, 1970. *The Violent Gang*. Baltimore, MD: Penguin Books.

Zahn, Margaret A. (ed.). 2009. *The Delinquent Girl*. Philadelphia: Temple University Press.

Zambrano, R. D. 2003. Menores amputaron mano a su víctima para robarle. *El Diario de Hoy*, November 13, elpais@elsalvador.com.

Zamudio Hermida, Benjamín. 2007. *La Verdad de la Mara Salvatrucha*. Mexico City: B. Zamudio Hermida.

Zilberg, Elana. 2002. A troubled corner: The ruined and rebuilt environment of a Central American *Barrio* in post–Rodney King riot Los Angeles. *City and Society* 14(2): 31–55.

Zilberg, Elana. 2004. Fools banished from the kingdom: Remapping geographies of gang violence between the Americas (Los Angeles and San Salvador). *American Quarterly* 56(3): 759–79.

Zimring, F. E. 1996. Kids, guns, and homicide: Policy notes on an age-specific epidemic. *Law and Contemporary Problems* 59: 25–38.

Zimring, F. E. 2004. Firearms, violence, and the potential impact of firearms control. *Journal of Law, Medicine and Ethics* 32(1): 34–38.

INDEX

....

Acceptance, 65
Abandonment, 38, 49–50, 70, 135
Adolescence, 59
Aguantar, to suffer in silence, 50
Alcohol, 60, 104, 139, 161
Anthropology, goals of, 5. *See also*
Ethnography

Belonging, 59, 64
Betrayal, infidelity, 119, 126, 131
  ratting out, snitching, 95–96,
    127–29, 131
Borders, without, meaning of, xi-xii
Boredom, 19, 100–104, 122, 200
Brincada, la Gloria, initiation, 56–57,
    71 n. 6, 125. *See also* Joining
Bullies, at school, 54–55, 61, 68
  on the soccer field, 73

Calmado, retirement, 97, 136–37,
    175–77
Capricious, decisions, 59–60
Caretaking, 135, 137–38
Church, 52, 79, 81, 190–91, 196
Civil war, El Salvador, 1, 31–32
Coleman, Chuck, 8

Compassion, 4, 179
Composite characters, 15–16, 79, 185
Confidentiality, 9–11, 15
Cora, anger, bravery, 145, 171 n. 2
Corte, 94, 100. *See also* Punishment
Coyotes, smugglers, 40–41, 43, 115
Cruz, Susan, xiv, 177
Culture, 52–53, 62. *See also*
    Ethnography

Dating, 62, 68–69, 99–100, 119, 124–25
  desirable mates, 134
  enemy gang members, 131–32
Death squads, El Salvador, 6, 46 n. 16
DeCesare, Donna, xv; photographs, 32,
    34, 37, 56, 61, 118, 144
Democratic anarchy, type of leadership,
    91, 93–94. *See also* Gangs,
    leadership
Deportation, 41, 44, 75
Disappearances, 46 n. 15
Discrimination, racial, 54, 68, 73–74,
    172 n. 13
Disillusionment, 136, 176, 180–82
Dress, cultural differences, 54
  of gangster, 60, 77, 83, 113, 156

227

rules, enforcement, 100, 181. *See also* Corte

taboos, 95–99

types of, 76, 83, 86, 88, 106. *See also* Stoners

Gangster, meaning of, 63

Generation gap, 52

Grief, 165–66

Guilt, feelings, 163, 166, 177, 185–86, 190, 200

Guns, 61–62, 165

Hardcore gang members, 4, 12–13, 16–17. *See also* Gang members

Heart connection, between members, 7, 178–79

Identity, as a 'gangster,' xii, 57, 59–60

as an undocumented immigrant, 52

sense of belonging, xii

Immigrants, 63

Immigration, undocumented, 1, 38, 40–42, 45, 47 n. 19, 114. *See also* Deportation; Uprooted

Initiation, into gangs, 56–59

Jealousy, 14, 154

Jobs, 114–115, 176, 192–93

Joining, gang initiation, 56–57. *See also* Recruitment

predictors for, 66

reasons for, 2–4, 55, 60–64, 66–69, 118–119

risk factors, 66–68

Kennedy, David, 198–99

Kickin' it, hanging out, 61, 103–104

Klein, Malcolm, xiv, 21 n. 12, 110 n. 11, 172 n. 20

Language, acquisition, 52–54, 112, 116

Salvadoran accent, 43, 53

La vida loca, crazy life, 2

Law enforcement, 74, 98, 129, 142 n. 27, 151–53, 156, 172 n. 18, 199 n. 2

attitudes toward gang members, 154

framing gang members, 187

Machismo, within gangs, 19, 77

Mara Salvatrucha, (MS), cities in the U.S., 91, 168

crimes, 167–69

economic endeavors, illicit, 111 n. 42, 170–71

in other countries, 168

meaning of the name, 76

numbers of members, 91

organization, level of, xi, 170

reputation, world's most dangerous gang, 167–69

Maxson, Cheryl, xiv, 10, 21 n. 8

Memories, of El Salvador, 17, 22, 24, 45

Names, alternate terms for gang members, 16

nicknames, placasos, 23, 25, 27, 32–34, 102, 113

ridicule, 54, 113, 141 n. 2

Parenting, 35–36, 49–51, 100, 136, 158, 193

abuse, 52, 68

Participant-observation, 8–9, 14

Partying, 60, 62, 105

Paying one's dues, 97, 177, 185

PNC (National Civil Police), El Salvador, xiv, 10. *See also* Law enforcement

Posttraumatic stress disorder, PTSD, 157

Pregnancy, 121, 134–37

Prevention, gang, 64. *See also* Joining, Recruitment

Prison, 150–51, 185, 189, 197

Prostitution, 109

Protection, 55, 59, 65, 73, 107, 185